BUILDINGS & LANDSCAPES

JOURNAL OF THE VERNACULAR ARCHITECTURE FORUM

VOLUME 18 | NUMBER 2 | FALL 2011

Buildings & Landscapes (ISSN 1936-0886) is published twice a year in the spring and fall
by the University of Minnesota Press, 111 Third Avenue South, Suite 290, Minneapolis,
MN 55401-2520. http://www.upress.umn.edu

Published in cooperation with the Vernacular Architecture Forum (VAF). Members of
the VAF receive the journal as one of the benefits of membership. For further information about membership, contact Gabrielle Lanier, VAF Secretary, Vernacular Architecture
Forum, P. O. Box 1511, Harrisonburg, VA, 22803-1511, or visit us on the Web at http://
www.vafweb.org.

Postmaster: Send address changes to *Buildings & Landscapes*, University of Minnesota
Press, 111 Third Avenue South, Suite 290, Minneapolis, MN 55401-2520.

Manuscript submissions should be prepared to conform to the *Chicago Manual of Style*.
Contributors agree that manuscripts submitted to *Buildings & Landscapes* will not be
submitted for publication elsewhere while under review by the journal. Please feel free
to direct any inquiries to either editor via email: Marta Gutman, Associate Professor of
Architecture, Spitzer School of Architecture, The City College of the City University of
New York, 141 Convent Avenue, New York, NY 10031, mgutman@ccny.cuny.edu; Louis
P. Nelson, Associate Professor of Architectural History, School of Architecture, Campbell
Hall, University of Virginia, Charlottesville, VA 22904-4122, Lnelson@virginia.edu.
Please send submissions to both editors, preferably in electronic form, illustrations
included. Please see http://vafweb.org/publications/ for author guidelines.

Address subscription orders, changes of address, and business correspondence (including requests for permission and advertising orders) to *Buildings & Landscapes*, University
of Minnesota Press, 111 Third Avenue South, Suite 290, Minneapolis, MN 55401-2520.

Subscriptions: Regular rates, USA: individuals, 1 year, $60; libraries, 1 year, $125. Other
countries add $5 for each year's subscription. Checks should be made payable to the
University of Minnesota Press. Back issues are $37.50 for individuals and $78 for institutions (plus $5.00 shipping for the first copy, $1 for each additional copy inside the U.S.A.;
$9.50 shipping for the first copy, $5 for each additional copy, outside the U.S.A.). For
issues 1–13, please contact the Vernacular Architecture Forum. *Buildings & Landscapes*
is a benefit of membership in the Vernacular Architecture Forum.

Buildings & Landscapes is available online through Project MUSE, http://muse.jhu.edu,
WilsonWeb Journal Directory, http://vnweb.hwwilsonweb.com/hww/Journals/, JSTOR,
http://jstor.org, and from other online vendors.

THE VERNACULAR ARCHITECTURE FORUM is the premier organization in the United
States studying ordinary buildings and landscapes. Established in 1979–80 to promote
the appreciation of and scholarship on vernacular structures, it is an interdisciplinary
organization composed of scholars from many fields, including history, architectural
history, geography, anthropology, sociology, landscape history, preservation, and material-
culture studies. Since its founding, the VAF has played a major role in the academic study
and preservation of common buildings. The VAF holds an annual meeting, publishes a
newsletter and a journal, and maintains a Web site.

BUILDINGS & LANDSCAPES

JOURNAL OF THE VERNACULAR ARCHITECTURE FORUM
VOLUME 18 | NUMBER 2 | FALL 2011

LOUIS P. NELSON AND MARTA GUTMAN

Editors' Introduction

The articles in this issue of *Buildings & Landscapes* address a wide range of subjects: bathrooms in early twentieth-century workers' housing, floating houses in Cambodia, sidewalk cafes in Philadelphia, and the neighborhood of Bogside in Derry, Northern Ireland. Yet, even in the midst of their wide differences, these articles clarify a number of key interpretive themes that have animated the field of vernacular architecture studies in recent years.

The first and foremost is a focus on spaces rather than objects. Each of these articles engages as its primary subject a space or a set of spaces: bathrooms, domestic interiors of houseboats, sidewalks, and neighborhoods. By focusing on spaces we resist the fetishism of the object and we enter into deeply engaging discussions of the public and private spheres. Two authors directly take on the nature of public space. Stephen Nepa's discussion of the sidewalk cafes of Philadelphia examines the phenomenon of the appearance of more than three hundred sidewalk cafes in the past decade, when before there were almost none. He argues that these new cafes "provided Philadelphians and their visitors a higher degree of cosmopolitanism, a more pronounced feeling of safety, places for gathering, and an appealing way to experience the city," showing that these new spaces have participated in the transformation not only of the city's physical landscape but also its civic identity and sense of place. Yet he also questions whether these cafes are not stages for the performance of a new public, one that leads to the exclusion of the heterogeneous public from publically owned property. He notes that the cafes appear only in upper-middle-class neighborhoods that created safe "public" spaces, which were "seemingly impenetrable to the protracted problems of infrastructural decay, abandoned properties, and crime" that plagued other

regions of the city. And, as he shows, these spaces occasionally became flashpoints for disagreements over the use of public space.

Sara McDowell and Catherine Switzer offer a new perspective for our journal by analyzing the implications of violence on vernacular spaces. They walk us through the history of the neighborhood of Bogside in Derry, Northern Ireland, first through its massive physical transformation in midcentury redevelopment, then through the three years of street violence in the late 1960s and early 1970s now called the Northern Ireland Troubles that culminated in Bloody Sunday (January 30) of 1972, and finally, the more recent process of memorializing those events in the landscape. Although it takes place in a landscape filled with buildings, their story focuses on streets and open spaces where violence broke out and where people were killed. More tragic than Nepa's, their narrative shares his concern with the parameters of public space. Who has the right to represent the civic good and whose side of the resulting conflict is memorialized? They examine both "the organization of memory [and] the organization of silences." Drawing on de Certeau's examination of the practice of everyday life (also the title of his seminal work) these authors understand the space of the city "as a place controlled and resisted."

Kim Hoagland scrutinizes the emergence of the early twentieth-century bathroom: she uses a rigorous microstudy of working-class houses in a copper mining district of northern Michigan to examine the slow transformation of houses to accommodate the individual fixtures of sink, bath, and toilet in a single space called the bathroom. Refuting earlier claims that the modern three-fixture bathroom emerged fairly rapidly as a room in middle-class American houses, Hoagland demonstrates convincingly that "nearly all working-class houses nationwide acquired this new space, but its introduction was strategic, idiosyncratic, and incremental." She introduces us to families with sinks in their bedrooms, toilets in their basements, and privies outside their homes. Families often installed indoor toilets, bathtubs, and sinks as individual fixtures before there was a dedicated space in the house to receive them. While many families began by locating fixtures in basements of older houses, some experimented with putting toilets in closets. Hoagland also notes how the removal of the toilet from the yard transformed that space as well; family members no longer needed to take several daily trips through the yard to the privy—with an especially despised job of hauling the night's slops outside. At about the same time laundry moved indoors, refrigeration reduced the need for gardening and tending animals, and central heat eliminated the necessity for piles of firewood in yards. As a result, the yard lost many of its work-associated functions.

Our fourth article is Tijen Roshko's article on the floating dwellings of Chong Kneas. Transformed by seasonal rains, dry seasons and monsoons, the Tonle Sap Lake and its tributaries are home to thousands of families who have lived in floating houses for more than a century. Her research began by focusing on the houses of these communities as social and spatial objects. Through the careful recording of twelve examples, she reveals some shared characteristics of the subdivisions of these typically 40-foot-by-20-foot boats into spaces for work, food preparation, protecting unmarried daughters, and honoring one's ancestors. She also works to understand the urban morphology of a floating city, where seasonal changes require the moving of houses on at least a monthly basis. Who is able to put a house on the main "street"? How are ethnic minorities incorporated or marginalized? And finally she reports that these floating cities have negative spaces shaped by both climate and cosmology, where occupants cannot go.

If space is a critical lens in vernacular architecture studies, another long-standing theme in our field is an assessment of the margin. Early studies in vernacular architecture tended to focus on buildings that represented economically or culturally marginal groups. In this issue, the essay closest to that tradition is on the floating dwellings of Cambodia. Roshko focuses on the dwellings of those at the economic margin and engages issues of ethnically marginalized communities. While this way of defining the marginal remains an area of interest, the focus on the margin in these pages takes on new dimensions in other articles. The aggregation of the sink, the bath, and the toilet into a single indoor space—by its association with bodily uncleanness and waste—created a marginal space in the early twentieth-century house. This marginal quality is reinforced by the paucity of attention this space receives in the historical literature. Hoagland points out that the emergence of the bathroom is given almost no attention in the popular or professional literature of the period. Nepa's sidewalk cafes quite literally stand simultaneously on the margins of privately held land and the public street, a liminal condition that opens them to contest among multiple parties. And Bogside, as McDowell and Switzer make clear, was a highly charged politically marginal space. The practice of memorialization is complicated by the continuously shifting material landscapes—moving margins—that work against the practice of establishing a fixed place for memory preservation.

These articles also bring to the fore the instability of vernacular spaces. While the earliest scholarship in vernacular studies romantically embraced "the vernacular house" as a stable fixture in an ever-changing landscape, these articles remind us that no cultural production is ever stable. While the houseboats of Chong Kneas demonstrate a number of shared characteristics, the literal fluidity of that place and the instability resulting from changing seasons reminds us what we already know—that cities are never stable places and water cities even less so. The arrival of the bathroom was also not a direct, clean, or stable process. The rigorous investigation of this discrete case study undermines sweeping generalizations about narratives of stable, cohesive change over time. Change over time in real places is messy and unstable. And both articles about cities remind us that the "public" of public space is also unstable; it is itself a socially constructed space. Philadelphia's sidewalk cafes might appear to be stable places, but only for a certain sector of society and only for a season. Bogside's history is one of profound instability, and the challenges of memory-making destabilize the present place. We have come to recognize that instead of fetishizing the "stable vernacular type," focusing instead on instability is the stuff of great scholarship.

Spaces, margins, and instability are, of course, great fodder for great stories and it is to stories that Ryan Smith turns our attention in "Viewpoint." Some of our readers will remember Smith's paper on this same subject delivered at last year's Washington, D.C. conference. The intensity of discussion immediately following made it clear that this was to be our next "Viewpoint." Smith goes straight for the VAF jugular by criticizing our penchant to write for one another rather than for a broader audience. He pits our general practice of presenting analytical and technical structures requiring patience if not specialized knowledge against a narrative structure that draws readers into a *story*. He examines the practice of a few from our ranks who have employed imagined vignettes or narrative bookends but still criticizes the standard differentiation—even in these examples—between the story and the *real scholarship*. He challenges us to migrate toward a full embrace of narrative-as-scholarship by developing characters and establishing plot sequences, taking a lead from John Demos in *The Unredeemed Captive* and Henry Glassie in *Passing the Time in Ballymenone*. But then there is the challenge of invention—invented dialogue and scenes, the representation of events or conversations that *might* have happened as fact, and so forth. Can we as scholars adopt the liberty of fiction? As the editors of *Buildings & Landscapes,* we are intrigued but skeptical—as the highly analytical bent of this very volume demonstrates. But Smith concludes by asking how we—a subfield so purportedly democratic—can "ignore a technique that so plainly reaches a wider audience?" We ask you, the readership, to consider finding ways to engage narrative without compromising the scholarly rigor we value.

In loving memory
Pamela Hemenway Simpson, 1946–2011

Pam Simpson,
Jamaica, June 2011.
Photo by Jennifer Baughn.

RYAN K. SMITH

Viewpoint: **Building Stories**

Narrative Prospects for Vernacular Architecture Studies

A Beginning

In 2008, Charles E. Pattillo III, a retired architect in Jacksonville, Florida, self-published his first novel. Titled *St. Dunstan's & John,* the book is set along Florida's St. Johns River and tells two parallel stories. The first follows two earnest main characters—an architect and an Episcopal priest—in their modern-day rediscovery of hidden Confederate treasure; the second (told in flashback) recounts the hiding of that treasure during the waning days of the Civil War. The book has many flaws; the story is far-fetched and the dialogue is wooden. For example, one Florida man exclaims to a federal officer in 1863: "Even though our political beliefs are not in agreement and you are representatives of the enemy, we will stand true to our heritage of hospitality and welcome you to this community."[1] Even worse, Pattillo's tale inexcusably romanticizes the Confederate cause. But the book offers more than this tale, for it also works as an exquisitely detailed introduction to the seventeen Carpenter Gothic Episcopal churches actually built along the river from 1854 to 1891. These small, board-and-batten churches, constructed largely with Northern funds amid riverside cypress and palm trees, are architectural gems (Figures 1, 2, and 3). Pattillo explains his historical intentions in the preface. His project was "Originally planned as a guidebook on the history of small wood frame Episcopal churches built along the river." In the end, though, "I decided a novel would be more interesting and enjoyable than a dry recitation of architectural design facts."[2] So as the Confederate cavalry rides, and the modern-day architect and priest go about their search, the reader encounters passages like this:

"The others are close to that," replied Charlie. "The consistent use of a wood structural frame, vertical wood siding with small triangular wood battens to cover the joints, the slope of the roof, the pointed or lancet windows appear to be from a standard plan."

"Would that be from Richard Upjohn's book?"

"For sure."[3]

Or this:

Harry Drake carefully checked the location of each screw jack to insure placement beneath the perimeter sill beam and the center, or summer, beam of the church. Before any actual load of the church was transferred to the crossbeams, Ed Foley removed the windows and placed diagonal wood braces from wall to the floor inside the church.[4]

Or this:

Pushing the low bushes aside, Charlie removed a small section of protective screen between two brick piers and crawled under the church. He turned on his flashlight, pulled his tool bag alongside and inched his way toward the center. Some evidence of mechanical and electrical additions plus the sacristy addition were obvious. . . . He reached up to touch, with appreciation, circular saw marks on the wood framing made over one hundred years ago by a steam powered circular saw.[5]

Thus Pattillo's tale is no ordinary Confederate romance. Not only does it provide detailed explanations of the churches' construction, it also goes on to explore the theological significance

Figure 1. St. Mary's Episcopal Church, Green Cove Springs, Florida, photograph circa 1885. Completed in 1880, this is one of the seventeen churches along the St. Johns River that form the subject of Pattillo's book. PR04015, Florida Photographic Collection, State Archives of Florida.

Figure 2. St. Mary's Episcopal Church, Green Cove Springs, Florida, photograph circa 1966. RC04716, Florida Photographic Collection, State Archives of Florida.

of their designs and their adaptation to the local environment.

The book is packed with so much architectural information of the type encountered in *Buildings & Landscapes* or the *Vernacular Architecture Newsletter* that it could easily have been reworked into a useful, standard article. Yet, pleading readership, Pattillo chose not to.

With a little reflection, it would be easy to add to the list of storytellers who have likewise explored historic architecture in their work. There are much bigger players than Pattillo. Novelist Dan Brown has become a publishing sensation with his fast-paced, Hollywood-ready forays into art history set within, in his words, "entirely factual" representations of buildings and landscapes in Rome, Paris, and Washington, D.C. Also on the bestseller lists, Ken Follett has had success with his fictionalized accounts of medieval cathedral construction, which have lately led to a television miniseries. The efforts of such popularizers have brought new audiences to appreciate and debate architectural issues. For example, one can now take "Lost Symbol" tours of Washington on a Segway, or hear actors discuss what Salisbury Cathedral means to them.[6]

But surely more is at stake here than mere popularization. Pattillo's choice still haunts. His preface notwithstanding, he is responding to something more profound; his choice to offer a novel rather than a guidebook or article is not just about the prospect of wider audiences. For in stories, we *experience* historic structures differently. In Pattillo's hands, we can see these churches

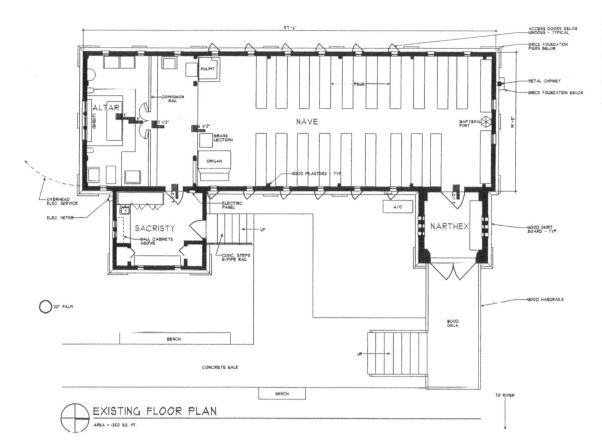

Figure 3. Plan of
St. Mary's Episcopal
Church, Green Cove
Springs, Florida. Drawn
by Kenneth Smith
Architects.

being raised, we can touch the old saw marks as we lie on our backs, the melodrama of the plot connecting the buildings to our emotions. More fundamentally, the fields of psychology, religion, literature, and folklore have demonstrated that humans make meaning of their lives and the world through narratives. Those fields suggest that storytelling serves essential purposes, beyond something "interesting and enjoyable." Given the power and attractions of such techniques, how have the Vernacular Architecture Forum (VAF) and related scholars interested in the built environment employed stories? In this, I am not considering general narratives of change over time. Rather, how have practitioners used flesh-and-bones constructions that feature the more potent tools of character, setting, plot, and perspective?

For over twenty-five years, the VAF and other practitioners have developed an impressive list of accomplishments. They have opened the canon of architectural history, developed a rigorous field-based methodology, and provided the his-

toric preservation movement with essential tools with which to weigh the values of our built heritage. But these practitioners have chosen, by and large, not to tell stories.

This is understandable. Traditional historians and art historians have not been interested in telling stories either, after the death of master narratives in the 1960s. By now we have all seen how these once staple narratives—linear tales with heroes and villains—functioned as props for nationalism, racism, sexism, and other privileged positions in addition to the fact of their often being wrong. Further, Henry Glassie has shown how the method of narrative history can be philosophically unsound, calling it "a serial array of literary scraps that give the reader the sensation of progress." On the other hand, Hayden White and many others have observed that it is impossible for historical scholarship to avoid stories on some level. We all are generally engaged with the metanarratives inherent in all of our studies: stories of progress, of resistance, of comedy, of tragedy. Still, the analytic has become the default writing mode for most scholars studying the past.[7]

And this is especially true for the VAF, a group formed in reaction against the congratulatory tales of high-flying architects and patrons. In this new forum, ordinary builders and their objects took center stage, but only via active theoretical and methodological mediation by researchers. The essays published over the years in *Perspectives in Vernacular Architecture* illustrate the point. Almost every one, from 1982's initial "The Stanley-Lake Barn in Topsfield, Massachusetts" by Robert Blair St. George to current issues of *Buildings & Landscapes,* relies on analytical/technical structures and explication to move the reader through an understanding of their subjects. I have found only three essays in *Perspectives* that come close to an "it was a dark and stormy night" approach. The most notable is Alison K. Hoagland's "The Boardinghouse Murders: Housing and American Ideals in Michigan's Copper Country in 1913," published in 2004, which uses the sources generated from a murder trial to explore ethnicity in mining town housing. In her first paragraph we follow a group of striking miners home, where a shoot-out between boarders and deputies occurs. The story itself is of historic interest to Hoagland, but its main value for her lies in the sources generated by the subsequent court case, which she uses to tease out complex human relationships involving the town and company property. Her narrative voice essentially ends halfway through the article. To be fair, there are not many more stories found in, say, *The Journal of American History* for the last few decades.[8]

Yet there has been some growing unease in regard to the recent scarcity of stories. It has been notably enunciated by arch-social historian John Demos in the opening plea of *The Unredeemed Captive.* In the first line, he tells us, "Most of all, I wanted to write a *story.*" A certain yearning for the novelist's technique lingers. A number of vernacular architecture scholars have joined those traditionalists, social historians, and even archaeologists who, like Pattillo, have increasingly turned to living, breathing stories to explore their subjects through plot structure.

Their accomplishments suggest the promise and the difficulty of the technique.[9]

A Middle

There are several ways in which practitioners have applied the technique to the study of historic buildings. One of the most common has been the *imagined vignette,* in which the researcher describes a hypothetical scene set within the broader study. In many cases, documents or other evidence indicate that such a scene took place, but the scholar must consciously construct the timing, the details, and the emotional tone of the vignette. This approach was made famous by James Deetz, who often began his works with imagined vignettes of individuals in the past going about routine tasks, so that the reader could get a sense of Deetz's findings in their original contexts and become invested in them as products of real people. "Ebenezer Soule set down his hammer and chisel." So Deetz began *In Small Things Forgotten,* imagining a moment in colonial Plympton, Massachusetts. "It was late evening, but he had completed the gravestone that he had been carving and that now stood before him." Deetz's subsequent profiles of farmer Jacob Mott, cook Mary Andrews, banjoist Wade Ward, gentleman William Rand, and an unnamed appraiser are similarly quaint and illustrate in the most general way the subjects and origins of the evidence to follow in the rest of the book. These scenes invite the reader inside, but the ephemeral moments they portray are not essential to Deetz's research or conclusions. They are friendly introductions for the reader.[10]

Imagined vignettes become more central when scholars use them as devices to illustrate how a particular landscape or social group operated. In *Lost Words and Lost Worlds,* Allan Pred explored late nineteenth-century industrial Stockholm, Sweden, by meditating on the language that shaped workers' lives there. In one chapter emphasizing the force of the city's geography, specifically its docks, Pred reconstructed a fictional "docker's daily path." Nilsson from Sörmland starts his hypothetical mid-May morning at 5:00 a.m. with the sun's rays reaching into his one-room apartment. He moves past his housemates and puts on his clothing, topped with a *Vega* cap. He visits the outhouse and begins his trek to work, traced visually on the book's accompanying map with chronological markers. Pred uses specific period photographs from along this path to involve his readers here, stating that from one viewpoint Nilsson "would have approached you, the viewer, along the shaded side of the street." Pred's narration continues, following Nilsson's sense impressions as he observes shops and cafes; smells sour beer and gutters; hears horses' hooves and trolley bells. Nilsson arrives at the harbor, has a beer, joins the work of unloading a ship, takes breaks for food and drink, interacts with his comrades and waitresses, and eventually leaves work by 6 p.m. to head to a public bar. Brief, invented dialogue spills out afterward into the night street until Nilsson heads home to bed before 10:00 p.m. Pred describes this episode as a "verbal montage." The effect uniquely complements his other linguistic attempts to recover the experiences of the city. Lisa C. Tolbert, in *Constructing Townscapes: Space and Society in Antebellum Tennessee,* expands on this technique by following through Tennessee towns the movements of people with various and sometimes conflicting perspectives—young white men, young white women, and slaves—demonstrating the ability of vignette to work "against a single interpretation of the townscape." Tolbert also ups the ante by reconstructing the documented movements of real, not hypothetical, figures. For Pred and Tolbert, these are not neutral invitations; even if they stop short of actual plot, they do convey character and setting.[11]

Perhaps the most powerful use of the imagined vignette occurs when it fully crystallizes the essence of an interpretation. For example, Dell Upton deployed a tour-de-force assortment of interpretive devices in his study of colonial Virginia's Anglican parish churches in *Holy Things and Profane,* but perhaps the most memorable was his opening tale. In it, he followed the imagined tobacco farmers Zachariah and Rebecca Sneed to a Sunday service at their church. The Sneeds are common farmers and they are somewhat out of place in the church. They enjoy mixing

with friends in the churchyard, but once the service starts they sit uncomfortably in the public benches in the back. Vivid things happen—a commotion arises because "Crazy Jacob had tried to sit in the vestry's pew again"—while Zachariah worries about the taxes associated with plans for a new church building and their relation to the handsome glebe house nearby. He and Rebecca also connect the church building and its furnishings with the powerful burgess's house. Finally, Zachariah's mind wanders during the sermon until he is shaken with the joyful realization that the service is ending and his chore is over. The rest of the book develops these themes analytically, visually, and theoretically, only returning to the Sneeds briefly at the beginning of part two. And while few critics have questioned Upton's presentation of the buildings themselves, they have doubted his reading of what the buildings *meant* and how they operated in their communities. The story of the Sneeds embodies his reading, which Joan Gundersen seizes upon in her review of the book for the *William and Mary Quarterly,* calling his vignette "a devastating reconstruction of the Sunday trip to church by a fictional small planter." Upton acknowledges that the buildings' meanings are the critical points; "I have been taught by my teachers that buildings are really only as interesting as the people who made them and used them," he stated in his introduction. His story of the Sneeds clarifies, for himself and for his critics, what his analysis ultimately suggests.[12]

Deetz, Pred, Tolbert, and Upton show the continuing attraction of storytelling for scholars, in the technique's ability to humanize and open perspectives into its subjects. Still, each author uses the technique at arm's length. There is a clear delineation in their work between the "imaginary" scenes and the actual research. Like a potent spice, the narratives are used sparingly and temporarily.

We get closer to full-fledged stories with another approach, exemplified in the work of archaeologists Ivor Noël Hume and, later, William Kelso. These scholars turned their own winding investigations of historic buildings into the story itself, an approach we might call the *researcher's journey.* Hume's discovery of English close helmets at Martin's Hundred and Kelso's landing on the original walls of the Jamestown fort impart an Indiana-Jones, come-along-on-the-ride-with-me feel, which highlights the important role of the researcher in his or her own findings. Though such stories can be sustained and suffused throughout a work, they rarely advance our understanding of the objects in their original contexts. Still, the approach holds some possibilities, as demonstrated recently by Margaret Ruth Little in *Carolina Cottage: A Personal History of the Piazza House.* Little, so familiar with the analytical demands of a vernacular architecture audience, supplements her explication of the rise of the piedmont cottage form with her own personal experiences (and indeed love) of living in such a house and touring those near her. In doing so, she is able to approach that most slippery aspect of our studies—the subjective. Can we prove that the form made people happy? Perhaps only through story.[13]

A third approach involves the use of the technique as a *frame,* a bookend, a thematic thread with which to tie an investigation together, as in Hoagland's "The Boardinghouse Murders." The promise of such an approach was demonstrated clearly in Bernard L. Herman's *The Stolen House,* a study of the lower Delaware landscape in the early American republic that employed the curious court case of the title as a hook and as a source of evidence. This approach is widespread and more compatible with research, for it does not require imaginary scenarios nor an undue focus on the researcher as narrator. Still, the countless studies that employ this approach risk not taking their own technique seriously enough. As much as I remember the Christopher orphans' stolen house predicament, I remember chewing over the frustrations of the book's reviewers, such as Donald Friary in the *Journal of Southern History,* who lamented that "a provocative title and story are insufficiently exploited." Herman had mastered his subject and put forth a fresh explanation of the human landscape; still, Friary is frustrated by the seemingly false promise of the title. Indeed, in an anticlimax, the reader reaches the conclusion of the book only to find that the titular

"stolen house" suit was dismissed by its judge. Herman's next book, *Town House,* embraced the challenge more, with thematic chapters organized around the individual predicaments of "The Burgher's Dilemma," "The Servant's Quarter," "The Widow's Dower," "A Traveler's Portmanteau," and on. These stories are more satisfying, even if Herman turns to "the poetic" by way of conclusion.[14]

There does exist a class of architectural studies perched between Pattillo's fictionalizations and Herman's thematic framing devices. These tell singular, sustained stories about buildings and landscapes. On the bestseller list, Ross King and Erik Larson, respectively, have drawn on secondary sources to guide readers through Brunelleschi's Dome in Florence and Chicago's White City exhibition. Less blockbuster but more research-oriented studies include: Nancy Lusignan Schultz's *Fire and Roses,* J. Ritchie Garrison's *Two Carpenters,* Andrew S. Dolkart's *Biography of a Tenement House in New York City,* Scott W. Berg's *Grand Avenues,* Jane Kamensky's *The Exchange Artist,* and, to a lesser extent, Ann Smart Martin's *Buying into the World of Goods.* Though many of the above lean heavily on individual life stories, none are straight biographies. True, they all artificially arrange the slosh and noise of time into an unnatural coherence, and they risk sentimentalizing their subjects. But they also engage readers with a palatable style and help us confront the past through an explicitly human perspective. They take us through the experiences of their subjects, if we can still the postmodern doubts for a moment, in the order in which they were experienced in time. Even more, they reveal the limits of what we know about the past. This is no small feat. In Ann Smart Martin's terms, what did the slave Suckey's purchase of a mirror from John Hook's store in 1774 mean?[15]

Perhaps the issue of medium is relevant here, for there are vernacular architecture practitioners outside academia who already deal with sustained storytelling on a daily basis. Surely almost every historic house museum has had to engage with the stories its own guides and exhibits tell. In my city alone, Richmond, Virginia, visitors can hear the tug between particular family tales and their broader historical contexts in the tours of the John Marshall House, the John Wickham House at the Valentine Richmond History Center, Jefferson Davis's "White House of the Confederacy," the Dooleys' Maymont House, the Maggie L. Walker National Historic Site, and, now, Robert Lumpkin's slave jail, among others. When stories do not survive to animate important aspects of their exhibits, as in the service spaces at the Wickham House, the curators often create composites to illustrate likely scenarios. And their three-dimensional spaces help propel the tales; the Virginia Holocaust Museum places visitors in the midst of its subject by inviting them to experience the event bodily; guests "can crawl through a replica of an actual hiding place where 13 people hid during World War II for nine months," in the words of its website. Just down the road, Colonial Williamsburg has pitched an entire village with countless subplots set within the narrative frame of the mid-1770s. We might ask: How have these institutions' storytelling strategies shaped their research agendas and their landscapes? And what can individual scholars learn from this interplay?[16]

The stakes involved in such questions are high. We need only witness the evasions and denials of slavery built in to the presentations at many plantation house museums in the South, where for years most of the stories told involved the sites' few white owners. Such stories do not always flow from the institution down; in public spaces, visitors join in as authors. Pamela H. Simpson has charted the recurring "old house stories" that, despite the best efforts of well-informed docents, forever reappear on tours, such as the wall openings through which residents supposedly defended themselves against Indians and the minimal closets attributed to imagined taxes. Visitors' influence can also be seen in the recent market-driven spread of "ghost tours" in historic areas far outside Salem, Massachusetts, in which visitors and their guide share evening frights centered on particular stories, with the local landscape serving as an essential prop. When there are competing ghost tours in staid Williamsburg, Virginia, as has come to pass

in the past decade, we know that visitors are driving new genres.[17]

A Twist

Personally, I had my own John Demos "Most-of-all-I-wanted-to-write-a-story" moment after my first book was published in 2006. The book was organized thematically, and though its reception in my field was generally positive, I was predictably frustrated that it seemed to be such a chore for my nonacademically inclined friends to approach it. Also, I harbored a lot of the evangelicalism of the VAF/material culture movement: I wanted my next project to push material culture under the noses of even the most object-averse historians and thought that telling a ripping story might help my chances. Finally, I started to listen to the drumbeat I regularly tapped out for my students: even the blandest historical sources reveal an inherent perspective; they convey the particular persuasions of their authors. If this was true for eighteenth-century tax records, then why not for all varieties of modern scholarship? In other words, as Upton has demonstrated, I could launch a thesis inside a story as in any other vehicle.[18]

So, for my current project, I landed on a subject that I thought addressed substantive historical and material culture questions while having narrative potential. That is, American founder Robert Morris and his ill-fated "Folly," the grandiose Philadelphia mansion designed by Peter Charles L'Enfant. I had already studied the Folly and was intrigued by its French-inspired design, its enormous costs, and the spectacular reaction it drew from the community. It stood in the center of an entire block near the city's core, in sharp contrast to Philadelphia vernacular row house traditions. Morris was attempting to build the mansion just as his financial speculations began to unravel in the 1790s (Figure 4). His financial overreaching landed him in debtor's prison in 1798, whereupon his creditors and scavenging citizens tore down the nearly finished Folly with glee (Figure 5). The tale lived on in local lore as a cautionary tale. Thus Morris's financial and architectural fortunes seemed to intertwine; the house presented a more meaningful symbolic

Figure 4. A view of Robert Morris's "Folly" in its most advanced state of completion, immediately prior to its demolition. Plate 14, "An Unfinished House, in Chesnut Street Philadelphia," William Russell Birch, Thomas Birch, and W. Barker, *The City of Philadelphia, in the State of Pennsylvania, North America: As it Appeared in the Year 1800* (Philadelphia: W. Birch, 1800). Courtesy of the Library Company of Philadelphia.

Figure 5. William Sansom's row house project, which took the place of Morris's Folly. Thomas Carstairs, "The Plan and Elevation of the South Buildings in Sansom Street, in the City of Philadelphia," circa 1800. Courtesy of the Library Company of Philadelphia.

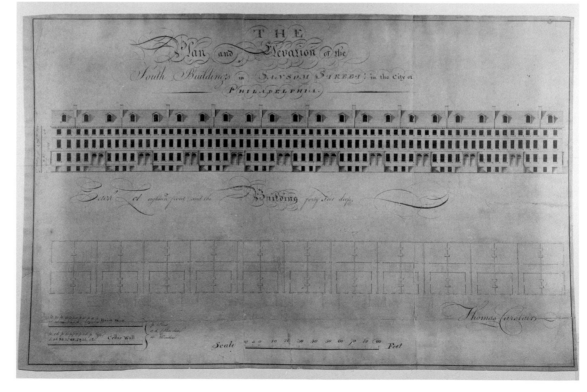

platform for the public than Morris's tangled accounts. I felt the episode could be used to highlight important boundaries and anxieties in the early republic. And the story runs perfectly against the grain of most "Founding Fathers" myths, especially those of the studiously modest, rags-to-riches Benjamin Franklin and of the seemingly power-cautious George Washington. If nothing else, in the Folly, I could dramatize a building as a fundamental historical character, something like Morris's double.

Writing in this mode has been great fun. I have adopted as my mantra Douglas R. Egerton's rationale for storytelling in his study of Gabriel's attempted slave rebellion near Richmond in 1800: "It would be a nearly criminal act if the story did not unfold for the reader as it did for those who lived through it." However, in the process I am bumping up against the problems every nonfiction storyteller encounters. There are plentiful sources although only a few physical remnants survive, which include two mantelpieces and two sculpted reliefs believed to be from the house. Morris left a great deal of correspondence and private account books that shed light on his activities in the 1790s. And of course a fair amount of the more traditional streetscape has been amply recovered and studied. Yet when retelling the story, I still find the necessary ingredients scant. There is simply no way to compete with fiction in this regard. For example, to serve the plot it would be useful to provide a sense of Morris's or L'Enfant's initial dialogue or intentions. I can address the backgrounds of both, with Morris's ambitions and appetites for worldly pleasures and L'Enfant's colorful design history. But the best I can do for the period directly before the two broke ground is to place L'Enfant in Philadelphia and in Morris's acquaintance by early 1793, with this kind of narration:

> It would have been easy for the enthusiastic L'Enfant to match Morris's vision, both for the nation and for Morris's place within it. And Morris could relate to L'Enfant's tales of unwarranted persecution. Presumably, over veal, shad, and claret, the two put aside any remaining disagreements [from previous fiscal matters], and began to

plan. L'Enfant, though never one to be bound by budgets, quoted Morris an estimate for the whole project—perhaps $60,000—and Morris, flush with his recent sales, accepted.

He had certainly engaged the Major by May 9, 1793, when he sent a gently sarcastic letter to L'Enfant expressing his eagerness to move forward: "Dear Sir, I had like to have stopped my House for fear of wanting money, that difficulty being removed, it will now be stopped for want of Major L'Enfant." The next month L'Enfant walked away from the Paterson project, and the thing was begun.

I have the typical academic distaste for invented dialogue. And here we see that even the voluminous manuscripts of a famous man are a weak substitute for true dialogue.[19]

Historians have handled this particular challenge in several ways. Egerton fell back on broad context and then tiptoed toward fiction in critical scenes, as when the slaves Charles and Frank stood trial: "Off Charles stumbled, hurried along by the guards, even as two more warders nudged Frank forward." Note the absence of any conjecturing language in these details. Going further, John Demos famously leapt into the breach in *The Unredeemed Captive*. In a key scene, he narrates a meeting between the young girl captured by Mohawks a decade earlier and a representative from her father, a New England minister. The recorded exchange is minimal and gives little sense of the feelings and motivations of Demos's primary subject. "We can only speculate—only imagine—but that much, at least, we must try," Demos concludes. He proceeds to give her a voice: "*With a clarity born of old bitterness, she remembered the last times she had seen [her father]. She remembered his coming to the village when she was still a small child—feeling scared and strange, and gripped inside by the ties of her old life* [italics in the original]." On the other hand, most historians have backed away from this leap, sometimes maddeningly. Jon F. Sensbach painstakingly reconstructs the life story of Rebecca Protten, an eighteenth-century Moravian missionary who was once enslaved on St. Thomas, but he is careful not to do violence with her silences. In one of the few remaining letters purportedly written by her, Sensbach properly concludes that the words "might have been framed entirely, partly, or not at all by her, and thus might have expressed either what she felt or what she was expected to feel. Perhaps the most we can say is that the letter was designed to express certain sentiments for a particular audience." True, but then with what are we really left?[20]

In my manuscript, I try to solve such problems by using details to the fullest when they are available. Through the sustained tale, I believe my sense of Morris's and L'Enfant's characters comes through. In any case, I pitch the story toward its climax, even while other questions emerge along the way. How do I handle the relatively long cast of characters? How do I convey the voice of Morris's wife Mary, who was actively involved but quiet in the documents? And, in the end, will my main audience—you—become frustrated by the lack of an explicit thesis and overt historiographic orientation?

Clearly, it is easier to call for more stories than to deliver them within the constraints and purposes of scholarly journals, National Register nominations, and museum exhibits. In 1997, Mary Praetzellis coordinated a panel on the theme of "Archaeologists as Storytellers" at the Society for Historical Archaeology's annual conference, with comment by James Deetz. The complete set of papers was published the following year in the journal *Historical Archaeology*. The papers were not explicitly theoretical or methodological in their focus; they were all practical in demonstrating storytelling techniques, and many adopted the liberties of fiction in their interpretive stories. The initiative proved so popular that Praetzellis soon organized a follow-up panel at a subsequent conference, and *Historical Archaeology* presented a roundtable on the topic in 2000. In it, James G. Gibb headed an attempt to make sense of the movement's sudden flowering and provide it with more theoretical focus. The storytelling technique, Gibb insisted, provides "a powerful analytic tool, [a] means of exploring archaeological and archival data." Others agreed, and a number of explicitly story-oriented books followed, such as Rebecca Yamin's *Digging in the City of Brotherly Love: Stories from Philadelphia Archaeology*. Yet a cursory glance at recent issues of *Historical Archaeology* reveals that the movement does not truly threaten to destabilize the analytic or technical as the dominant scholarly mode.[21]

There are reasons for this beyond the limitations of evidence discussed above. Among the other critical drawbacks to the storytelling mode, perhaps foremost is that the technique lacks the efficiency and freedom of thesis-driven analysis. It is simply easier to construct our own, more flexible frameworks. And though the twentieth century introduced a dazzling array of examples showing how one might subvert a traditional narrative form, the technique still tends to emphasize a linear and limited flow of time. Even worse, the technique of storytelling seems to prioritize drama over evidence, with the logical extreme becoming something like a Dan Brown novel: exciting and a page-turner, but deeply suspect.

Further, there is a more stubborn problem. Even if practitioners wanted to tell more stories, the technique itself can be difficult to master. Witness Pattillo's wonderfully researched but green novel. Writing a successful story is not a self-evident process. And graduate programs are not spending much time preparing future researchers for this kind of craft. As the system is now set up, we can expect exquisite critiques of books or exhibitions from students, or thorough architectural surveys, but few experiments with stories.

In the end, we might wonder if focus on the technique is worth it. Can it even deliver its most basic promise of connecting our work with a wider audience of nonspecialists? As demonstrated by the lone review of Pattillo's book on Amazon.com, maybe we just cannot have it all. The reviewer, an acquaintance of the author in Jacksonville, Florida, and a self-described "history buff," writes, "I must admit the extensive architectural interpretation was beyond me a little (or a lot), but up to a point it too was interesting." Surely this is damning with faint praise. What readers of this journal would judge as an initial exploration of the buildings, the lay reader finds beyond him. Nor do the story's architectural his-

11. Allan Pred, *Lost Words and Lost Worlds: Modernity and the Language of Everyday Life in Late Nineteenth-Century Stockholm* (New York: Cambridge University Press, 1990), 291 (quotation), 229–35. Lisa C. Tolbert, *Constructing Townscapes: Space and Society in Antebellum Tennessee* (Chapel Hill: University of North Carolina Press, 1999), 10. For another example, see Billy G. Smith, *The "Lower Sort": Philadelphia's Laboring People, 1750–1800* (Ithaca, N.Y.: Cornell University Press, 1990).

12. Dell Upton, *Holy Things and Profane: Anglican Parish Churches in Colonial Virginia* (New York: Architectural History Foundation/MIT Press, 1986), xxii (last quotation), 3–4 (first quotation), 101; Joan R. Gundersen, review of Upton, *Holy Things and Profane* in *William and Mary Quarterly* 46 (April 1989): 378–82 (second quotation, 380).

13. Ivor Noël Hume, *Martin's Hundred* (New York: Knopf, 1982); William M. Kelso, *Jamestown: The Buried Truth* (Charlottesville: University of Virginia Press, 2006); Margaret Ruth Little, *Carolina Cottage: A Personal History of the Piazza House* (Charlottesville: University of Virginia Press, 2010). Little states her intent for the technique in the introduction: "I hope my story helps readers to see clearly the significance of the Carolina cottage and how an architectural style has helped me shape and understand the person I am," xiii.

14. Bernard L. Herman, *The Stolen House* (Charlottesville: University Press of Virginia, 1992); Donald R. Friary, review of *The Stolen House*, in the *Journal of Southern History* 60 (February 1994): 125–26; Bernard L. Herman, *Town House: Architecture and Material Life in the Early American City, 1780–1830* (Chapel Hill: Published for the Omohundro Institute of Early American History and Culture, Williamsburg, Va., by the University of North Carolina Press, 2005).

15. Ross King, *Brunelleschi's Dome: The Story of the Great Cathedral in Florence* (New York: Penguin, 2001) and Erik Larson, *The Devil in the White City: Murder, Magic, and Madness at the Fair that Changed America* (New York: Crown Publishers, 2003). We might also add, among many more, John Berendt, *Midnight in the Garden of Good and Evil* (New York: Random House, 1994), given its impact on Savannah. Also, Nancy Lusignan Schultz, *Fire and Roses: The Burning of the Charlestown Convent* (Boston: Northeastern University Press, 2002); J. Ritchie Garrison, *Two Carpenters: Architecture and Building in Early New England, 1799–*

1859 (Knoxville: University of Tennessee Press, 2006); Andrew S. Dolkart, *Biography of a Tenement House in New York City: An Architectural History of 97 Orchard Street* (Santa Fe, N.M.: Center for American Places, 2006); Scott W. Berg, *Grand Avenues: The Story of the French Visionary Who Designed Washington, D.C.* (New York: Pantheon Books, 2007); Jane Kamensky, *The Exchange Artist: A Tale of High-Flying Speculation and America's First Banking Collapse* (New York: Viking, 2008); and Ann Smart Martin, *Buying into the World of Goods: Early Consumers in Backcountry Virginia* (Baltimore: Johns Hopkins University Press, 2008), 173. See also Catherine W. Bishir, "Jacob W. Holt: An American Builder?" *Winterthur Portfolio* 16 (1981): 1–31 (reprinted in Upton and Vlach, ed., *Common Places*, 447–81); and Daniel J. Vivian, "'A Practical Architect': Frank P. Milburn and the Transformation of Architectural Practice in the New South, 1890–1925," *Winterthur Portfolio* 40 (Spring 2005): 17–46.

16. "Explore the Museum," www.va-holocaust.com, accessed January 17, 2011. Other curatorial examples abound. For discussion of Williamsburg's research agenda and narrative choices, see Cary Carson, "Colonial Williamsburg and the Practice of Interpretive Planning in American History Museums," *The Public Historian* 20 (Summer 1998): 11–51, as well as the rest of that issue.

17. E. Arnold Modlin Jr., "Tales Told on the Tour: Mythic Representations of Slavery by Docents at North Carolina Plantation Museums," *Southeastern Geographer* 48 (November 2008): 265–87; Pamela H. Simpson, "Windows, Closets, Taxes, and Indians: Old House Stories We Have Known and Loved (Redux)," *Vernacular Architecture Newsletter* 119 (Spring 2009): 1–7; Pamela Simpson, "Windows, Closets, Taxes, and Indians: Architectural Legends and Myths" *ARRIS* 3 (1992): 23–34. For a recent study of the ghost tours, see Glenn W. Gentry, "Walking with the Dead: The Place of Ghost Walk Tourism in Savannah, Georgia" *Southeastern Geographer* 47 (2007): 222–38.

18. Ryan K. Smith, *Gothic Arches, Latin Crosses: Anti-Catholicism and American Church Designs in the Nineteenth Century* (Chapel Hill: University of North Carolina Press, 2006).

19. Douglas R. Egerton, *Gabriel's Rebellion: The Virginia Slave Conspiracies of 1800 and 1802* (Chapel Hill: University of North Carolina Press, 1993), x.

Some fine print for reconstructing the above narration: The quote comes from Robert Morris to Major [Peter Charles] L'Enfant, May 9, 1793, James Dudley Morgan collection of Digges-L'Enfant-Morgan Papers, Manuscript Division, Library of Congress. John Watson, Philadelphia's early annalist who drew much of his source material from hearsay, recorded four decades later that a "gentleman was present at R. Morris's table when L'Enfent [sic] was there, and first broached the scheme of building him a grand house for 60,000 dollars." Watson did not name the year of the anecdote. Watson continued: "Mr. Morris said he could sell out his lots and houses on High street for 80,000 dollars, and so the thing was begun." John F. Watson, *Annals of Philadelphia and Pennsylvania, in the Olden Time: Being a Collection of Memoirs, Anecdotes, and Incidents of the City and its Inhabitants, and of the Earliest Settlements of the Inland Part of Pennsylvania, from the Days of the Founders* vol. 1 (Philadelphia: Penington and Hunt, 1844), 409. This story of L'Enfant's proposal over dinner did not appear in the earlier 1830 issue of Watson's work. Morris did indicate later that L'Enfant had given him an initial estimate for the total cost. See Robert Morris to Major C. L'Enfant, September 25, 1795, Robert Morris Papers, Library of Congress; in which Morris writes that a single stone contractor "alone has received from me a sum equal to what you told me in the outset the whole Building would cost."

20. Egerton, *Gabriel's Rebellion*, 87; Demos, *The Unredeemed Captive*, 108. For a similarly active approach, see Simon Schama, *Dead Certainties: Unwarranted Speculations* (New York: Knopf, 1991); and the comments of Otis L. Graham, Jr. in "Editor's Corner: History + Fiction = Faction/Miction," *The Public Historian* 16 (Winter 1994): 10–13. Also, Jon F. Sensbach, *Rebecca's Revival: Creating Black Christianity in the Atlantic World* (Cambridge, Mass.: Harvard University Press, 2005), 63.

21. James G. Gibb, "Imaginary, But by No Means Unimaginable: Storytelling, Science, and Historical Archaeology," *Historical Archaeology* 34 (2000), 1–6 (quotation, 3); "Archaeologists as Storytellers," *Historical Archaeology*, 1–96; "Forum," *Historical Archaeology*, 1–24; and Rebecca Yamin, *Digging in the City of Brotherly Love: Stories from Philadelphia Archaeology* (New Haven: Yale University Press, 2008). See also Dan Mouer, *Digging Sites and Telling Stories: Essays in Interpretive Historical Archaeology* (New York: Plenum, 1998).

22. Comment from E. Cobb Harbeson, June 22, 2008, Amazon.com, accessed October 4, 2010.

23. Yamin, *Digging in the City of Brotherly Love*, 211.

24. Henry Glassie, *Folk Housing in Middle Virginia* (Knoxville: University of Tennessee Press, 1975); Henry Glassie, *Passing the Time in Ballymenone: Culture and History of an Ulster Community* (Philadelphia: University of Pennsylvania Press, 1982), xiv.

25. St. George, "The Stanley-Lake Barn in Topsfield, Massachusetts," 17. Carson himself has taken our field to task for its complacent insularity and proposed overarching frameworks of inquiry to move us forward rather than a particular method. See Cary Carson, "Material Culture History: The Scholarship Nobody Knows," in *American Material Culture: The Shape of the Field*, ed. Ann Smart Martin and J. Ritchie Garrison, 401–28 (Winterthur, Del.: Henry Francis du Pont Winterthur Museum, 1997).

ALISON K. HOAGLAND

Introducing the Bathroom

Space and Change in Working-Class Houses

The introduction of the bathroom in the late nineteenth and early twentieth centuries was probably the single greatest change to the architecture of middle- and working-class houses. The bathroom was a dedicated space that did not previously exist. Within a few decades, it appeared in new houses and old, urban and rural, sprawling suburban cottages and tiny apartments. The bathroom did not arrive equally, of course: middle-class homeowners before working-class renters, urban houses before rural farms, architects' plan books before real buildings. Its arrival was revolutionary, affecting—among other things—women's work, servants' work, standards of cleanliness, perceptions of status, circulation patterns, design, and ideas of convenience.[1] A room with such ramifications merits an examination of how it came to be, although Americans' reluctance to discuss such a personal space makes the bathroom an understudied part of the house. Working-class American housing offers new perspectives on the desirability yet difficulty of acquiring a bathroom.

Contrary to the assertion of Siegfried Giedion, who held that the bathroom rapidly attained its modern form of a room containing a bathtub, toilet, and sink, the development of the bathroom was slow and multivalent (Figure 1).[2] Possession of bathroom fixtures was a factor of money and, as such, a bathroom helped to define class. As historian Maureen Ogle has shown, in the nineteenth century the upper class attained the different fixtures at different times and tended to isolate them. The sink, replacing a water pitcher and basin, was first located in the bedroom,

while the bathtub received its own room adjacent to the bedroom. The toilet, however, was placed elsewhere, in a separate room, due to odors associated with its use. Beginning in the 1870s, public health professionals encouraged the consolidation of the three fixtures into a single room in order to simplify the network of pipes and traps that ran through the house.[3] Needing a name for this room, building professionals took the most innocuous function, the bath, and named the room after that. The term "bathroom," written as two words or hyphenated into the twentieth century, was an accepted term for this multipurpose space by the 1880s.[4] By the end of the nineteenth century, most upper-class houses had three-fixture bathrooms.

Middle-class homeowners, who began to attain bathroom fixtures around 1900, also adopted the preference for concentrating the fixtures in one room. They had three avenues for obtaining a bathroom: buy a new house, add a room to an existing house, or appropriate an existing room for this new use. Most new house plans indicated bathrooms.[5] Even as early as 1884, a plan book of "medium and low cost houses" stated, "no house should be without a bath-room, large and conveniently located."[6] But most Americans lived in houses that were already built, and for these two solutions presented themselves: adding a room or taking a room.[7] The problem of retrofitting a bathroom into an existing house received little attention in the press, although it must have occurred with staggering frequency. Of the 16 million households in the United States in 1900, probably a quarter of them were in houses that

Figure 1. Laurium
Hardware, 317–19
Hecla Street, Laurium.
The three fixtures of
the bathroom—sink,
toilet, and tub—
are exhibited in this
basement showroom of
a hardware store in the
early twentieth century.
Courtesy of Mr. and
Mrs. Jack Browning.

would receive a bathroom in the next quarter century.[8] Surprisingly, there was no discussion of this remodeling in the professional and popular press.[9]

Working-class houses had constraints not experienced by the middle class. Their occupants could not afford to build new houses or add new rooms, nor could they afford bathroom-equipped houses financed by someone else. And they had no extra room to appropriate for bathroom use; crowded already, working-class houses had a minimal number of rooms. Yet these were the people who would have benefitted the most, because working-class women performed their own domestic chores, unlike middle-class women who hired servants (i.e., working-class women). Due to these spatial constraints, the complete bathroom came slowly to working-class houses; instead, the three fixtures of a bathroom—sink, toilet, and bathtub—arrived at different times, into different spaces, but for very different reasons than for the upper-class homeowners. Historian Joseph Bigott attributes the gradual acquisition to cost; indeed, fixtures were

a considerable expense for a low-income family.[10] In 1913 one estimate for installing a bathroom in a preexisting house was $140: $100 for the fixtures and plumbing, and $40 for the carpentry.[11] But introducing a bathroom into a preexisting house was not only an issue of cost; it was also a spatial issue and working-class houses did not have the space to spare, nor their owners the means to create new spaces. High cost and lack of space caused bathroom fixtures to arrive incrementally in working-class houses.

The bathroom's spatial implications have been little studied, although other aspects of the bathroom are more familiar. The technology of plumbing and toilets has received some attention, as have changing attitudes toward cleanliness.[12] Historians such as Ruth Schwartz Cowan and Susan Strasser have taken these two factors further, examining how these new technologies and changing attitudes affected women's work.[13] Other historians view bathrooms through the lens of systems, tracing utilities and drawing houses into larger networks of water supply, sewage, electricity, and food processing.[14] Thomas

Hubka and Judith Kenny link the acquisition of the bathroom to status and class, arguing that the bathroom was a middle-class amenity gradually acquired by the working class in the early twentieth century.[15] The change in the form of the house as a result of this addition, though, has not received much attention.[16] Where this new room went and the way in which it arrived—the working class's piecemeal acquisition—indicate how its new owners conceived this new facility.

With water and sewer services arriving to rural and urban settings—even within cities—at greatly different times, and with the three fixtures also arriving at separate times, there is no consistent narrative as to how the bathroom was accommodated in working-class houses.[17] Homeowners adopted these services in ad hoc and idiosyncratic ways. Given the variety of experiences, the introduction of domestic technologies into working-class houses must be assessed on a case-by-case basis. Accordingly, this article will examine the transformations of modest houses in one working-class community—a microstudy to shed light on the larger issue.

In the copper-mining district of northern Michigan known as the Copper Country, the building stock is well preserved, with the physical fabric that marks the transformation still visible in many houses. Corporate copper mining began on the Keweenaw Peninsula of Lake Superior in the 1840s, and by 1910 the population was just shy of 100,000, with about 15 active mining companies.[18] At that time, nearly 90 percent of the population was foreign-born or born to foreign-born parents.[19] Winters are severe, with snowfall averaging more than 200 inches. On company land, the houses—some 3,200 built by the mining companies, plus another 1,750 built by the occupants themselves on a ground-rent system—were clustered in communities that fell between urban and rural.[20] Outside of company land, incorporated villages accommodated the rest of the workforce as well as many commercial and institutional functions. Study of this area also benefits from a written record, including several hundred letters in which company-house tenants requested the installation of indoor toilets and other amenities, often citing reasons.

Mining companies were forced to contend with the provision of sinks, indoor toilets, and bathing facilities. The situation may have been unique, but the task of retrofitting domestic technologies into existing houses was common.

The Sink

The sink, in the sense of a receptacle for water attached to a wall or pedestal, was nearly universal in houses by the early twentieth century, although not necessarily located in the bathroom. Sinks were placed in kitchens, where they served the full range of food-related and personal-cleanliness needs. Sinks appeared even in houses without running water, being filled with water from buckets (Figure 2). Drains, though, were essential, because if there were no pipe to drain a sink, a portable basin would be preferable. A sewage system was not necessary; the "gray water" of a sink could drain under the house or into the yard.[21]

Once a house received running water, it would be piped first and foremost to the enameled-metal sink in the kitchen (Figure 3). While upper-class householders might have been accustomed to pitchers and basins in their bedrooms before their houses had running water, that kind of convenience was dependent on servants. Working-class residents would have washed up in the kitchen or in the nearby yard. Once water was piped indoors, if there were only one sink in the house, the kitchen sink served the functions of a bathroom sink. Shaving mirrors and toothbrush holders found in the kitchens of houses without bathrooms—but occupied into the late twentieth century—indicate the versatility of these kitchen sinks.[22]

Figure 2. Kitchen, house 18, Mandan. Piped-in water is not a requirement for a sink, as seen in this house built in 1907. Photographed by author in 1998.

Figure 3. Putrich House, Seeberville, Painesdale. In this house owned by the Champion Copper Company, a sink with one faucet—indicating cold running water—was photographed in 1913. Courtesy of Michigan Technological Archives and Copper Country Historical Collections, Acc. 06–087A01–07–10.

nies in Michigan, drew water from an inland lake for its steam needs but built a separate system for potable water. In 1889, the company constructed a waterworks on Lake Superior, pumping lake water four-and-a-half miles to a high point inland; then distributing it to the 764 houses it owned, as well as to the thousand houses owned by occupants but located on company land. It also distributed water to two incorporated villages on land that it did not own. The company did not charge its tenants for water, but it charged the villages substantially.[23] Calumet & Hecla was one of the better-equipped companies, though; only a little more than half of the company houses in the Copper Country had running water in 1913.[24] This compares favorably to Homestead, Pennsylvania, an industrial community in which the companies did not generally own the housing, where in 1910 slightly more than half of the English households surveyed had running water but only three of the 239 Slavic families did, reflecting the poorer living conditions of non-English-speaking immigrants.[25]

The Bathtub

Bathtubs were omnipresent before running water; a large, portable container could be brought out as necessary, filled with water from pails, and used where convenient. For the upper class, this was in the bedroom, to which servants would bring the water. For the working class, the kitchen served this purpose. Bathing once a week was considered sufficient and, because of the difficulty of transporting, heating, and disposing of the water, the bathwater was shared among family members. Once the tub was attached to pipes, however, it needed a permanent location, usually in a dedicated space. Workers' houses rarely had such a space available.

Increasingly through the nineteenth century, the frequency of bathing correlated with social status. Historians Richard Bushman and Claudia Bushman traced a "culture of cleanliness" that developed in the nineteenth century. Although bathing was hardly seen as desirable at the end of the eighteenth century, its popularity grew due to a combination of religious acceptability and medical imprimatur; by the early nineteenth

Running water was by no means universal in the early twentieth century. Running water—water piped into a house from a centralized source—was most easily obtained in urban areas, where the density of households provided efficiencies. Mining towns are remote but dense, thus requiring city services on a small scale, and it fell to the mining companies to equip these settlements with utilities for company houses and noncompany houses alike. Needing a steady water supply to create steam to power massive engines, mining companies were experienced with piped water. Calumet & Hecla (C&H), the largest and most profitable of the copper-mining compa-

century cleanliness was regarded as a mark of gentility. The middle class took up routine personal washing by the mid-nineteenth century, to the extent that it became a sign of civilization and a moral force.[26] As Boston mayor Josiah Quincy declared, "The advance of civilization is largely measured by the victories of mankind over its greatest enemy—dirt."[27] By the late nineteenth century, middle- and upper-class Americans were looking askance at "the great unwashed," and reformers encouraged bathing opportunities for the masses. The influx of eastern and southern European immigrants into the United States at the turn of the century meant that the immigrants were often associated with the unwashed, their class and ethnicity conflated. While some reformers believed that cleanliness would elevate them morally, others equated it with their assimilation as Americans. In an article entitled "Americanization by Bath," Albert Wilhelm argued that daily bathing "had a very beneficial effect upon the foreign element. . . . It has tended to make them more cleanly in their homes, also in the shops and factories, and has undoubtedly made them more self-respecting. . . . They are neater in their attire, and the women take more pride in the appearance of their homes."[28] Wilhelm believed that bathing would somehow inculcate immigrants with middle-class American values.

But as Anzia Yezierska pointed out, immigrants bathed rarely because they did not have the facilities and opportunity, not because they did not desire to be clean. Yezierska, who wrote searingly about her experience as a Russian immigrant, also took the guidance that was given her—"Soap and water are cheap. Anyone can be clean"— and pointed out that cleanliness was a superficiality that one class used to exclude another. She described "agents of clean society" dismissing her from consideration for jobs because of her shabby clothes and personal appearance. The low wages she earned prevented her from getting better clothes, and the long hours she worked did not leave time for a luxury like a bath, even if her house had had a bathtub.[29]

Alternatives to private bathtubs included commercial bathhouses, which seem to have been lo-cated in every city and small town. Commercial bathhouses were available in the Copper Country as early as 1862 and probably even earlier, and continued to be built into the twentieth century. In 1906, Samara Gennette built a new building in Hancock that contained a saloon on the first floor, apartments on the upper floors, and a barbershop and bathhouse in the basement. As the newspaper described it, "Connected with the barber shop is a number of bath rooms, which are first-class in every respect and include regular tub baths, steam and sweat baths with dressing and cooling rooms adjoining. The dressing rooms are provided with individual lockers for the use of the patrons of the place, and it is Mr. Genette's [sic] plan to provide sleeping rooms for those of the patrons who wish them."[30] This bathhouse probably had an exclusively male clientele, which may have been true of other commercial bathhouses as well.

The Finnish population, the largest ethnic group in the region, composing 13 percent of the county's population in 1910, preferred the use of steam baths known as saunas.[31] Rather than being solely for achieving cleanliness, saunas also served a social purpose important in Finnish culture, with people bathing together for a shared experience. Individual families built saunas, as circumstances permitted, and bathed together. Childbirth, the administration of folk therapies, and laundering also occurred in saunas.[32] A commercial sauna, where men and women bathed separately, survived in Calumet into the 1990s. Saunas remain a popular diversion in the Copper Country. They also remain essential to some; in the 1990s one elderly resident nearly refused substantial government-funded renovations to his house because the state agency insisted on installing a bathtub. The resident was content with his sauna and saw no need for a bathtub.[33]

Companies also provided bathing facilities for their workforce. At each mine shaft, or sometimes between two shafts, companies built dry houses (also called change houses), which were changing rooms for their employees. At minimum these buildings contained a place to hang work clothes so that they could dry before the next day, a place to change, and washbasins to wash in.

Increasingly, in the early twentieth century, the companies built these dry houses with bathing facilities, especially showers. The Copper Range Company, for example, built a dry house at its Baltic mine in 1907 that included twelve showers and six tubs.[34] Similarly, the North Kearsarge Shaft No. 4 dry house plans from 1913 included five showers for the men, two for the shift bosses, and one for the mine captain.[35] Dry houses were not standard in other mining districts. Coal mining, in particular, was extremely dirty work and companies rarely provided washing facilities at the mine site until required to by legislation in the 1920s.[36] Before then, the burden fell on women to provide washing facilities in their house or yard for their husbands and boarders. Copper-Country women were relieved of this chore due to the prevailing regional custom of companies providing dry houses.

Schools provided another alternative, at least for some children. Painesdale High School, which opened in 1909, included a gymnasium, locker rooms, and showers. Students were required to shower every Monday, an interesting enforcement of the "clean body, clean mind" dictum.[37] The desire to cultivate students who were morally elevated, not only by academic education but also by personal cleanliness and exercise, was clear here, especially when considering that most of the high school population were children of immigrants—the very population that middle-class Americans thought most needed instruction in middle-class American mores.

Workers desired private bathtubs; as one labor official said, "the workers like to have bathrooms in their houses and leisure time enough to use them."[38] The companies were reluctant to supply workers' houses with bathtubs, seeing it as an expensive undertaking. Not only would the company have to purchase an enameled-metal tub, but a hot-water boiler—not previously supplied in company houses—was implied by the installation of the tub. Piping and drains would add to the cost. So the more established companies opted for a centralized solution: public bathhouses for the use of employees and their families. The three largest companies put these bathing facilities in the basements of buildings that had other facilities for workers: Calumet & Hecla in the basement of its $40,000 library, built in 1898; Copper Range Consolidated Company in the basement of its library, built in 1903; and Quincy Mining Company in the basement of its clubhouse, which also contained a small library, in 1916–17. In 1911, Calumet & Hecla built a separate bathhouse.

These company-provided bathhouses shared many similarities with municipal bathhouses, which were built in this period at the urging of reformers. Like those, the company bathhouses were constructed for the general benefit of the population, not for profit—Calumet & Hecla operated its bathhouse at a loss of about $7,000 per year, not including the $45,000 cost of construction.[39] The companies also had other motives consistent with corporate paternalistic behavior designed to keep their workers loyal. But company management was affected by trends in urban reform as well.

Because of the association of cleanliness with moral uplift and civilization in the middle-class mind, Progressive reformers latched onto public bathhouses as a municipal obligation. Toilets and sewage systems also received some attention, but they did not have the cachet or acceptability in public discourse that bathhouses did, so they appeared more rarely in Progressive literature. The reformers' efforts were impressive: by 1912 more than forty cities operated bathhouses year-round.[40] Historians have explored various aspects of this public effort. In 1979, David Glassberg presented bathhouses as a civic effort emblematic of Progressive Era reform but rooted in Victorian Era concerns with morality. Public bathhouses, he argued, were designed to sanitize and control the poor, not introduce them to middle-class life.[41] In 1991, Marilyn Thornton Williams examined various permutations of bathhouses—outdoor and indoor, some with swimming pools, gymnasia, and laundries—in five major American cities. She found a diverse array of reformers and politicians involved in promoting bathhouses, suggesting a complexity of motivations.[42] More recently, Andrea Renner, in her study of New York City bathhouses, pointed out how the designs reinforced class divisions.

While bathhouses might have been seen as elements of social control by their proponents, she showed how the behavior of their working-class patrons undermined that control.[43]

For our purposes, though, the question is the extent to which these bathhouses filled the void created by the lack of a bathroom in working-class houses. Without first-hand accounts of the bathing preferences of these residents, study of the bathhouses themselves leads to some understanding about how they might have been used. There were some consistent aspects to these company bathhouses. Men's and women's usage of the facilities was strictly separated, with Calumet & Hecla and Quincy offering separate bathing rooms. At Copper Range men and women were assigned different days on which to use the four tubs in the library basement.[44] Calumet & Hecla, which provided more and better amenities for its employees than other companies, built the earliest and grandest bathing facilities. In its library, patrons descending to the basement were separated halfway down the stairs, channeled into their own gender-segregated bathroom (Figure 4). The tubs and showers for men and tubs for women were immediately popular; six months after opening, the company reported that they had "barely been equal to the demands made upon them by both men and women."[45] The original plans had allowed for expansion—apparently, Calumet & Hecla wanted to see how popular the bathing facilities were—and it soon added more bathtubs for men.[46] The custom of the weekly bath endured; the librarian noted that men were turned away every Friday and Saturday because of inadequate water supply. Nonetheless, the librarian reported that 24,675 men and 7,951 women used the facilities in 1906.[47]

The company's general manager soon began planning a purpose-built bathhouse and asked the head librarian, Marie Grierson, for advice. She recommended doubling the number of showers and baths and providing "comfortable waiting rooms."[48] Opened in December 1911, the bathhouse contained a swimming pool as well as bathing facilities (Figure 5). The raised one-story Italian Renaissance brick building had a low profile with a flat roof and broad eaves. Two

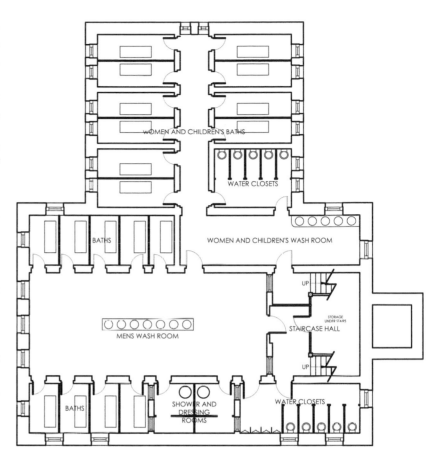

WOMEN AND CHILDREN'S BATHS

WATER CLOSETS

BATHS

WOMEN AND CHILDREN'S WASH ROOM

UP

STORAGE UNDER STAIRS

STAIRCASE HALL

UP

MENS WASH ROOM

BATHS

SHOWER AND DRESSING ROOMS

WATER CLOSETS

BASEMENT

SCALE

0   5   10   20 FEET

PLAN NORTH

Figure 4. Plan of basement, Calumet & Hecla Public Library. Built in 1898, the library had a bathhouse in the basement, offering toilets, baths, and showers to gender-segregated users. Courtesy of NPS, Keweenaw NHP, drawn by Quentin Peterson in 2004, based on original drawings.

Figure 5. Calumet & Hecla Bathhouse, Calumet. Opening in 1911, the company bathhouse was built in response to the popularity of the baths in the library. Courtesy of Michigan Technological Archives and Copper Country Historical Collections, Neg. No. 02389.

Figure 6. Basement and first-floor plans, Calumet & Hecla Bathhouse, 1910 and 1911. Women's facilities were on the right and men's on the left; both had access to the swimming pool. Courtesy of Michigan Technological Archives and Copper Country Historical Collections, C&H Drawings Collection.

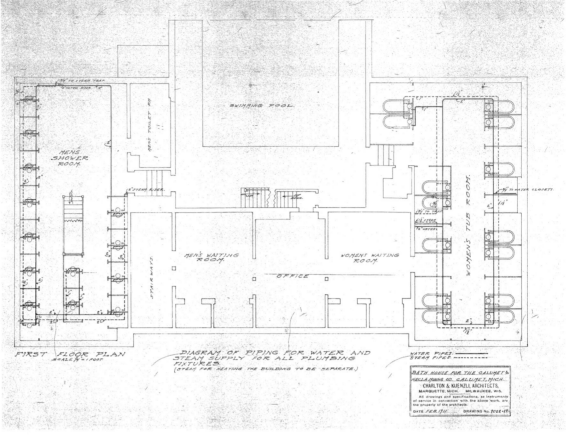

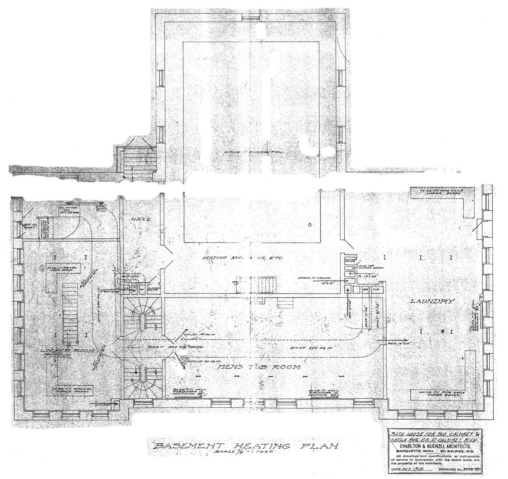

exterior stairways led into separate waiting rooms for men and women (Figure 6). Men were routed downstairs, either to the tub room or to the locker room, where they would leave their clothes before going upstairs to shower prior to going to the pool (Figure 7). The women's waiting room led to their tub room, which had fourteen bathtubs in private cubicles but no lockers or showers, despite Librarian Grierson's recommendation that a couple of showers in the women's department might be welcome (Figure 8). After a bath, the women could enter the pool room.

This fifteen-foot-high space, lit by a skylight as well as other windows, contained the 26-foot-by-40-foot pool (Figure 9). Use of the pool was strictly segregated by gender, and men and boys swam naked.[49] The motivation for the inclusion of a swimming pool in the bathhouse is suggested by the Progressive reformist literature, which identified two claims for swimming pools in bathhouses: exercise and cleanliness. On the one hand, reformer Josiah Quincy assured fellow reformers, swimming was recreation, and at a time when playgrounds were being urged as a municipal responsibility, swimming pools were certainly justified as a public expenditure. On the other hand, pools put people in the "habit of bathing," enticing nonbathers into the custom of immersion in water. Pools aided the cleanliness cause by getting people—especially boys—into water.[50]

A grand public bathhouse runs the risk of alienating the very people for whom it is intended. As Librarian Grierson cautioned, "the use of such a bath house will depend so much upon its location and its management."[51] Its location in Calumet was convenient: in the heart of the industrial district, next to the railroad roundhouse, near the library. To run the bathhouse C&H selected Mr. Evelyn Carter, who had been in charge of the baths in the library.[52] The bathhouse was open to all, not just Calumet & Hecla employees and their families. Charging three cents for men, two-and-a-half cents for boys, and nothing for women and children, and by offering coupon books to further reduce the rates, the bathhouse saw 40,413 bathers in its first year, 1912, and 62,286 in 1915.[53]

Figure 7. Men's showers, Calumet & Hecla Bathhouse, photographed circa 1912. The men's area was equipped with showers. The staircase in the center led to the lockers in the basement. Courtesy of Michigan Technological Archives and Copper Country Historical Collections, MS003 25A-48-03829.

Figure 8. Women's tub room, Calumet & Hecla Bathhouse, photographed circa 1912. The women's area had fourteen bathtubs in cubicles. Courtesy of NPS, Keweenaw NHP, Foster Collection, C&H Public Library Photo #355.

The company endeavored to respond to the needs of the bathhouse's patrons. Initially, the company charged five cents to users between 10:00 a.m. and 2:00 p.m., apparently to reserve this time for wealthier users. But the baths received little patronage then, so the bathhouse operator, Evelyn Carter, dropped the extra charge, seemingly not caring to be exclusive. Instead, he tried to attract more boys, proposing the addition of free hours for them. His justification for the open hours was that some boys wanted to swim so badly that they stole, as Carter put it, "on account of the questionable ways some boys obtain money and coupons for towels." The response of the company's general manager was apparently favorable, because the charge for boys was dropped entirely. Users of the pool were required to bathe first, and an attendant checked them for skin rashes and dirty feet before they were allowed in the pool.[54]

Figure 9. Swimming pool, Calumet & Hecla Bathhouse. Men and women were allotted separate hours for using the pool. Courtesy of Michigan Technological Archives and Copper Country Historical Collections, MS003–012–GN132.8.

Women were allowed to bathe free but here, as in most public baths, women were less frequent users. Women used the bathhouse at less than half the rate of men. They also had fewer hours allocated to them in the pool: originally only ten per week, as opposed to forty-seven for men and thirteen for boys. To some extent this reflected demand. Reformers mentioned several reasons for women's lesser rates of patronage, including modesty, household duties, and women's difficulty in drying their hair.[55] Another aspect of women's usage was that they were often accompanied by children. Children, defined in the bathhouse regulations as girls under the age of twelve and boys under the age of ten, had to be accompanied by an adult female. Originally the women's hours in the pool were limited to ten a.m. to noon, but Carter added afternoon and Saturday morning hours "during school season" to accommodate the children that women cared for. Further recognizing the presence of children, the bathhouse provided an attendant in the pool area "to safeguard against accident" during the women's and boys' hours, but not the men's.[56]

Despite the bathhouse's immense popularity, there was unevenness in public acceptance. As noted, women used the bathhouse less than men. In addition, non-English-speaking immigrants probably used it less than American and British residents. The bathhouse also benefited those who lived closer; the company provided no bathing opportunities to its more distant mine towns. Nonetheless, the company considered its obligations toward public cleanliness fulfilled with the construction of the bathhouse. There would be no tubs in company houses.

Instead, the working class took advantage of various alternatives—or none. They might have used the company-provided bathhouse, if it were close enough to be convenient. Finnish immigrants would have used saunas and some people might have used commercial bathhouses. Students, where required, would have showered at the high school and men would have washed—if not showered—at their workplace. Most people, though—especially women—would have washed at home in the kitchen. They might have filled a tub once a week, but more likely they washed face and hands regularly and took a sponge bath on occasion.

The Toilet

Before the introduction of the toilet into working-class houses, the privy was the most common receptacle of body waste. These wood-sided small buildings usually stood at the back of the yard. The vault would be cleaned out once a year or so, depending on the largesse of the company.[57] The privy looked orderly and seemed properly separated from the rest of the family's activities. One supplement to the privy, though, was the chamber pot, which would be used in the bedroom during the night. In the morning emptying it into the privy and cleaning it would be women's work, one of their most distasteful tasks. Sometimes no facility at all was used; in the iron range town of Sagola, Michigan, one young couple who rented a company house complained about the boardinghouse next door, where men urinated from the second-story windows into their yard.[58]

The toilet, a plumbed fixture that disposed of body waste, was the most difficult element of the three-fixture bathroom to acquire. Its waste had to be carefully disposed due to the threat to human health, so either a cesspool or a sewer system was involved. The toilet also demanded its own private location, much as the bathtub did. The challenge of finding space for the indoor toilet generated a variety of responses. In places where the climate permitted pipes to run under houses or porches without masonry foundations, toilets could be added in small closets on the rear porch. Geographer Paul Groth notes that these back-porch toilets were added after 1920 to pre-existing houses in West Oakland, California.[59] In 1917 in Birmingham, Alabama, the Republic Iron and Steel Company replaced privies along the alleys of Thomas, its company town, with flushing toilets. Not until private owners acquired the houses after 1949 were indoor toilets installed, along with other bathroom fixtures.[60] In the Copper Country, where freezing temperatures were a consideration, the most common solution was to put the toilet in the basement.[61]

Traditionally, the main function of the cellar was for cold storage for dairy products or fruits and vegetables. For many, that remained its function into the twentieth century, although urban and upper-class dwellers had long located kitchens and laundries in well-equipped basements.[62] By 1907, the treatise "Sanitation in the Modern Home" assumed that the cellar would contain a toilet, laundry, furnace, coal room, tool room, vegetable room, fruit room, and wine room, along with a cement floor, ample windows, and gas lighting.[63] By contrast, a 1914 bulletin, *Houses for Mining Towns,* recommended the construction of only a small cellar—8-foot square—for cold storage.[64] Clearly, cellars were a marker of social class, and greater incomes earned more rooms not only in visible spaces, but also belowground. In the Copper Country, cellars that had been built to keep the structure dry soon found a new use as the location of the toilet.

In 1914, tenants of nineteen houses owned by the Calumet & Hecla Mining Company petitioned for changes to their dwellings. Built in 1900, the nineteen houses were all alike: wood frame, two stories, gambrel roofs, and five rooms (Figure 10). They were small, with just 450 square feet of living space on each floor (Figure 11). The plan shows some extra spaces, such as the small front hall and upstairs closet, that reveal a subtle shift toward middle-class amenities. Over the next quarter century, working-class houses such as these would acquire not only bathrooms but also porches, dining rooms, more closets, and other markers of middle-class status.[65] Here, the

tenants asked that a room be added to each house and that a toilet be placed in the basement. They did not ask for the toilet to be put in the addition; they needed that room for additional living space. In response, the company agreed to put toilets in each basement, but declined to build additions.[66]

By 1914 all of Calumet & Hecla's houses had running water. The company had also built a sewer system and gradually began installing toilets and connecting them to the system, so that by 1914 nearly half of the company's houses had indoor toilets. Other companies were not so generous, though, and across the Copper Country only 15 percent of the company houses had sewage connections.[67] Sewers were not always a foregone conclusion, either. In 1897, residents of Laurium, a newly established village, considered the installation of sewers and initially voted against them. One advocate of rejection argued that for a village with a lot of houses not yet paid for, carrying a debt of $35,000 or $40,000 against the village would be too much. Secondly, because Laurium residents received piped water and did not use wells in their yards, the use of privies was less of a health concern. Finally, he pointed out that few residents could afford to have fixtures installed to take advantage of the sewer system; he put the cost at $100 to $150 per house. Laurium soon reversed itself, however, and sewers were under construction a few months later.[68]

Figure 10. Calumet & Hecla houses, photographed in 1913. Tenants of houses such as these requested the installation of toilets in 1914. Note the privies in the yards, along with a shared barn. Courtesy of Michigan Technological Archives and Copper Country Historical Collections, Neg. No. 02408.

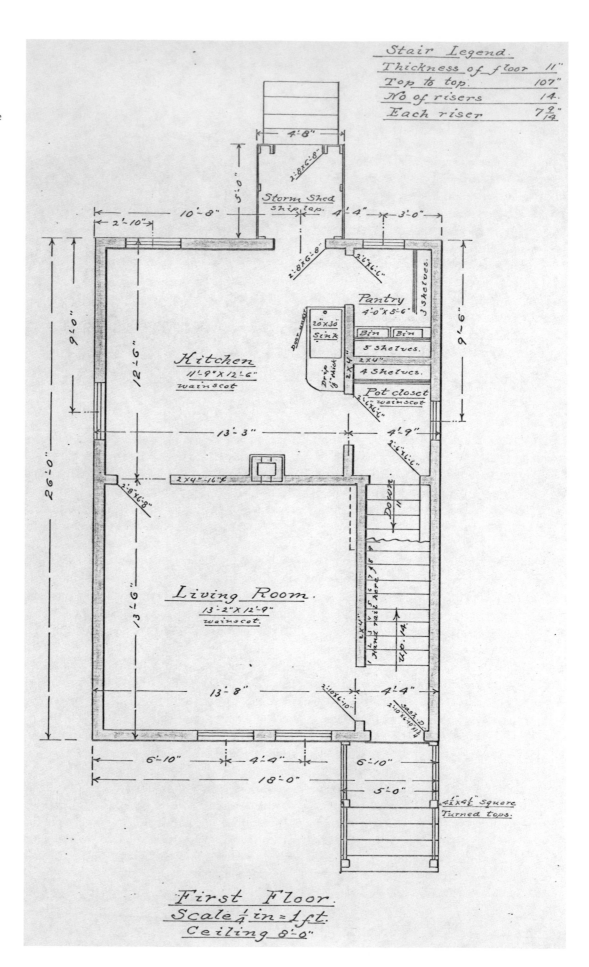

Figure 11. First- and second-floor plans, Calumet & Hecla houses, 1899. Plans of the 18-foot-by-26-foot houses shown in Figure 10 indicate the lack of space for a bathroom. Courtesy of Michigan Technological Archives and Copper Country Historical Collections, C&H Drawings Collection.

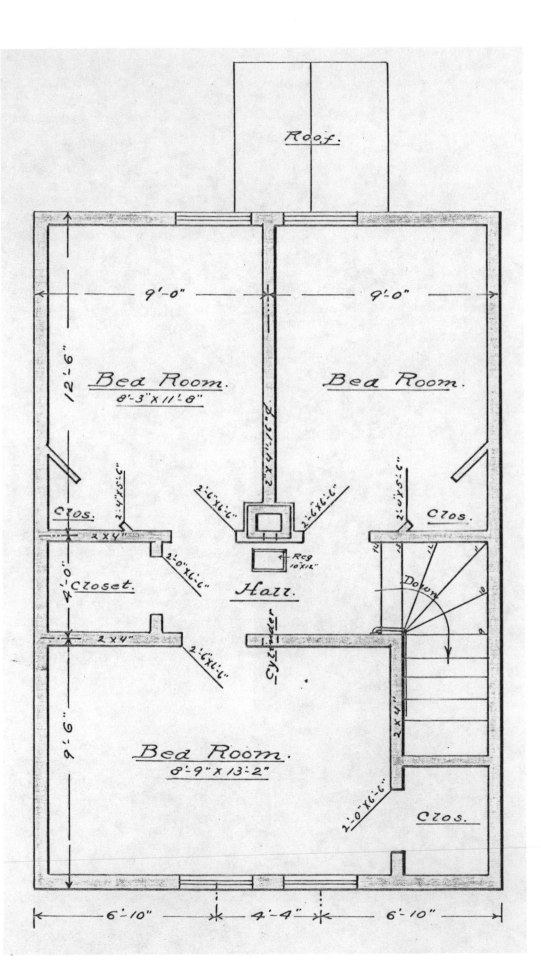

In Calumet & Hecla's company houses, most of the retrofitted toilets were placed in basements (Figure 12).[69] Toilets also appeared in the basements of houses of other mining companies, as well as in houses that had no connection to the mining companies. The basement toilet is not to be confused with those in houses of the elite, who put toilets in basements for the use of their servants who worked down there. Rather, these toilets were in the basement because installation was cheaper and there was, simply, no room elsewhere.[70] The toilet would have been enclosed in a wooden privy-like room.[71] The cellar remained dimly lit and dirt-floored; the stone walls were sometimes whitewashed. These dark and dank cellars were the opposite of the bright and sanitary bathroom promoted by reformers. There was often no room for a decent stairway to the basement, either; entry was usually through a trap door and down a steep flight of stairs (Figure 13).

It is difficult to find much discussion of toilets, or even bathrooms, for that matter, due to general squeamishness about such a highly personal matter. While advertisements and home-improvement magazines often give insight into middle-class behavior, those outlets were less interested in the working class, and it is hazardous to rely on reformers' understandings.[72] The collection of letters to Calumet & Hecla's general manager written by employees seeking to have toilets and other amenities installed is thus especially valuable.[73] Despite the difficulty of access and the downright creepiness of many dirt-floored basements, residents thought of these toilets as conveniences, and that is the word they used in their written requests for installation.[74] Indoor toilets were not necessities; privies worked just fine, after all. But an indoor toilet was a convenience and an outdoor facility an annoyance. Engineer John Hicks explained, "It being very inconvenient for grown people (especially women folks) and almost impossible for small children (especially in the winter time), to use the old fashioned toilets now in the back yard." Miner Thomas Ellis wrote, "It would be more convenient for my family because I have three children." Patternmaker Thomas Cocking cited the burden the privy imposed on his wife: "I have four small children and it is very inconvenient for my wife to be running out side so many times a day." Only one used the word "necessity": "Will you please investigate and consider the absolute necessity of a toilet. . . .The one now in use is so near the back entrance so that in the summer months it is very disagreeable." Several others commented on the inadequacy of the existing privy: "because the one we got now is all rotten"; "the out side toilet makes an awful odor at this time of the year"; "the old one which we have now is about 12 to 13 ft. away from the kitchen, which makes a very bad smell in the summer time and brings many flies"; "because the out house, cause such an awful smell in the warm weather on account of the box leaking."[75]

Figure 12. Toilet in basement, 19604 Sampson, Hancock. With so little space to spare, toilets were commonly placed in basements. Photographed by author in 2006.

Figure 13. Stairway to basement, 50802 Mesnard, Quincy Hill. Access to this Quincy Mining Company basement, which had a toilet, was through a trap door in the kitchen and down a steep flight of stairs. Photographed by author in 2005.

Some of the petitioners cited illness of someone in the family. Mrs. George Gipp wrote, "For my mother is with me and she is blind and it is pretty hard to lead her when you got your work to do." Brakeman Daniel Macdonald wrote, "My wife is troubled with rheumatism and being out in the cold bothers her." William Becker said, "My wife is in poor health and it [an indoor toilet] would be more convenient for her."[76]

Mrs. Fred Lebeau presented a particularly compelling case. The company initially refused her request because the sanitary sewer had not reached her location. Six months later, she wrote again, elaborating on her request. First, she mentioned her sick daughter: "The old one of my family has tuberculoses in the knee who walks with crutches she is a little better. But I think she will have it all winter with her crutches." Then she mentioned her own illness: "And another thing I have the same sickness in my right hand. It is seventine weeks. It is that I do not work with it, I have my hand rapped up like a broken arm." Then the difficulty of doing her housework: "You can see just one hand to do the work. And the care of seven children. The oldest one aged 13 years is sick since one year." She also took in two boarders out of need: "So that I can pay the expenses of my washing outside and a dressmaker to repare the clothes of the family. You see it is very hard for me to do my work." She made a final plea: "I want to ask you again to put the Water Closet in the house because to send the children outside in the Closet it is impossible." She then addressed the technological challenges: "You have already told me that the sours [sewers] were not good [i.e., the nearest sewer was not sanitary] but I think if you want it isn't for one Closet more [meaning, one more hook-up will not add too much to the non-sanitary sewer]." In reply, the general manager noted again that the sanitary sewer had not arrived in her neighborhood, and he declined to add any sewerage to the other line: "There is so much sewage going into the Calumet Pond at the present time we cannot possibly increase it." He held out hope that the sanitary sewer would be extended to her street the following spring.[77]

Mrs. Lebeau's situation was extreme, but her letter raises several points. The presence of illness, young children, and boarders added to housework, and an indoor toilet lessened that burden. Negotiating an outdoor privy with the sick or disabled, or supervising children's use of a privy, were additional difficulties. Existing privies were too far away in winter and too close in summer, when the smells were overwhelming. They were, most of all, inconvenient. These householders desired the convenience of indoor plumbing and, for most, placing a toilet in the basement was convenient enough.

What if there was no basement? Many of the workers' houses had been built on wood posts, but as a means of protecting its investment the companies sometimes installed stone foundations after construction. A cold cellar could be easily enlarged by digging into the ground; these were, after all, miners accustomed to moving earth. In some houses, though, homeowners searched for other places to put the toilet. In 1960 new owners of one former company house, which the Huron Mining Company had built on wood posts in the late nineteenth century, abandoned the yard pump and privy. They installed running water in the kitchen and placed a toilet under the stairs, in the downstairs bedroom (Figures 14 and 15). Built as a five-room house, it was occupied until 2000 without ever having had a three-fixture bathroom installed. The

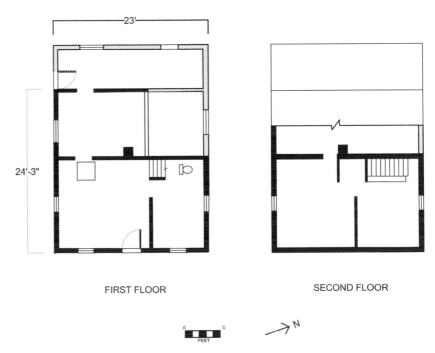

Figure 14. First- and second-floor plans, Huron Mining Company house, Frog Pool Lane, Houghton, probably built in the late nineteenth century. Beginning as an L-shaped, three-room plan, this house was expanded. In 1960 the toilet was added under the stairs; the house did not have a basement. Measured by Carol MacLennan and author in 2003, drawn by author.

FIRST FLOOR

SECOND FLOOR

Figure 15. Huron Mining Company house, Frog Pool Lane, Houghton. The small house never had a three-fixture bathroom installed, although it was occupied until its demolition in 2003. Photographed by author in 2003.

Figure 16. Calumet & Hecla houses, Ninth Street, Lake Linden. These houses built for stamp-mill workers did not contain any space for bathrooms. Photographed by author in 2009.

family, which included seven children, bathed and did laundry in a nearby stream.[78]

Another alternative was to place bathroom fixtures in newly acquired closets. This involved a different kind of trade-off, with one achievement, a storage area rarely found in nineteenth-century workers' houses, being sacrificed for the amenity of the toilet. In the one-and-a-half-story, 22-foot-by-26-foot houses owned by Calumet & Hecla, there were two closets on the second floor, one opening off the hall and one off of a bedroom (Figures 16 and 17). In at least one instance, the closet toward the front of the house was occupied by a toilet and the closet behind it by the bathtub. Each fixture filled up its allotted space, leaving no room for a sink; occupants used the one in the kitchen for all sink functions.[79]

The introduction of the indoor toilet changed not only the space it went into but also the space it left—the yard. In a sense, the introduction of domestic technologies caused the yard to move indoors. The disappearance of the privy was the most visible evidence of this shift. The elimination of this outbuilding also meant that several daily trips through the yard by every member of the family were no longer necessary. The introduction of running water also made the use of a well and pump unnecessary. With central heating, fuel as well as furnace was located in the basement, so a woodpile in the yard was no longer needed. Processed food and refrigeration gradually reduced the need for fruit and vegetable gardening as well as to tend animals.[80] Laundry moved indoors with the acquisition of new appliances.

At the cusp of all these changes, photographs of two yards in the company town of Painesdale illustrate their uses (Figures 18 and 19). Both yards are hard-packed earth, one with a bit of grass, and are enclosed by rough fencing. Both are occupied by fowl—chickens and ducks. One yard appears to accommodate a cow, which would have been taken to graze off-site. Privies are located in the rear of the yard—two privies for the double house and a single one for the small house that at one point was occupied by thirteen adults and four children.[81] Neither yard shows any evidence of gardening, despite a flowerpot in a window, but one occupant probably gardened on an adjacent vacant lot. In some photographs laundry hangs on a line. There is also a woodpile. The yard was indisputably a place of work.[82]

As Christopher Grampp has shown, as domestic functions moved indoors, yards increasingly became devoted to recreation and leisure, changing from a functional—even unsanitary—landscape into a decorative garden. But Grampp dismissed the nineteenth-century urban yard too easily; he called it "only meagerly habitable" and said it was "a neglected, utilitarian space with little or no value for gathering or socializing."[83] Yet photographs of Copper Country yards in 1913 and beyond indicate otherwise. In the yard of the boarding house, described above,

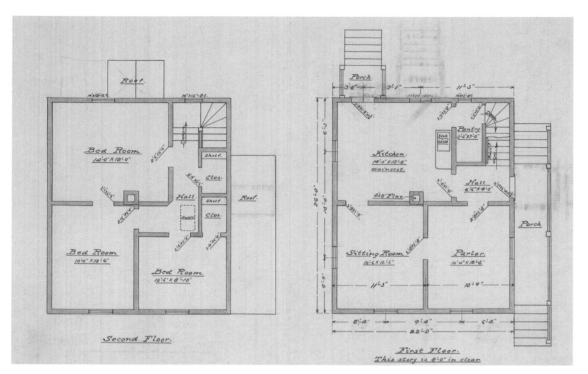

Figure 17. First- and second-floor plans of houses of the type pictured in Figure 16, undated Calumet & Hecla drawings. In at least one house of this type built on Ninth Street in Lake Linden, the tenants converted the closets on the second floor to their preferred uses. They put a toilet in the front closet and a bathtub in the rear one. Courtesy of Michigan Technological Archives and Copper Country Historical Collections, MS005–31A–17C–6271.

Figure 18. Unidentified double house. The fenced yard contained various outbuildings for livestock, as well as two privies. Courtesy of Michigan Technological Archives and Copper Country Historical Collections, Neg. No. 00351.

Figure 19. Putrich House yard. Seeberville, Painesdale, photographed in 1913. The back of this single house shows livestock, a washtub, and firewood. Food preparation, laundry, and fuel would all move indoors in the next few decades. Courtesy of Michigan Technological Archives and Copper Country Historical Collections, Acc. No. 06–087A–01–07–07.

the men would bowl using a ball suspended from a tall pole. Although workers' houses were not equipped with porches, several yards had hammocks, indicating leisure use. Another, in a 1913 photograph, had a swing set.[84] With a 50-foot-by-100-foot lot as the norm, clearly Copper Country yards afforded more space than urban working-class districts, yet we should not underestimate the multiple functions that a yard could serve.

Nonetheless, bringing various yard functions into the house changed the yard dramatically. And just as the house was figuratively pulling into itself, it was also reaching out through various technological systems. Plumbing, sewerage,

gas, and electricity all tied the houses into larger, often invisible networks. Eventually, after incremental achievements and partial solutions, these systems would facilitate the creation of a new space.

The Three-Fixture Bathroom

This examination of bathroom fixtures demonstrates that the three-fixture bathroom was a step removed from bringing water and sewer to a house. Connecting a house to piped water and a sewage system or cesspool did not automatically produce a bathroom. Working-class occupants were anxious to receive the conveniences of sink, toilet, and bathtub, but the installation of these items was not predicated on the availability of a room for these functions, nor did it instantly produce such a room. The indoor toilet, the private bathtub, and the sink for personal cleanliness were achievements separate from the appearance of a bathroom.

Working-class residents did desire three-fixture bathrooms, although it was usually the children or grandchildren of the generation that received basement toilets who finally obtained the complete bathroom. Companies were unwilling to build additions for bathrooms, but once the houses went into private ownership—which occurred in the Copper Country from the late 1930s to the present—the new homeowners made these additions. They took different approaches but the new bathrooms tended to be located on the first floor, still some distance from second-floor bedrooms, and somewhat cobbled together using a variety of materials. Reformers, designers, and advertisers urged sanitary finishes, convenient placement, and unified designs—qualities these retrofitted bathrooms did not have. But the three-fixture bathroom was increasingly seen as essential. Three houses illustrate the rising expectations for bathrooms.

Calumet & Hecla built a wood-frame house, 30 feet by 22 feet, divided in two units, some time in the late nineteenth century (Figures 20 and 21). In 1914, timberman John Messner requested that the company put a toilet in this company house "for the sake of Father," who apparently lived with him. The cellar was 6 feet 10 inches high, reached through a trap door in the kitchen. There were few options for placement: the 550 square feet of his half of the first floor of the house were occupied by a parlor, dining room, kitchen, and pantry; on the second floor there were two bedrooms under the low gable roof. The general manager granted Messner's request, and the company installed a toilet in the basement, underneath the dining room.[85] At some point, a shower and a sink were also installed in the basement, although underneath the kitchen, not adjacent to the toilet. An interior stairway to the basement was added, easing the trip to this sprawling bathroom. After the company had sold the house in the late 1930s, the new homeowner

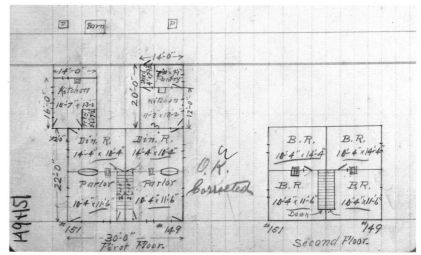

built a small bathroom, with just a sink and toilet, in the rear of the kitchen. It was not very conveniently located, but at least it was a first-floor toilet. In 1970, a new owner acquired both halves of the double house, converting it into a single unit, a fairly common treatment of these small double houses. He changed the 11-foot-by-13-foot room that had been one unit's kitchen into a three-fixture bathroom. It was next to the former dining room, which he used as a bedroom.

Likewise, in a similar double house, 94–96 Pine Street, originally equipped with privies, Calumet & Hecla installed toilets in the basements, which were reached through trap doors in the kitchens. After the house went into private ownership, the two owners took different approaches to installing bathrooms. (Figure 22) In the right half, 96 Pine, Henry Huhtala, a widower, bought the house he had rented for years and lived there with his two bachelor sons. At some point they installed a three-fixture bathroom by taking space from the kitchen, entering

Figure 20. First- and second-floor plans, 149–51 Calumet Avenue, Calumet & Hecla notebook, 1901. A company employee documented a number of extant houses in a small notebook. Here, he indicated the dimensions of rooms in this double house, as well as the location of the privies and the shared barn. At the tenant's request, the company installed a toilet in the basement of the unit on the left. Courtesy of NPS, Keweenaw NHP, Foster Collection, Records of Calumet & Hecla, Dwelling records.

Figure 21. 151 Calumet Avenue, Calumet. After the company sold off the double house, it was converted to a single residence and one kitchen converted to a bathroom. Photographed by author in 2005.

Figure 22. First- and second-floor plans, 94–96 Pine Street, Calumet, documented 1996. In a double house similar to that pictured in Figure 21, homeowners took a different approach to installing bathrooms. One put it in the kitchen and the other in the dining room. The connecting doors between the two units were added much later. Courtesy of Donna Zimmerman.

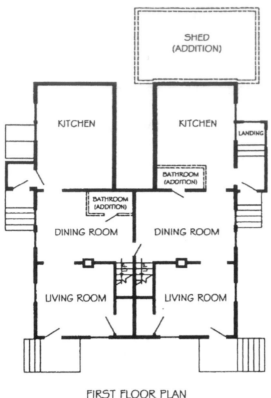

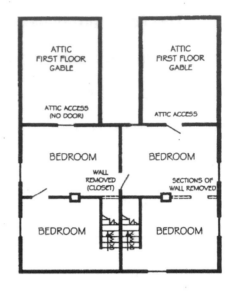

FIRST FLOOR PLAN

0   5   10
SCALE IN FEET

SECOND FLOOR PLAN

0   5   10
SCALE IN FEET

Figure 23. Isle Royale Mining Company houses, No. 2 Location, Houghton, built circa 1899. The house documented in Figure 24 was one of several dozen lining a muddy street in this 1913 photograph. Courtesy Archives of Michigan, Neg. No. 18845.

the bathroom through the dining room. The fixtures—a toilet, a sink, and a stall shower—were aligned along the long wall in the 7-foot-by-4-foot space. The walls were covered with a fiberboard that had a tile-like imprint up to the 4-foot level, imitating a wainscot. Linoleum covered the floor. Next door at 94 Pine, in 1939 Rupert and Kate Laakso bought for twenty-five dollars the company house they occupied. They installed a bathroom in a corner of the dining room, severely limiting the utility of that space. The 7-foot-9-inch-by-3-foot-4-inch bathroom had a toilet, sink, and stall shower, each piped through a different wall. The room was paneled in wood, the ceiling was acoustical tile, and the floor remained tongue-and-groove wood.[86]

Isle Royale Mining Company built five-room, 22-foot-by-25-foot houses near its No. 2 Shaft in 1899–1900 (Figure 23). The company sold off the houses in the 1940s and when the grandson of one of the purchasers moved into the house in 1975, it had been little altered. In 1980, though, the area received water and sewer systems, replacing the need for the hand pump at the kitchen sink and the privy in the yard. The residents carved a 5-foot-6-inch-by-13-foot-6-inch bathroom out of the room that had served as a first-floor bedroom, adding a closet and extending the kitchen into the other part of the former bedroom (Figure 24).[87] The two bedrooms on the second floor were adequate for their needs; the bathroom was much more important to the homeowners than a downstairs bedroom.

In these examples, the bathrooms that resulted were far from the ideals of convenience and aesthetic coherence. They were on the first floor, while bedrooms were on the second (until one resident moved his bedroom to a former dining room). They were awkward spaces—some too big, some too small. They were finished with a variety of materials, ceramic tile not among them. They appear to have all dated after World War II but the prosperity that much of America experienced in the 1950s and 1960s eluded the Copper Country. Homeowners modernized their houses, but not in dramatic or expensive ways.

Also, these examples demonstrate that the

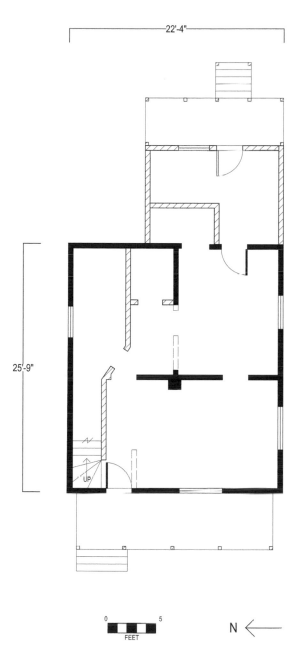

Figure 24. First-floor plan, Isle Royale Mining Company, 47596 Second Street, Houghton. Hatched lines indicate walls added, while dotted lines indicate walls removed. Homeowners put a bathroom in the left rear corner, in what had formerly been a bedroom. Measured by Larry Mishkar, Alicia Valentino, and author in 2002; drawn by author.

three-fixture bathroom was attained at the expense of other rooms: a larger kitchen, a functional dining room, an additional bedroom. Just to obtain the individual fixtures, without a whole bathroom, residents were willing to give up private bedrooms and closets, other hard-won spaces. In small houses every achievement involves a trade-off—one that can reflect the residents' priorities. The three-fixture bathroom was not an easy accomplishment for working-class householders. The mining companies provided baths, but at a public facility. The companies also provided indoor toilets, although in inconvenient spaces. It was the homeowners who built bathrooms for themselves. Three-fixture bathrooms were important to working-class homeowners—so important that they sacrificed other spaces for them and settled for less-than-ideal locations and configurations.

The bathroom's use tends to be a subject that is little discussed. As Ruth Schwartz Cowan has explained, the bathroom changed woman's work, giving her another place to keep clean. It also changed standards of cleanliness, making it easier to take baths more frequently than weekly and demanding a certain level of sanitation.[88] Bathrooms also made houses modern, giving them the latest technologies and housing them in a new, dedicated space.[89] More importantly, bathrooms changed how residents moved through their houses and yards. The letters that deplore the inconvenience of going outside to a privy, maneuvering on crutches, or taking care of young children indicate the importance of a convenient indoor facility. But the bathroom also serves as a significant accomplishment for working-class householders. Examining the methods that workers in one mining community used to get bathrooms reveals the importance they attached to those fixtures and, ultimately, to that space. Nearly all working-class houses nationwide acquired this new space, but its introduction was strategic, idiosyncratic, and incremental.

NOTES

I would like to thank Marta Gutman, Tom Hubka, Louis Nelson, Mark Schara, and Pam Simpson for their suggestions and assistance, as well as the homeowners who let me into their bathrooms. I gave versions of this paper at meetings of the Society for American City and Regional Planning History and the Society for the History of Technology, and I would like to thank those colleagues for their comments.

1. On women's work, see Susan Strasser, *Never Done: A History of American Housework* (New York: Pantheon, 1982); and Ruth Schwartz Cowan, *More Work for Mother: The Ironies of Household Technology from the Open Hearth to the Microwave* (New York: Basic Books, 1983). On status see Thomas Hubka and Judith T. Kenny, "Examining the American Dream: Housing Standards and the Emergence of a National Housing Culture, 1900–30," *Perspectives in Vernacular Architecture* 13, no. 1 (2006): 49–69. On design see Ellen Lupton and J. Abbott Miller, *The Bathroom, the Kitchen, and the Aesthetics of Waste: A Process of Elimination* (Cambridge, Mass.: MIT List Visual Arts Center, 1992). On convenience, see Maureen Ogle, *All the Modern Conveniences: American Household Plumbing, 1840–90* (Baltimore: The Johns Hopkins University Press, 1996).

2. Siegfried Giedion, *Mechanization Takes Command: A Contribution to Anonymous History* (New York: Oxford, 1948), 682, 697.

3. Ogle, *All the Modern Conveniences*, 62, 141.

4. Wm. Paul Gerhard, "Sanitary Questions," in *Cottages; or, Hints on Economical Building*, ed. A. W. Brunner (New York: William T. Comstock, 1884), 46. Merritt Ierley, *The Comforts of Home: The American House and the Evolution of Modern Convenience* (New York: Clarkson Potter, 1999), 142, also notes that J. L. Mott Iron Works' 1884 catalog, titled *The Bath Room Illustrated,* included bathtubs, toilets, and sinks.

5. Gail Caskey Winkler, "Introduction," in *The Well-Appointed Bath: Authentic Plans and Fixtures from the Early 1900s*, ed. Charles E. Fisher III (Washington: Preservation Press, 1989), 15, notes that, of course, these houses cost more. Eight of the thirteen villas pictured in A. J. Downing's *The Architecture of Country Houses* (New York: D. Appleton and Co., 1850) had bathrooms, but only one of the thirteen cottages. Similarly, Gwendolyn Wright found that in 1904 a three-fixture bathroom for a $2,000 house cost $150 to $300. She attributed the absorption of these costs to the growing popularity of smaller, simpler dwellings. Gwendolyn Wright, *Moralism and the Model Home: Domestic Architecture and Cultural Conflict in Chicago, 1873–1913* (Chicago: University of Chicago Press, 1980), 337–38, n. 17.

6. Brunner, *Cottages,* 16. Nonetheless, fifteen of the twenty-three plans published in this book did not include bathrooms.

7. Ierley, *Comforts of Home,* 175, discusses an instance of appropriating a room: David and Ida Eisenhower converted a small first-floor bedroom into the house's first bathroom some time after 1908.

8. Calculating the installation of indoor toilets is a difficult, if not impossible, task. The U.S. Census did not collect this data until 1940, by which time only 55 percent of U.S. households had a bathroom. Ierley, *Comforts of Home*, 220. Some additional figures indicate the scope of the change in the early twentieth century. In 1893, 53 percent of New York's households, 70 percent of Philadelphia's, 73 percent of Chicago's, and 88 percent of Baltimore's had outside privies only. In the late 1920s, 71 percent of urban households and 33 percent of rural ones had indoor toilets. Strasser, *Never Done*, 97, 102–03. In Leifur Magnusson's survey of company towns published in 1920, 93.9 percent had a water system and 60.3 percent had a sanitary sewer. Magnusson, *Housing by Employers* (U.S. Bureau of Labor Statistics, Bulletin No. 263, 1920), 39.

9. Of course, it is difficult to prove a negative. I surveyed the following journals: *Popular Science Monthly* (checked indices, 1900–15); *Domestic Engineering* (skimmed 1905; index for 1910); *Popular Mechanics* (skimmed 1902, indices for 1907 and 1910); *Good Housekeeping* (skimmed first half 1905, first half of 1906, all of 1912); *The House Beautiful* (indices 1900–03, table of contents 1903–05, skimmed 1912–13); *Cosmopolitan* (table of contents 1899–1906); *Journal of Home Economics* (indices 1909–25); *The Engineering Record* (which prior to 1887 was *The Sanitary Engineer*: indices 1894–1905). Also *Engineering Index*, 1884–1906, *Industrial Arts Index*, 1913–21, and *Avery Index*, 1880–1930. Nor did retrofitting appear in manuals, such as Frank E. Kidder, *The Architect's and Builder's Pocket-Book* (New York: John Wiley & Sons, 1908), or R. M. Starbuck, *Modern Plumbing Illustrated* (New York: Norman W. Henley, 1907).

10. Joseph C. Bigott, "Bungalows and the Complex Origin of the Modern House," in *The Chicago Bungalow*, ed. Dominic A. Pacyga and Charles Shanabruch (Chicago: Chicago Architectural Foundation, 2003), 35.

11. J. S. Cocking to James MacNaughton, September 26, 1913, MS-002, Box 47, Folder 501, Michigan Technological University and Copper Country Historical Archives (hereafter MTU). The estimate was in response to a request from Thomas Hall, a mining captain. Bigott, "Bungalows and the Complex Origin," 49, points out that Mott Iron Works offered complete sets in 1914 that ranged from $70 to more than $800, although Sears advertised them in 1910 for as little as $39.

12. On the technology, see Ogle, *All the Modern Conveniences*; and Bigott, "Bungalows and the Complex Origin." Ierley, *The Comforts of Home*, is an example of a more popular work that focuses on the "firsts" in its examination of the available technology. Lawrence Wright, *Clean and Decent: The Fascinating History of the Bathroom and the Water Closet* (New York: Routledge, 1960), looks at the technology in Britain and the United States. On cleanliness, see Richard L. Bushman and Claudia L. Bushman, "The Early History of Cleanliness in America," *Journal of American History* 74, no. 4 (March 1988): 1213–38; they concentrate on the early nineteenth century in tracking changing attitudes. Suellen Hoy, *Chasing Dirt: The American Pursuit of Cleanliness* (New York: Oxford, 1995), examines cleanliness from a public policy perspective.

13. Cowan, *More Work for Mother*; Strasser, *Never Done*.

14. Martin V. Melosi, *The Sanitary City: Urban Infrastructure in America from Colonial Times to the Present* (Baltimore: The Johns Hopkins University Press, 2000); Charles David Jacobson, *Ties That Bind: Economic and Political Dilemmas of Urban Utility Networks, 1800–1990* (Pittsburgh: University of Pittsburgh Press, 2000); Thomas P. Hughes, *Networks of Power: Electrification in Western Society, 1880–1930* (Baltimore: The Johns Hopkins University Press, 1993); Mark H. Rose, *Cities of Heat and Light: Domesticating Gas and Electricity in Urban America* (University Park: Pennsylvania State University, 1995). David E. Nye, *Electrifying America: Social Meanings of a New Technology, 1880–1940* (Cambridge: MIT, 1990), on the other hand, sees electricity as more of a social construction.

15. Hubka and Kenny, "Examining the American Dream," 49–69.

16. One exception is May N. Stone, "The Plumbing Paradox: American Attitudes toward Late Nineteenth-Century Domestic Sanitary Arrangements," *Winterthur Portfolio* 14, no. 3 (Autumn 1979): 283–309, in which she considers the placement of bathrooms in New York row houses in the 1880s.

17. Olivier Zunz, *The Changing Face of Inequality: Urbanization, Industrial Development, and Immigrants*

in Detroit, 1880–1920 (Chicago: University of Chicago Press, 1982), 91–128, discusses the uneven distribution of utilities in an urban setting. Reformers' efforts concentrated on New York tenements, on which there is extensive literature. For a good description of retrofitting one such tenement, see Andrew S. Dolkart, *Biography of a Tenement House in New York City: An Architectural History of 97 Orchard Street* (Santa Fe, N.M.: Center for American Places, 2006).

18. I have previously written about this area in *Mine Towns: Buildings for Workers in Michigan's Copper Country* (Minneapolis: University of Minnesota Press, 2010); this article is drawn from that work. For more on the history of the Copper Country, see Larry Lankton, *Cradle to Grave: Life, Work, and Death at the Lake Superior Copper Mines* (New York: Oxford, 1991); and Larry Lankton, *Hollowed Ground: Copper Mining and Community Building on Lake Superior, 1840s–1990s* (Detroit: Wayne State, 2010).

19. Arthur W. Thurner, *Rebels on the Range: The Michigan Copper Miners' Strike of 1913–14* (privately printed, 1984), 21. Out of a population in Houghton County (the largest of the three counties that make up the Copper Country) of 88,098, just 9,446 people were native-born of native-born.

20. Walter B. Palmer, *Michigan Copper District Strike* (U.S. Department of Labor, Bureau of Labor Statistics, Bulletin 139, 1914), 113–14, 117.

21. Ogle, *All the Modern Conveniences*, 3, makes this same point about toilets; an extensive water system was not necessary for a toilet.

22. For an example of a sink that was never connected to running water, see House no. 18 at Mandan. Shaving mirrors and toothbrush holders were observed in 2004 in the house at 49937 U.S. 41, and the one at 720 (50802) Mesnard, both on Quincy Hill.

23. In 1905 Calumet & Hecla sold 10 percent of its water to the villages of Laurium and Red Jacket and to the Hecla & Torch Lake Railroad, but these three entities paid 54 percent of the cost of the water. In 1908 the company lowered the rate from twenty-five cents per thousand gallons to eighteen cents; the company's cost was less than ten cents. MacNaughton to Agassiz, May 29, 1905, Folder 18; MacNaughton to Agassiz, June 13, 1908, Folder 3; and Agassiz to MacNaughton, June 17, 1908, Folder 3. Letters in MS-002, Box 53, MTU.

24. Palmer, *Michigan Copper District Strike*, 114.

25. Margaret F. Byington, *Homestead: The Households of a Mill Town* (1910; repr., Pittsburgh: University of Pittsburgh Press, 1974), 136–37. The Copper Country was not necessarily any less biased. Recent immigrants were less likely to inhabit company houses, so the company-house statistics inherently favor English-speaking households. See Hoagland, *Mine Towns*, 39, 52–53.

26. Bushman and Bushman, "The Early History of Cleanliness."

27. Josiah Quincy, "Playgrounds, Baths, and Gymnasia," *Journal of Social Science* 36 (December 1898): 142.

28. Albert Wilhelm, "Americanization by Bath," *Literary Digest* 47 (23 August 1913): 280–81. This was an abridged version of the article Wilhelm wrote in *Modern Sanitation*; it is not known what the article was titled in that journal.

29. Anzia Yezierska, "Soap and Water and the Immigrant," *The New Republic* 18, no. 225 (February 22, 1919): 117–19.

30. "New Building Nearly Finished," *Daily Mining Gazette,* November 28, 1906, 2.

31. Arnold R. Alanen and Suzanna E. Raker, "From Phoenix to Pelkie: Finnish Farm Buildings in the Copper Country," in *New Perspectives on Michigan's Copper Country*, ed. Alison K. Hoagland, Erik C. Nordberg, and Terry S. Reynolds (privately printed, 2007), 62.

32. Alanen and Raker, "From Phoenix to Pelkie," 62.

33. Kim Stoker, personal interview in Houghton, Michigan on December 10, 1996.

34. *Engineering & Mining Journal* 94, no. 26 (December 28, 1912): 1230.

35. MS-005, Drawer 199, MTU.

36. Margaret M. Mulrooney, *A Legacy of Coal: The Coal Company Towns of Southwestern Pennsylvania* (Washington, D.C.: Historic American Buildings Survey/Historic American Engineering Record, National Park Service, U.S. Department of the Interior, 1989), 22–23; Crandall A. Shifflett, *Coal Towns: Life, Work, and Culture in Company Towns of Southern Appalachia, 1880–1960* (Knoxville: University of Tennessee Press, 1991), 56.

37. "Painesdale High School an Efficient Institution," *Daily Mining Gazette,* March 21, 1912, 2.

38. Cited by Luke Grant, report of February 27, 1914, U.S. Commission on Industrial Relations, Daily

Reports on Congressional Hearings, Copper Strike, Hancock, Michigan, February–March 1914.

39. Calumet Baths for Years 1913 and 1915, MS-002, Box 212, Folder 33, MTU. U.S. House, Subcommittee of the Committee on Mines and Mining, *Conditions in the Copper Mines of Michigan,* 63rd Cong., 2nd Sess. (Washington, D.C.: GPO, 1914), 1452.

40. Marilyn Thornton Williams, *Washing "The Great Unwashed": Public Baths in Urban America, 1840–1920* (Columbus: Ohio State University Press, 1991), 39. Note that the text says "1922" but the footnote makes it clear that it should be 1912.

41. David Glassberg, "The Design of Reform: The Public Bath Movement in America," *American Studies* 20, no. 2 (Fall 1979): 5–21.

42. Williams, *Washing "The Great Unwashed."*

43. Andrea Renner, "A Nation that Bathes Together: New York City's Progressive Era Public Baths," *Journal of the Society of Architectural Historians* 67, no. 4 (December 2008): 504–31.

44. Jane C. Lucchesi, *History of Sarah Sargent Paine Memorial Library* (privately printed, 1978), 8.

45. Calumet & Hecla Mining Company, *Annual Report for 1899* (privately printed, 1899), unpaginated.

46. "A Boon to the Community!" *Copper Country Evening News,* September 16, 1898, 5.

47. Grierson to MacNaughton, February 19, 1907, MS-002, Box 45, Folder 351, MTU.

48. Grierson to MacNaughton, February 19, 1907, and MacNaughton to Charlton, February 23, 1907, MS-002, Box 45, Folder 351, MTU.

49. Bruce Norden, interviewed by Jo Urion, January 14, 2003, and John and Eleanor Buckett, interviewed by Jo Urion, March 27, 2002, Keweenaw National Historical Park. One reformer, mayor of Boston Josiah Quincy, thought that the need for bathing suits discouraged poor people from using pools, so his city provided bathing suits to children for free and to adults for a small charge. Others thought that removing the requirement for bathing suits entirely was a neater solution. One reformer noted, it "adds extensively to the interest that is taken in the amusement and perhaps even to its benefits." Quincy, "Playgrounds, Baths, and Gymnasia," 146.

50. Quincy, "Playgrounds, Baths, and Gymnasia," 139; Robert E. Todd, "Municipal Baths of Manhattan," *Charities and the Commons* 19 (October 19, 1907): 897; Glassberg, "The Design of Reform," 6; Williams,

Washing "The Great Unwashed," 25–26; Renner, "A National that Bathes Together," 505–06.

51. Grierson to MacNaughton, November 17, 1909, MS-002, Box 45, Folder 351, MTU.

52. Carter to MacNaughton, May 1, 1911, MS-002, Box 212, Folder 33, MTU.

53. Bath reports, MS-002, Box 212, Folder 33, MTU.

54. Carter to MacNaughton, December 18, 1913, MS-002, Box 212, Folder 33, MTU; "Calumet Baths, April 1914," MS-002, Box 212, Folder 33, MTU. Jeff Wiltse, *Contested Waters: A Social History of Swimming Pools in America* (Chapel Hill: University of North Carolina Press, 2007), 40, points out the impact of entrance fees on class stratification. The C&H bathhouse regulations defined boys as males between the ages of ten and sixteen. "Rules of the Calumet Baths of the Calumet & Hecla Mining Company," December 1911, MS-002, Box 353, Folder 006C, MTU. My thanks to Sarah Heald, Heather Lindquist, and Carol MacLennan for making this rule book available to me. Norden and Buckett interviews.

55. Williams, *Washing "The Great Unwashed,"* 136. Marta Gutman, "Race, Place, and Play: Robert Moses and the WPA Swimming Pools in New York City," *Journal of the Society of Architectural Historians* 67, no. 4 (December 2008): 536, 538, also discusses particular restrictions on girls' public bathing and swimming, especially among immigrant families.

56. "Rules of the Calumet Baths," Carter to MacNaughton, December 18, 1913, MS-002, Box 212, Folder 33, MTU.

57. Palmer, *Michigan Copper District Strike,* 115.

58. Paula Stofer, "An Examination of the Socio-Cultural Roles of Boardinghouses and the Boarding Experience on the Michigan Mining Frontier, 1840–1930," (PhD diss., Michigan State University, 1997), 236.

59. Paul Groth, "Workers-Cottage and Minimal-Bungalow Districts in Oakland and Berkeley, California, 1870–1945," *Urban Morphology* 8, no. 1 (2008): 17.

60. J. Lewis Shannon, "Thomas Worker Housing," HAER (Historic American Engineering Collection, Library of Congress) no. AL-121 (1992): 7.

61. Mulrooney, *Legacy of Coal,* 99, notes that in the southwestern Pennsylvania coal country homeowners installed toilets in the basement after acquiring their houses from the company in the 1940s.

62. By the 1880s, sanitation experts advised having a cellar with no function but general sanitation;

one expert recommended a clean, dry cellar and sturdy foundation walls for the general health of the house and its occupants. Gerhard, "Sanitary Questions," in Brunner, *Cottages*, 35–37. If neglected, vegetables stored in cellars would rot; hence the emphasis on cleanliness and light, so that the vegetable matter could be seen. James C. Bayles, *House Drainage and Water Service in Cities, Villages, and Rural Neighborhoods* (New York: David Williams, 1884), 262–63, quoted Henry F. French, *Farm Drainage,* published in the 1860s. While Bayles acknowledged that the description was "drawn with the free hand of caricature," he said it was not greatly exaggerated: "No child whoever saw a cellar afloat during one of these inundations will ever outgrow the impression. You stand on the cellar stairs, and below is a dark waste of waters of illimitable extent. By the dim glimmer of the dip candle a scene is presented which furnishes a tolerable picture of chaos and old night, but defies all description. Empty dry casks, with cider barrels, wash tubs and boxes, ride triumphantly on the surface, while half-filled vinegar and molasses kegs, like water-logged ships, roll heavily below. Broken boards and planks, old hoops and staves, and barrel heads innumerable, are buoyant with this change of the elements, while floating turnips and apples, with here and there a brilliant cabbage head, gleam in the subterranean firmament like twinkling stars, dimmed by the effulgence of the moon at her full. Magnificent among the lesser vessels of the fleet, like some tall admiral, rides the enormous mash-tub, while the astonished rats and mice are splashing about at its base in the dark waters like sailors just washed at midnight from the deck by a heavy sea." John M. Bacon, "Cellars, Garrets, and Related Spaces in Philadelphia Houses, 1750–1850" (Independence National Historical Park, 1991), 21–24. Bacon (165–67) also discusses the various usages of *cellar* and *basement,* conceding that their meanings are commonly undifferentiated today. *Cellar* more commonly referred to a place of storage, while *basement* implied an inhabited story. Similarly, Carl R. Lounsbury, *An Illustrated Glossary of Early Southern Architecture and Landscape* (New York: Oxford, 1994), 24 and 66. Some building codes differentiate between cellar and basement today, with relation to grade being the distinction.

63. Jno. K. Allen, *Sanitation in the Modern Home* (Chicago: Domestic Engineering, 1907), 64–82.

Similarly, Charles E. White, "Often Neglected Opportunities: Basement and Attic," *The House Beautiful* 32, no. 4 (September 1912): 101–02, suggests, in addition to laundry, cool room, and heating apparatus: storage for empty trunks, garage, dustless coal bin, workshop for boys, racks for screens and storm windows, darkroom for photography, and a play room for children.

64. Joseph H. White, *Houses for Mining Towns* (U.S. Department of the Interior, Bureau of Mines, 1914), 37–38; he described this as "a cool place to keep milk and butter, as ice is not available in most mining towns, and furnishes a storage place for vegetables for use during the winter."

65. Hubka and Kenny, "Examining the American Dream," 49–69.

66. MacKenzie et al. to MacNaughton, undated, and MacNaughton to MacKenzie et al., March 28, 1914, MS-002, Box 48, Folder 533, MTU.

67. "List of Company Houses with Inside Closets," October 1911, MS-002, Box 544, Folder 002, MTU. Palmer, *Michigan Copper District Strike,* 114. This compares to Homestead, Pennsylvania. Of the 90 English-speaking households that Margaret Byington surveyed in 1908, 15 had indoor toilets; of the 239 Slavic families she surveyed, none had an indoor toilet. Byington, *Homestead,* 54, 137.

68. "Sewers or No Sewers," *Copper Country Evening News,* March 4, 1897, 8; *Portage Lake Mining Gazette,* August 5, 1897, 3. The sewer system was completed in 1899 but replaced by a new system in 1901. "Sewers Finished," *Hancock Evening Journal,* November 1, 1901, 5.

69. Of the 278 surviving letters concerning toilets, 39 asked that the toilet be put in the basement. It is unclear if that is where the tenant really wanted it, or if that is where he thought the company would put it. Miner Nels Olsen wrote, "I understand the Calumet and Hecla Mining Company is willing to install toilets in the basements of its houses." Nels E. Olsen, April 20, 1914, MS-002, Box 47, Folder 517, MTU. Similarly, miner Michael Sullivan began his letter, "Hearing that the toilletts are being installed in the basements of the homes of those who wish them . . ." Michael Sullivan, May 1, 1914, MS-002, Box 47, Folder 517, MTU.

70. Cost was probably a serious consideration. Ronald Hyrkas, a plumber who has practiced in the Copper Country for thirty years, estimated that it would cost

40 percent more to put a toilet on the second floor—rather than in the basement—of a preexisting house. Personal interview, Houghton, September 10, 2010.

71. Few of these enclosures survive due to the deterioration in wood caused by dampness. Examples survive, among other places, in the Yarbrough House on First Street in Laurium. The prevalence of these enclosures is indicated by the chief carpenter at Calumet & Hecla telling his boss that his staff built "rooms for inclosing" the 162 toilets that were installed in company houses in 1915. J. S. Cocking to James MacNaughton, March 8, 1916, MS002, Box 49, Folder 613, MTU.

72. For example, "The Care of the Bath-Room," *The House Beautiful* 14, no. 2 (July 1903): 124; Russell Fisher, "The Service End of the House," *House and Garden* (August 1910): 94–95; Lizabeth Cohen, "Embellishing a Life of Labor: An Interpretation of the Material Culture of American Working-Class Homes, 1885–1915," in *Common Places: Readings in American Vernacular Architecture*, ed. Dell Upton and John Michael Vlach, 261–78 (Athens: University of Georgia Press, 1986).

73. 278 letters regarding toilets survive; 85 of them were written in response to requests that do not survive. They date between 1912, when the head plumber requested that a policy be outlined, and 1917. "Occupant . . . wants to buy a water closet for same. Are you willing that he should put one in, if so, what are to be the conditions?" Wm. Phillips on behalf of Samuel Jordan, September 27, 1912, MS 002, Box 47, Folder 487, MTU. Letters are in MS-002, Boxes 47 and 48, MTU.

74. Ogle, *All the Modern Conveniences*, 17–18, explains the principle of "convenience." The use of this word favored by domestic advisers suggests that these ideas had filtered down to the working class.

75. John Hicks, April 2, 1914, Box 47, Folder 517; Thomas Ellis, December 2, 1915, Box 48, Folder 572; Thomas F. Cocking, May 5, 1914, Box 47; Fred Cudlip, April 21, 1914, Box 47, Folder 517; Peter Sterk, May 14, 1915, Box 48, Folder 572; James H. Berryman, March 30, 1914, Box 47, Folder 517; Philip Miller, May 5, 1914, Box 47, Folder 517; Alex A. Brown, May 11, 1914, Box 47, Folder 517. All in MS-002, MTU.

76. Mrs. George Gipp, May 1, 1914, Folder 517; Daniel Macdonald, May 2, 1914, Folder 517; William Becker, March 19, 1914, Folder 501. All in MS-002, Box 47, MTU.

77. Lebeau to MacNaughton, October 22, 1913; MacNaughton to Lebeau, October 28, 1913. Her first request in Lebeau to MacNaughton, March 14, 1913. All in MS-002, Box 47, Folder 487, MTU.

78. The family member, whom I interviewed by telephone on November 11, 2003, and in person on November 15, 2003, requested anonymity.

79. Brian Geshel, personal interview in Houghton on October 3, 2005, discussing a house on Ninth Street in Lake Linden.

80. Elizabeth Collins Cromley, *The Food Axis: Cooking, Eating, and the Architecture of American Houses* (Charlottesville: University of Virginia Press, 2010), discusses some of this spatial transformation.

81. This single house is the one that I wrote about extensively in "The Boardinghouse Murders: Housing and American Ideals in Michigan's Copper Country in 1913," *Perspectives in Vernacular Architecture* 11 (2004): 1–18.

82. Photographs of unidentified double house found in Keweenaw Digital Archive, MTU neg. nos. 00350, 00351, 00355, 00359. Photographs of the single house: Acc. 06–087A–01–0705, –06, –07, and State Archives of Michigan Negs. 11836 and 18842. All at MTU.

83. Christopher Grampp, *From Yard to Garden: The Domestication of America's Home Grounds* (Chicago: Center for American Places, 2008), 13. See also J. B. Jackson, "Ghosts at the Door," *Landscape* 1, no. 2 (Autumn 1951): 3–9, and Paul Groth, "Lot, Yard, and Garden: American Distinctions," *Landscape* 30, no. 3 (1990): 29–35.

84. MTU Neg. 05922, MTU. State Archives of Michigan Neg. No. 18848, Lansing, Michigan.

85. John Messner, 16 May 1914, MS-002, Box 47, Folder 517, MTU. C&H notebook, House #149–151, Keweenaw National Historical Park. There is still a toilet in the basement today.

86. At 96 Pine, the toilet bore a date of 1981, but the other fixtures appeared to be earlier. At 94 Pine, no date was visible in the toilet tank or lid. Drawings of this house are found in Donna Zimmerman, "From Paternalism to Privatization: The Evolution of a Corporate Mining 'Location' in the Copper District of Michigan's Keweenaw Peninsula" (master's thesis, University of Wisconsin-Madison, 2000), 182–83, and Arnold R. Alanen and Katie Franks, ed. *Remnants of Corporate Paternalism: Company Housing and*

Landscapes at Calumet, Michigan (Calumet: Keweenaw National Historical Park, 1997), 45–49. My thanks to Richard Dana for allowing access and for sharing correspondence from previous owners.

87. Larry Mishkar, Documentation of Destrampe House (2002), MS-046, MTU.

88. Cowan, *More Work for Mother*, 88–89.

89. As Mira Engler wrote, "Plumbing embodied the idea of modernity—invisibility, central authority, efficiency, and hierarchy." Engler, *Designing America's Waste Landscapes* (Baltimore: The Johns Hopkins University Press, 2004), 43.

TIJEN ROSHKO

The Floating Dwellings of Chong Kneas, Cambodia

This study focuses on the community of Chong Kneas, Cambodia—primarily its floating houses—in order to understand the ideas of place making, identity development, sense of belonging, and the crucial role that built environments and object placement play in defining these concepts. The study first discusses social rules and relationships and appropriation practices as the processes that link people to their domestic environments. Next, the paper discusses symbolic oppositions related to gender, age, and kinship; how they are expressed in Cambodian cosmology and in the physical domestic space; and how these oppositions enculturate occupants who live and move through their home environments. The discussion simultaneously deals with dwellings in terms of their structural and cosmological aspects. In a broader framework, this vernacular study investigates the dialectic relationship between the rhythm of the lake and the culture of its inhabitants.

Tonle Sap Lake is the largest freshwater lake in Southeast Asia and lies in the central plains of Cambodia. The main tributary of the lake, the Tonle Sap River, exhibits an extraordinary hydrological phenomenon. As the rainy season commences, the excess water from the Mekong River is diverted into both the South China Sea and the river. In the latter case, this excess water actually reverses the direction of flow of Tonle Sap River and leads, as a consequence, to the inundation of 1.25 million hectares of forest and agricultural land for several months each year. During this period, the surface area of the lake more than quadruples from 2,500 square kilome-

ters to 11,000 square kilometers, and its depth increases from one meter to ten meters.[1]

Periodic flooding has rendered the entire area one of the most fish-abundant regions in the world and, as a consequence of its rich biodiversity, UNESCO declared the area a biosphere reserve in 1997. The people of Cambodia have relied upon the abundance of fish and the agricultural richness of Tonle Sap Lake and the surrounding area for their livelihood for centuries. Tonle Sap Lake plays a key role in shaping the cultural identity, the economic health, and stability of the Cambodian people. The rhythm of the lake defines the rhythm of the culture. The vast majority of the population in the Tonle Sap area lives in poverty; livelihoods depend solely on the resources that the lake has to offer.[2]

The population density around the Tonle Sap area has varied greatly over the centuries. At the turn of the nineteenth century, the Tonle Sap region was only sparsely populated. However, toward the middle of the nineteenth century, the Khmer people began to move onto the lake for purposes of subsistence fishing. They moved into the area when the fishing season was most favorable and, once they had harvested enough fish for their yearly consumption, returned to their villages. Subsistence fishing was easily learned and required only a very small initial financial investment. Inexpensive gillnets and dip nets were used to catch fish and, once the amount for daily consumption was set aside, the rest of the catch was sold to buy rice. Khmer presence at the lake became more prominent after the Khmer Rouge regime disbanded. The trend toward increased

Figure 1. Vietnamese houseboat, 2007. Photograph by author.

Figure 2. Typical Chong Kneas house assembly, 2007. Photograph by author.

are rudimentary, Chong Kneas acts as a transfer point for transporting fish that are caught on the lake. Dry shipments across the lake also come through Chong Kneas. In addition, it is one of the main transportation hubs for local traffic and for passengers travelling from Phnom Pen. There is significant tourist boat traffic resulting from visits to Prek Toal Wild Life Sanctuary and the water-inundated forest at Kompong Phlunk.

The floating houses of the village are of various sizes and types, and shift location with the changing water level (Figures 1, 2, and 3). Some of the houses are built on platforms, while others are designed like rafts and simply float when the water level rises. Still others are designed as small boats, which reside permanently on the water. The buildings, simple timber post-and-beam structures, are built predominantly from lightweight bamboo, mangrove, and wood. The flooring is made of timber plank or plywood sheet. The roof structure is mostly bamboo leaf thatching, although corrugated sheet metal applications are often used as a substitute. Exterior and interior non-load-bearing partitions are filled in with bamboo or light timber material that allows the integration of full-length louvered windows to provide much-needed ventilation. The homeowners renew their houses approximately every three years, and each occupant generally adheres to the same materials and forms in order to maintain their cultural and economic position within the community. On average, floating houses are twelve meters long and six meters wide, surrounded by a half-a-meter-wide patio and docking area.

The village proper contains not only floating dwellings but also educational and recreational facilities. Most of the commercial and educational facilities display greater permanence by utilizing timber plank exterior cladding and corrugated metal and timber roofing materials. Some of the commercial and retail activities are conducted in mobile stores, which float from house to house. Floating churches serve members of the Catholic community. The sound of the muezzin calling the faithful to prayer can be heard from the floating mosque.

A typical domestic setting consists of an indi-

settlement in floating villages continues today; reasons include lack of land tenure, family disputes, economic issues, and lack of education and skills. An estimated 80,000 people live in floating villages around Tonle Sap, and the Khmer population makes up the majority.[3]

While Cambodian villages are predominantly located on the land surrounding Tonle Sap Lake, a substantial number of Cambodians also reside in floating villages. Chong Kneas, a collection of some of these floating villages, exhibits its own unique rhythm in response to the changing seasons. The villages have their own enclosed communities that encompass diverse cultural groups, including the majority ethnic Khmer, as well as the Vietnamese, Cham Muslim, and Chinese minorities. Chong Kneas serves as the main harbour for Siem Reap, the capital city of Siem Reap province. Even though its landing facilities

vidual floating house flanked by the supporting family boats, which are used for fishing and additional storage. Some houses also support family-scale fish farms, and these fenced enclosures are located close to the main house. Together, they create small-scale family compounds that contain the main house, several fishing boats and canoes, and the fish farm or a floating animal pen (Figures 2 and 3).

During the wet season, the residents of Chong Kneas cluster around the base of a mountain called Phnom Krom, which is a rocky outcrop rising 140 meters above the seasonal flood lines. During the dry season, the movable boathouses are clustered at a boundary zone (or ecotone) between the lake and the plains. Changes in location occur in approximately twelve distinct stages. The mobility of the village collective enables the occupants to move freely between the lake and higher ground. The village composition is therefore less structured than those of the rice farmers' villages of the upper plains.

Chong Kneas also contains migrant fishermen who come from the lower Mekong River basin, primarily from Vietnam. Fishing on the lake is limited to the period between December and May. Migrating fish spawn from June to September, and high winds and storms make October to December a dangerous time to venture out onto the flooding lake.[4] Approximately 1,100 families live in Chong Kneas in their floating structures. The predominantly Khmer population of the village is around 5,800.

At first, one is struck by the complex mixture of types of floating structures. On the lake there are banks, barbershops, general stores, tailors, churches, mosques, schools, and pig and fish farms. Upon close inspection, the houses look homogenous in size and form. There seems to be no governing logic to the alignment of the houses at each of the temporary stopping places in the perpetually moving village. The locations of these stopping places between house movements are somewhat arbitrary and depend solely on natural conditions and the changing floodwater levels (Figure 4).

However, further investigation of the sociocultural structures and the cosmological beliefs

of the community reveals that there is indeed a logic to the configuration of the village at each stopping place. I will first discuss the sociological aspects and then the cosmological elements that determine the village alignment and assembly. The village layout discussed here is based on its location during the 2007 dry season.

Ordering the Landscape
Social rules encompass a wide range of dynamic relationships, affective and emotional bonds, cultural norms and practices, and communications.

Figure 3. Typical Khmer floating house in Chong Kneas, 2007. Photograph by author.

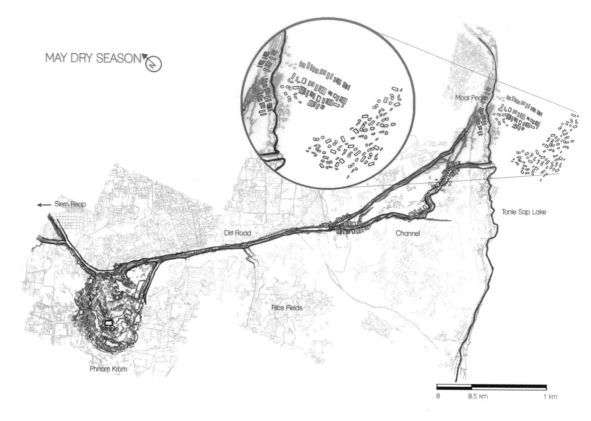

Figure 4. Chong Kneas, May (dry season) 2007. Most of the village is situated on the lake during May. In order to respond to the upcoming wet season and rising floodwaters, some residents have already positioned floating houses along the channel. Drawing by Nicolette Lane and author.

MAY DRY SEASON

← Siem Reap

Dirt Road

Channel

Moat Peam

Tonle Sap Lake

Rice Fields

Temple

Phnom Krom

0   0.5 km   1 km

Figure 5. Chong Kneas and Tonle Sap Lake during the dry season, 2007. The figure shows a view from the intersection of the channel and the dirt road leading to Moat Peam. The Vietnamese section is separated from the main part of the floating village, as seen in the oval on the top right of the image. Photograph by author.

In Chong Kneas, the socioeconomic status of the occupants is one determining factor in the spatial alignment of the floating dwellings. Economically viable families and commercial and regulatory agencies occupy the first row along the "main street" in a relatively orderly manner, without any ethnic differentiation. The main street allows fisherman and the village occupants to access Moat Peam, where the fish are brought to shore and processed. Access to the land from Moat Peam via a dirt road is also available during the dry season. Less economically solvent families occupy the second and third rows, and these streets show more emphasis on ethnic and extended family clustering. In general, kinship structure determines the grouping of the dwellings. It is an uxorilocal society, meaning that various members of a clan cluster together near the home of the wife's parents. The back rows have no distinguishing features with respect to alignment.

Within the village proper, ethnic groups cluster. In particular, the Vietnamese group is distinct and located far away from the other ethnic groups due to ongoing political and economic tension between Cambodia and Vietnam. Religious clustering is also evident in the village. Cham Muslims cluster around the mosque and occupy the second row of the main street (Figure 5).

The fixed elements in the village include educational structures and some of the commercial structures. The school location is fixed along the channel leading the way to Phnom Krom,

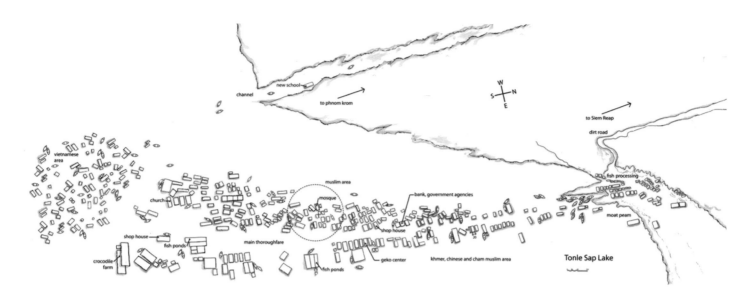

independent of the movements of the village. Another fixed element is the Crocodile Farm, a main tourist destination (Figure 6).

Tourist boats access the village at the center point through the channel and create noise and water pollution on their way to the Crocodile Farm and other destinations on the lake.

The cosmological belief system defines the parameters of village orientation. Theravada Buddhism is the official religion of the Cambodian people. However, Buddhist beliefs are generally superimposed onto the traditional animistic beliefs. Furthermore, Buddhist and animistic beliefs coexist with Hinduism.[5] Animism is the oldest belief system in Cambodia and offers a pantheon of supernatural beings. Buddhism encourages the integration of society on all scales, from family to village to nation, in order to create harmony, respect, and affection among believers. Buddhism is tolerant of other religions and, while it explains the existential questions of life and the afterlife, it is animism that provides a coping mechanism to deal with the day-to-day activities of the present. The Cambodian people greatly respect the invisible powers called Neak ta (ancestral spirits). They are the guardian spirits that protect the welfare of the thing or the area they inhabit. Cambodians believe that these spirits inhabit large trees. This has significant implications for the selection of timber for house construction. The construction of space on any scale depends on the beliefs and practices for appeasing the ancestral spirits. In common with other Southeast Asian and Austronesian societies, Cambodians believe all inanimate objects and animate beings possess a soul and interact with each other to create cosmological harmony.[6]

The Cambodian term phum refers to "a village," or "a group of houses," or even to a single house, but with an underlying connotation of sacredness.[7] In order to establish harmony between people, nature, and the spirits from the village, Cambodians follow certain rituals in house construction. Specific animistic beliefs, such as orientation according to cardinal points and the hierarchical notions of high to low and up to down, directly influence house construction and village layout.[8]

The residents of Chong Kneas generally orient their houses according to the cardinal points. They align the narrow sides of the rectangular houses that contain the entrance to face east since Cambodian traditional folk belief, following Buddha's instruction, perceives the East as auspicious and the West as inauspicious. The ridge pole of each house, which is a horizontal beam at the ridge of the roof, is aligned with the flow of the sun. This arrangement of the village is maintained during each temporary stopping place and does not vary from year to year or from season to season. The intersections of roads, rivers, and cardinal axis points are considered to be unlucky and are usually left unoccupied.[9]

There is a distinct gap, or unoccupied space,

Figure 6. Chong Kneas Settlement plan. The sketch is extracted from aerial photographs taken on May 27, 2007. The narrow sides of the rectangular houses are aligned to face east since Cambodian traditional folk belief perceives the East auspiciously and the West inauspiciously. The Vietnamese ethnic group is located in the southern part of the village (left in the figure) and is distinctly separated from the rest of the community. Their houseboats and houses do not adhere closely to the cosmological orientation rules. Drawing by author and Kristie Spencer.

in the village layout between the main village proper and the Vietnamese section. There are several possible reasons for this separation. The village elders determine the location of the center point of the village, which is called *phchet phum* (village naval). Villagers consider this location to be inauspicious and leave it unoccupied. This belief, along with the persistent political tensions, leads to a distinct spatial separation of the Vietnamese ethnic group from the rest of the community. Practical reasons, related to the provision of easy access for fishing and tourist boats to the processing harbour located at the end of the channel close to Phnom Krom, contribute as well. The Muslim minority in the village collectively orients its mosque and houses so as to face the direction of Mecca. In contrast with the rest of the village occupants, the Vietnamese section of the village observes the rules of orientation only loosely (Figure 6).

In summary, the prevailing factors that determine village morphology are socioeconomics, sociopolitics, ethnicity, the direct effect of the family kinship structure, and finally cosmology. Furthermore, village morphology drastically changes from dry to wet seasons, although somewhat similar layouts are executed from year to year for each season.

In the upper dry lands, villagers choose the location of a new settlement with consideration and care. The initial step is to delineate the wild from the domesticated and to protect village dwellers from the invisible forces that inhabit the wild. This is the sine qua non for both secular and religious entities of the village. While the forest is unknown and wild, the village is where people and spirits live in harmony; it is constructed with different levels of domestication and order. Regardless of the absence of physical boundaries around the village, every villager would recognize the line separating wild and domesticated.[10] In Chong Kneas, the lake replaces the forest and there is once again a clear understanding of the delineation between the wild and the domesticated. The landscape is one of the primary elements that determines settlement morphology and, in broader terms, the way of life in Chong Kneas. During the dry season,

the hot tropical climate of Chong Kneas is conducive to expansive, calm vistas on Tonle Sap Lake. By contrast, the incessant monsoons, wind, and tropical storms that characterize the wet season render the great lake formidable, wild, and claustrophobic. In the following segment I examine the broader context (the landscape) and its dialectical relationship to the inhabitants.

James Fernandez, in his work on the Fang and Zulu people, asserts that the relationship between people and their environment is reciprocal and mutually assertive. Environment influences people who acquire or take in qualities of that environment. This process is critical to the creation of meaningful cultural metaphors. It initiates identification with place and shapes identity. Once individuals have absorbed the qualities of a larger context (landscape), they will in turn project them onto built environments, settlement plans, and objects.[11] Fernandez further discusses the architectonics of landscape and its reflection on the Fang and Zulu people of Africa. He finds correlations between village morphologies and the physical experiential aspects of landscapes among African tribes. He emphasizes the contrasting nature of man-made and natural environments in which tribes live—the wide-open savannahs of South Africa in the case of the Zulu, and the dense rainforest of Gabon in the case of the Fang. According to Fernandez, Fang culture shows centrifugal tendencies in its rectilinear open settlement plans and architectural forms, while Zulu culture exhibits centripetal qualities in its circular built environments and settlement plans.[12] Chong Kneas, with its multiethnic, multireligious fabric, moves location without any physical territorial division and assumes different forms during different seasons. By using Fernandez's framework, it is possible to employ the architectonics of landscape to gain insight into the settlement arrangements of Chong Kneas. The general morphology of the village is isomorphic with its context and respectively centripetal and centrifugal in the dry and wet seasons. Environmental pressures on Chong Kneas are heightened during the wet season, a hostile, enclosed environment. Consequently, the village is dispersed around Phnom Krom Mountain. On the other hand, the tranquil vastness of Tonle Sap Lake during the dry season is manifested in the centripetal village form.

Fernandez also asserts that people project the qualities of the natural environment onto buildings as part of the larger "architectonics" of landscape.[13] The Zulu create round buildings, while the Fang create huts that are rectilinear in shape. However, contrary to these findings, the rectangular shape of the individual houses in Chong Kneas remains constant in spite of dramatic seasonal changes in the architectonics of the landscape.

The House

In order to understand the cultural makeup and built environment of Chong Kneas villages, anthropological methodologies were combined with architectural research techniques. Ethnographic observations were documented through photography, video, and field sketches. Specifically, the study gathered qualitative and quantitative data in the areas of environment, materials, resources, production services, decoration and symbolism, and typologies and uses.

I completed the first stage of the fieldwork during the end of the dry season in April 2007. During this period I visited twelve houses (three from each of the four dominant cultural groups), drew and documented the physical environments, and interviewed each head of the household. I limited the sample to twelve houses since the pattern of data was established by the end of the second set of four houses. Interviews with the community leaders also provided a political and structural perspective. The interviews revealed that the community of Chong Kneas was comprised of 1,101 families with a total population of 5,800 people. The cultural matrix was composed of 776 Khmer, 278 Vietnamese, 37 Cham, and 10 Chinese families.

The data-gathering process consisted of three distinct segments. First, I used a questionnaire to collect household information from each ethnic group about education, economic structure, ownership, family makeup, and social engagement. Second, I used photographs and video to record architectural elements, space planning,

decorations, uses, and functions along with materials and production. Finally, I measured and drew plans and elevations of representative floating structures; these documents provided in-depth information about architectural elements, interior planning and functions and, to a degree, space-use patterns. I selected three households at random from each ethnic group. An English-speaking guide from Siem Reap and two local guides from Chong Kneas supplied transportation and translation. The local guides also provided cultural and traditional introductions to the individual homes. In addition to gathering data in Chong Kneas, I investigated the northern shores of Tonle Sap Lake and documented a few similar floating villages, including Prek Toal and Kompong Plunk. Aerial documentation of the overall village layout supplemented the body of the research.

The first step in the analysis consisted of translating field drawings into working drawings in order to understand the subtle differences between the forms and the floor plans (Figure 7). The data showed similar basic needs—such as protection, gaining a livelihood, comfort, and shelter—for all ethnic groups. However, Khmer house plans were characterized by a single interior partition and clearly established the fundamental unit plan for all the structures of the remaining cultural groups (Vietnamese, Cham Muslims, Chinese), with the exception of two or three bay additions (Figure 8).

House forms and roof lines also showed parallel unit aggregations of form. A close inspection revealed that the unit form was predominantly adopted by the economically deprived Khmer households. Pierre Clement, in "The Lao House among Thai Houses," identified a "simple" Lao house in the Vientiane area, which had an interior partitioning system and a front entry location similar to the basic Khmer unit house in Chong Kneas.[14] Sophie Charpentier's extensive work in the Vientiane and Luang Prabang areas of Thailand also showed similarities in house form and interior partitioning system to a Khmer floating house (Figure 9).[15] One exception was stilts, which were replaced by floater systems in the dwellings of Chong Kneas. The

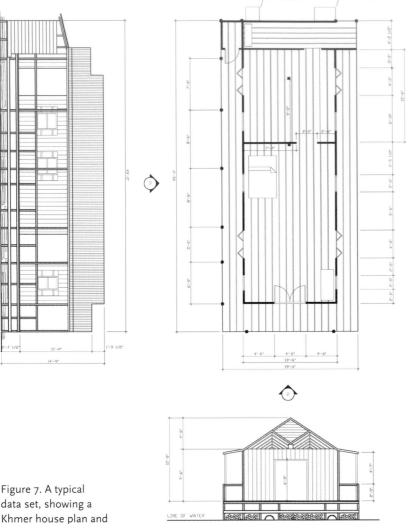

Figure 7. A typical
data set, showing a
Khmer house plan and
elevations. Drawing by
author and Randy Wong.

around porch that accommodates boat and canoe landings (Figure 10).

In his work on Berber houses, Pierre Bourdieu argues that the social structure of the house is a reflection of the social world at large.[17] He discusses homological relations between house and universe, both of which are governed by the same oppositional organization. For both, the processes and the forms of space use provide a potentially powerful means to decipher sociocultural aspects of society. In his study of Berber houses, he grafts certain spatial oppositions to encode opposed social categories such as female/male, senior/junior, kin/stranger. Bourdieu gives these categories a visual expression by mapping them onto spatial contrasts such as front/back, up/down, left/right, inside/outside. Although Bourdieu's main focus is gender relations in the Berber house, I will use a similar approach to understand Chong Kneas and its built environments; by that, I mean that I employ space-use patterns to illuminate the notion of place making (Figure 11).

I have selected the Khmer because they constitute the dominant cultural group; their houses create the base unit for the spatial developments of the community. Understanding the Khmer house from a structural and cosmological perspective will provide a unit or baseline of understanding for the rest of the built environments of Chong Kneas. Furthermore, one can only discuss the Khmer house in terms of a combination of the process of construction and cosmological properties since it is nearly impossible to separate these two defining elements.

An animistic belief system is the predominant determining element of house construction, from timber selection to location, from interior layout to overall building alignment. The energy of the spirits, which inhabit the trees, infuses the house and its occupants with vitality and well-being. Therefore, dealing with timber from the time of cutting to selection requires special attention. Cambodians usually cut during the dry season because it is considered to be an auspicious time. They only select straight trees with smooth surfaces and, during construction, builders erect columns in the same order as that of tree growth,

multiethnic fabric of the village is quite conducive to the adaptation of house forms from neighbouring regions; therefore, the basic house form of South East Asia finds continuity in Cambodia.

Home owners in Chong Kneas observe and reflect their social status in the aggregation of units. Occupants with higher economic power and social status— into which the Chinese minority falls—have opted for house plans with two or three unit additions. The Khmer interior configurations also have similarities to Kantaing houses, which migrants from China developed and introduced into Cambodian culture via Vietnam.[16] In Chong Kneas, the typical back porch of the Kantaing house has become a narrow wrap-

with the root end at the bottom and the branch end at the top of the column. These rules governing timber orientation and selection are significant for two main elements of house construction: *mé sâsâr* (the central column) and *mé dâmbaul* (the ridge beam).[18] The central column is where the spirit of the male ancestor lives, and it acts as protection against evil spirits. It is the defining element of the male domain, which is the public part of the house. The ridge beam hosts *mneang phteah* (the lady guardian) of the house and is adorned with *yantra* (a piece of red fabric with a diagrammatic drawing that provides protection from evil spirits coming from eight directions).[19] The female domain is where the domestic activities such as washing, cooking, and sleeping are dominant; it corresponds to the private section of the house and is reinforced by the presence of *mneang phteah*.

Houses in Chong Kneas are built with three rows of columns. *Sasar choeng rieng* (side columns) are shorter than the row of central columns, which is known as the ridge column row. In most floating dwellings, the central column row consists of two or three columns that are sometimes freestanding and, at other times, are embedded in the partitioning wall, thereby rendering the whole wall assembly sacred. This is where occupants display photographs of family ancestors. Additional side columns are fastened onto the base of the structure to support the roof of the surrounding porch. Usually, builders select the trunk of a tree for the most sacred components of the structure, the ridge beam and the central column. In general, the rest of the post-and-beam structure of the house is a mixture of available lumber and bamboo. Nevertheless, lumber use throughout the house is not uncommon.

Body metaphors similar to those of Austronesian cultures are incorporated into the design of the structural elements of the house, such as the *sâsâr trung* (column of the chest) or *thvear* (the main entry door), a term that makes direct reference to female anatomy.[20] The house is a female domain, while prayer halls and monasteries are the male realm. Men are expected to leave the house to engage in fishing or other income-generating activities. Women remain in the house

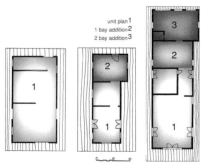

unit plan 1
1 bay addition 2
2 bay addition 3

plan. unit plan and additional bays

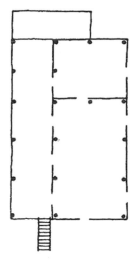

and undertake child-rearing and all other domestic activities. However, due to the unpredictability of subsistence fishing—as well as for other economic reasons—most of the family members, regardless of gender and age, take part in family income generation. Although the sacred

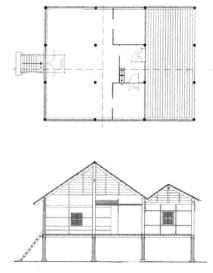

Figure 8. Unit plan and additional bays. Drawing by author and Kristie Spencer.

Figure 9. Simple Lao House in Vientiane. Drawing reproduced from "The Lao House among the Thai Houses: A Comparative Survey and Preliminary Classification," in *The House in East and Southeast Asia: Anthropological and Architectural Aspects*, ed. K. G. Izikowitz and Per Sorensen, Scandinavian Institute of Asian Studies Monograph Series 30 (London: Curzon Press, 1982), 72. Courtesy of Curzon Press.

Figure 10. Kantaing House plan and side elevation. Drawing reproduced from Prak Vireak, "Wooden Houses of the Early Twentieth Century: Settlement Patterns, Social Distinction, and Ethnicity," in Tainturier, *Wooden Architecture of Cambodia: A Disappearing Heritage*, ed. Francois Tainturier (New York: Rockefeller Foundation, 2006), 84. Courtesy of the Center for Khmer Studies.

Figure 11. Khmer Interior.
Drawing by Maggie
Khounthav, author,
and Kristie Spencer.

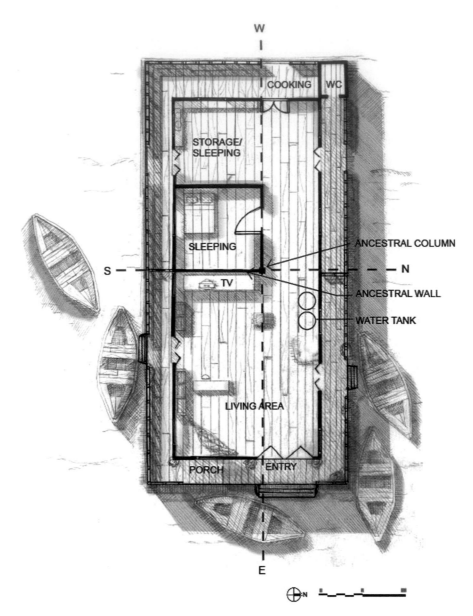

wall demarcates female and male domains, there is diffusion between the two domains, and similarly for the gendered attributes of inside and outside and day and night.

The building process is not arbitrary; builders measure and achieve correct proportions according to the function of the building, the status of the occupant, and the type of construction.[21] Essentially every male member of the family is informed about the basics of building *khtòm* (a hut); however, the construction of a robust floating house requires an expert house builder or carpenter.

In Cambodia the basic social unit is the nuclear family, the building block of social life. All members of the nuclear family live under the same roof, and the dwelling itself is the primary context for family life wherein the family can live in harmony with people, nature, and invisible spirits.[22] Therefore, the ritual of home building—requiring careful consideration of the selection of materials, time of construction, location and morphology—provides an additional opportunity for dwellers to bond with invisible spirits, the community, and members of the household.[23]

In general, two main types of dwellings in Chong Kneas, *phteah* (a house) and khtòm, are distinguished by construction materials (Figures 12, 13, and 14).

A house usually employs wood, bamboo, corrugated metal, prefabricated sheet goods, medium density fiberboard (MDF), or laminated particleboard, while a hut is made mostly of bamboo, sugar palm leaves, and wood. The traditional land-based Cambodian wooden house has a limited life span (materials are usually chosen not to exceed the life span of the owner) and a certain level of mobility (tongue-and-groove construction without nails allows owners to relocate the house if necessary). Dwellers of Chong Kneas lead a much more precarious existence.[24] They renew their homes every three years to combat environmentally induced wear and live in a state of constant mobility. Their material selection is less discriminating and they use nails throughout construction.

Journey to and through a Floating House

The typical journey to a Khmer house starts from the shores of Tonle Sap Lake in a canoe or a motorboat. Upon reaching the landing area around the house, one must ask for permission to dock. Once the home owner grants it, the visitor must remove all footwear at the porch area prior to entering the interior. The porch area, often surrounded with a two-foot-high wood fence, contains all the plants and vegetables of the household, some of which are decorative. The fence acts as a boundary marker and delineates the private from the public domain and, more importantly, demarcates the point of entry into the house. At first glance, one perceives the floating dwelling of Chong Kneas as a single level, but closer inspection reveals the presence of an additional level below the floor. The house dwellers reserve the main floor for day-to-day activities, while they store domestic animals and additional household items in the space between the floorboards and the floats. Cambodians consider this to be a dark and dirty space, not suitable for human habitation.

The main floor is divided into small *bântup* (rooms). Two axes separate the Khmer floating house, the north-south axis and the east-west axis that intersect at the ancestral column. Based on this main division, I superimposed an abstract matrix on the house plan in order to analyze the

Figure 12. Khmer floating house in Chong Kneas, 2007. Photograph by author.

Figure 13. A front view of a Chinese shop house with a newly painted roof in Chong Kneas, 2007. Photograph by author.

Figure 14. Khtòm (a hut) is one of the principal types of dwellings in Chong Kneas, 2007. Photograph by author.

spatial organization in terms of space use and movements within the space, thus permitting a deeper understanding of the differentiation by gender, age, and kinship (Figure 15).

After crossing the house threshold, which is located at the narrow side of the rectangle facing

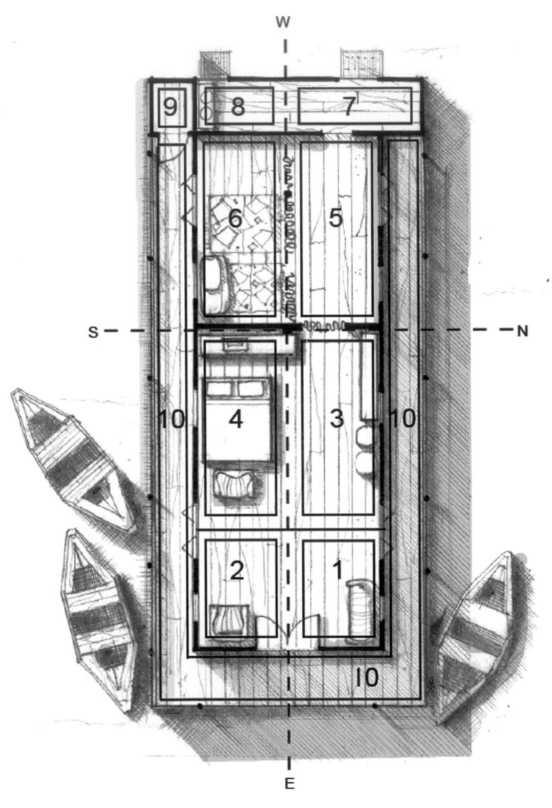

Figure 15. Khmer House analysis matrix. Legend: 1. Entry, public area; 2. Guest reception, family living area; 3. Passage from public to private realm/storage; 4. Dedicated to family religious activities/ sleeping area for the elder family members; 5. Storage; 6. Young daughters' bedroom; 7. Food preparation/ storage/pantry/ laundry; 8. Cooking; 9. Washroom; 10. Porch. Drawing by author and Kristie Spencer.

east, one finds oneself in the public area of the house (1 and 2 on the plan). This is where the family receives guests, serves dinners, and also stores tanks for potable water. It serves a multitude of family activities. This transitional area is where the family formalizes non-kin relationships. It has a direct view of areas 3 and 4. Small chairs or benches are located in this area for use by visitors. Area 4 is reserved as a sleeping area for the elder members of the family. It also contains mé sâsâr. A small altar, which holds the offerings to the spirit of the house to ensure protection, is mounted on this column on or near the ridge beam. The family permanently displays these religious icons in the public domain of the house at ceiling level, thus establishing the spiritual vertical axis of the interior. "Up" is auspicious while "down" is inauspicious. The family hangs various flowers and amulets from mé sâsâr for good luck and protection. They display ancestral photos on the partitioning wall and at or around mé sâsâr. It is the most spiritually charged area of the house.

Areas 3 and 4 contain most of the family objects, from hand crafts to family photographs and a television set. The TV, powered by batteries, is functional and is the most prominently located utilitarian object (Figure 16).

It reflects the social status of the family and is displayed on the sideboard, which also contains all other small-scale decorative and functional objects. It is a symbol of the occupants' identity and of their position in the community and, as such, they choose its location to provide the highest visibility. Furthermore, they align it with the most sacred element, the male ancestral column. The wall, within which the ancestral column is embedded, behaves as the area of intersection of all the religious and secular elements of the Khmer ethos (Figures 17 and 18).

Area 3 is a transitional space from the public to the most private realms of the house. Lace curtains separate the public realm from the private realm. Occasionally, doorframe decorations and flowers articulate this threshold of passage from area 3 to area 5. More family photos appear around this area, which also functions as storage for teacups and teapots. Area 5 is the multipurpose storage area for the family kitchen's tools

Figure 16. Television sets displayed in the living room. Both units, in working order, symbolize material accumulation and the financial solvency of the family. Photograph by author, 2007.

Figure 17. Secular objects like the television, fan, and VCR are located on the lower shelf, while the spirit house is placed along the spiritual axis, closer to the ridge beam. Photograph by author, 2007.

and utensils, which are displayed on the vertical surfaces of the north wall. Area 5 is also a transitional area to the outdoors, the porch, and the kitchen. It serves different functions depending on family occupation and structure; sometimes

Figure 18. Khmer floating house interior. The view was taken from an entry toward the ancestral wall as occupants took part in the field interview, 2007. Photograph by author.

with the exception of the designated sleeping area for young daughters. Once boys have transitioned from childhood to adulthood, they are expected to sleep wherever space is available—most often in the family boat or the canoe docked next to the house—to protect the family and their possessions. Roll-away floor mattresses provide sleeping areas within the dwelling for parents and the rest of the family at night. The arrangement and placement of the interior partitioned room in the back of the house reflect the cultural desire to protect family lineage and, consequently, the chastity of unmarried daughters. In all other respects, Khmer house plans are relatively open and uniform.

Food preparation, the responsibility of the eldest daughter or the daughter-in-law, takes place at the back of the house on or around the porches. This area is regarded as an exclusively female domain; there is a hierarchy among women of the household, based on age and marital status (area 7, 8). In some houses, the food-preparation area is located one foot below the main floor. Families store all kitchen utensils vertically on the walls and do their cooking in clay pots on an open wood fire. They serve daily meals at the front of the house and consume them mostly on the floor. Families with higher income usually replace the open-pit fire with modern butane-gas cooktops. All cooking and washing activities take place in and around these areas. The personal hygiene area (9) at the back of the house is limited to a three-foot-by-three-foot enclosure, with no infrastructure and limited privacy.

The narrow wraparound porch (10) plays a pivotal role in the social life of the community. It is a transitional space and the initial point of interaction with the social realm. It also acts as a privacy filter with respect to the public gaze. Most domestic chores and activities take place on or around the porch, which is covered at the roof level to provide protection from rain and sun. Activities such as personal hygiene, food preparation, and clothes washing move to the edge of the domestic enclosure. Thus the boundaries of the domestic domain expand to the exterior and transform the thresholds between interior and exterior into functional and habitable spaces. As a

it is used as a storage area for the family business and sometimes as a sleeping area for parents.

Area 6 is the only partitioned room of the dwelling. The most private area in here is the sleeping area. Located toward the left-hand side of the house when viewed through the front entrance, it is reserved for young daughters and is inaccessible to outsiders, non-kin guests, and males. The private part of the dwelling is not centered on an ancestral column like the public part and does not have a collective living area for the family.

The spatial development of house plans also reflects the family structure and the sociocultural makeup of the community. In general, sleeping arrangements are dispersed around the house,

consequence, a significant portion of social inter-actions and community connections take place on and around the semipublic domains of the porches. In principle, porches are considered a female domain; however, the movement and activities of male/female, kin/non-kin, and young/old are convoluted within these transitional spaces.

The fishing season has the most profound effect on the Khmer people and their environment. During the fishing season, house boundaries extend to accommodate fish-processing activities such as drying and cleaning. Families use the roof, porch area, and vertical surfaces of exterior walls. They erect bamboo structures to provide further surfaces to accommodate these activities. Interior spaces provide storage for fishing gear and nets. Daily homebound activities adjust to accommodate the fishing seasons. The boys' school cycle terminates so that they may help the adult men with their fishing activities. Daily routines adapt to a larger-scale cycle, men to a work cycle, children to a school and work cycle, women to both of these cycles and to the neighbors' and the community's cycles. Furthermore, these all adjust to a larger seasonal cycle. Thus, adaptation involves temporal cycles that are embedded hierarchically within one another. The other salient, overlapping, cyclic event is the change of flood levels: families move their houses an average of twelve times a year in order to provide protection against the monsoons and the wind. These two dominant cyclic events define the community, and all other activities, including personal cycles, adapt to these main salient cycles.

The objects displayed within the interiors play a significant role in place attachment (emotional or affective bond between people and place). Furthermore, they are the signifiers of the personal and cultural norms of occupants. During my visit, a Vietnamese doctor referred with pride to his diploma, which he had framed and displayed over the entry. The diploma has a salient presence and is a central object for establishing the owner's identity, social status, and place attachment. The diploma acts as a symbol that establishes the owner's superiority over others while referring to past, present, and possible future successes.

The salience of an object or a place in the home is variable. Its significance can rise and fall at different times, acting in a dynamic fashion. In particular, bucolic images, which are displayed in the living room as a reference to ancestral lands or as a reflection of yearning for the dry lands, can change in significance over time and be replaced by other objects or images.

The importance of social status in Khmer society is evident on every scale, ranging from alignment of homes, house plans, and forms of housing, to the smallest household object. Photographs of grandparents and wedding photographs of family members are also prominently located at and around the ancestral column (wall) and entry points; they create temporal references from past to present, with future implications of success. They are objects of social integration and forge the owners' relationship to the sociocultural context. Rituals and traditions of religious practices also contribute a vertical dimension to the spatial arrangement of the home. The positioning of religious objects and the objects themselves connect the owner to his religious group.

The object attachment (emotional or affective bonds between people and objects that are foundational to the definition of self) facilitates foundational processes such as identity development and place attachment, personal efficacies, and familial and cultural bonding. The temporary nature of the dwelling—in terms of construction, form, size, and mobility—renders interior spaces and objects within as the central elements of object attachment, which gives meaning to the built environment. Meanwhile, the land continuously moves and changes in Chong Kneas; only interior elements and objects remain fixed. Therefore the use of space, movement within the interior, and object attachments are the primary contributors to the identity- and place-attachment process.

Roxana Waterson studied the idea of the house as a "living thing" in Austronesian societies.[25] In Chong Kneas, the house is similarly infused with energy provided by spirits who inhabit trees. Rules and rituals observed during construction, coupled with a strong cosmological belief system, ensure that the house has a life force. Body metaphors reinforce the idea of the house as a "living thing." The house is an animate being with its own vitality and is united with spirits and occupants. Furthermore, Janet Carsten and Stephen Hugh-Jones propose that the house and the body are intimately connected, being extensions of each other.[26]

Nancy Munn defines space as conceptualized movement in a space–time continuum, rather than as a mere container.[27] Munn builds a notion of "mobile spatial fields" based on Lefebvre's concepts of "field of action" and "basis of action." The field of perception expands from the body and moves through locales, thereby creating mobile spatial fields. Munn argues that place making is a construct that originates simultaneously from the mind, land, custom, and bodily practice. The body as a mobile spatial field makes its own place in the world.[28] One can think of the limitations imposed on the land and the perpetual mobility of homes in Chong Kneas from a spatiotemporal point of view. Thus, the unified living house is a basis of action from which the spatial field of action extends. A social space moves with the house from locale to locale, and place making thus becomes a mobile notion centered on the house and its inhabitants. Therefore, within the continuum of time and space in Tonle Sap Lake, the sense of space is defined and redefined by the fluidity of the movement of its occupants.

During interviews, most of the time occupants did not answer the question, *"How do you determine where to go each time you move?"* Sometimes they answered with ambiguous comments like, *"We go to the same place."* Perhaps clarification of these vague answers lies in the interaction between restrictions induced by the landscape and the mobile field of action. Interdicted spaces on terrain defined by the shallow waters, the temperament of the climate, and cosmological beliefs carve out negative spaces. In turn, negative spaces create repeatable transient boundaries. The boundaries of these carved-out spaces define where occupants cannot go. Perhaps movement through these interdicted spaces is habitual and has established an obvious pattern of movement that rendered my field questions trivial to village occupants. Location determination requires fur-

ther study and specific empirical data. Boundaries define paths and, within these boundaries, place making or sense of space is not only defined by the act of moving through spaces as "mobile fields of action;" interiors and objects within also play an important role. They are the only constant elements, providing a sort of "frame of reference" within the fluidity of Chong Kneas.

Closing Remarks

In essence, the arrangement of physical space, the objects it contains, and the use of the physical environment reflect socioculturally defined behaviors and ideas. These collective behaviors and ideas are the definitive elements of the physical environment of a home. I have only touched on the greater meaning of Khmer domestic environments. In order to understand the cultural identity and its connectedness to the built environments, I studied social behaviors, space appropriations, and use through the filter of opposites such as male/female, young/old, upper/lower, secular/religious, inside/outside, kin/non-kin. I investigated the transactions between the material and immaterial world of domestic space on various scales, discussed how these transactions are modified, and showed how they affect each other. Interiors, centered on the ancestral wall, are pivotal in the day-to-day activities of the Khmer.

Built environments and their interiors are the central elements of a network of systems. They facilitate a form of identification and help engender a sense of belonging for the occupants of Chong Kneas in their fluid environment on all scales. However, I also argue that the act of moving through space also establishes a sense of place that is dependent on sociotemporal aspects of the land and its inhabitants. At present, as Chong Kneas challenges assumptions of fixed space and boundaries, it continues to maintain traditional built forms (although attenuated), building traditions, and the Khmer ethos.

NOTES

This project was funded by a research initiative grant provided by the University of Manitoba, UM/SSHRC, 2007. Thanks to my research assistants Amber Bewza,

Maggie Khounthav, Nicolette Lane, Andrea Sosa, Kristie Spencer, Satoko Takahashi, Zhi Weng, and Randy Wong for their enthusiasm and hard work. Special thanks to Carol Steer for invaluable editorial contributions. I am grateful to Dr. Roy Roshko for his active participation and encouragement at every stage of this project, from the fields of Cambodia to Canada. Finally, to the two anonymous reviewers for *Buildings & Landscapes,* your invaluable comments and directions were instrumental in the development of this article.

1. Renauld Bailleux, *The Tonle Sap Great Lake: A Pulse of Life* (Bangkok: Asia Horizon Books Co., 2003), 5.

2. Marko Keskinen, *Socio-Economic Survey of the Tonle Sap Lake Cambodia,* MSc Thesis (Helsinki University of Technology, 2003), 18–21.

3. Bailleux, *The Tonle Sap Great Lake.*

4. Ang Choulean, Eric Prenowitz, and Ashley Thompson, *Angkor: A Manual for the Past, Present, and Future* (Phnom Penh: APSARA, Royal Government of Cambodia, 1996), 123–39.

5. May Ebihara, *Svay: A Khmer Village in Cambodia* (PhD diss., Columbia University, 1968), 363.

6. Roxana Waterson, *The Living House: An Anthropology of Architecture in South-East Asia* (Singapore: Tuttle Publishing, 2009 edition), 115.

7. François Tainturier, "Building in Wood: Notes on a Vanishing Age-Old Tradition," in *Wooden Architecture of Cambodia: A Disappearing Heritage,* ed. François Tainturier (New York: Rockefeller Foundation, 2006), 12.

8. Fabienne Luco, "House-Building Rituals and Ceremonies in a Village of the Angkor Complex," in *Wooden Architecture of Cambodia,* ed. Tainturier, 92.

9. Luco, "House-Building Rituals," 98.

10. Tainturier, "Building in Wood," 12–14.

11. Setha M. Low and Denise Lawrence-Zuniga, "Locating Culture," in *The Anthropology of Space and Place: Locating Culture,* ed. Setha M. Low and Denise Lawrence-Zuniga (Malden, Mass.: Blackwell Publishing, 2007), 14.

12. James Fernandez, "Emergence and Convergence in Some African Sacred Places," in *The Anthropology of Space and Place,* ed. Low and Lawrence-Zuniga, 187–203.

13. Fernandez, "Emergence and Convergence," 187–203.

14. Pierre Clement, "The Lao House among the Thai Houses: A Comparative Survey and Preliminary Classification," in *The House in East and Southeast Asia: Anthropological and Architectural Aspects,* ed. K. G. Izikowitz and Per Sorensen, Scandinavian Institute of Asian Studies Monograph Series, no. 30 (London: Curzon Press, 1982), 72.

15. Sophie Charpentier, "The Lao House: Vientiane and Louang Prabang," in *The House in East and Southeast Asia,* ed. Izikowitz and Sorensen, 56–57.

16. Prak Vireak, "Wooden Houses of the Early Twentieth Century: Settlement Patterns, Social Distinction, and Ethnicity," in *Wooden Architecture of Cambodia,* ed. Tainturier, 84.

17. Pierre Bourdieu, "The Berber House," in *The Anthropology of Space and Place,* ed. Low and Lawrence-Zuniga, 134.

18. Tainturier, "Building in Wood," 16.

19. Tainturier, "Building in Wood," 16.

20. Tainturier, "Building in Wood," 18.

21. Sokol, "Sacred and Profane," 42.

22. Luco, "House-Building Rituals," 90.

23. Luco, "House-Building Rituals," 98.

24. Luco, "House-Building Rituals," 92.

25. Waterson, *The Living House,* 115.

26. Janet Carsten and Stephen Hugh-Jones, "Introduction: About the House: Lévi-Strauss and Beyond," in *About the House: Lévi-Strauss and Beyond,* ed. Janet Carsten and Stephen Hugh-Jones (Cambridge: Cambridge University Press, 1995), 2.

27. Nancy Munn, "Excluded Spaces: The Figure in the Australian Aboriginal Landscape," in *The Anthropology of Space and Place,* ed. Low and Lawrence-Zuniga, 102.

28. Munn, "Excluded Spaces," 92–107.

STEPHEN E. NEPA

The New Urban Dining Room

Sidewalk Cafes in Postindustrial Philadelphia

In 1997, Neil Stein learned the wine shop on Rittenhouse Square East was closing. Energized by the success of his restaurant, Striped Bass, the veteran restaurateur imagined for the space a French bistro that would "use the square as an asset."[1] His peers found the space too small to accommodate both a bar and dining room; where would his patrons *sit*? Unfazed, Stein simply said people would eat outside. This was a radical notion when there were few sidewalk tables in Philadelphia. After Rouge debuted in April 1998, Stein's gamble paid off. Packed on a daily basis, its black-clad waitstaff pushed through fashionable people mobbing the sidewalk tables, highline cars cruised by, and pedestrians interacted with those patrons sitting, creating a Felliniesque tableau. *Philadelphia Weekly* praised Stein's effort, proclaiming "the people watching is of such high caliber it could provide a distraction from the most mediocre food" and "romance is what Rouge is all about."[2] By offering what Stein defined as "theater on a piazza," Rouge became the central attraction of (and one of the few sidewalk

cafes ever to grace) Rittenhouse Square.[3] The following year, the *New York Daily News* announced Philadelphia's sidewalk cafe growth reflected its residents' "falling back in love with their space."[4] Since 1998, nearly 300 sidewalk cafes have appeared in Philadelphia. In block-by-block fashion, these cafes created a new urban dining room, magnetizing neighborhoods from East Passyunk to Northern Liberties and drawing people into a once forbidding postindustrial city.[5]

Though not without limitations, Philadelphia's sidewalk cafes were much more than welcoming spaces in which to dine. This analysis of their origins and recent surge in popularity shows that these cafes emerged as vital components of commerce and civic life in postindustrial Philadelphia. Commercially, they invigorated the local restaurant industry. In a civic capacity, they provided Philadelphians and their visitors a higher degree of cosmopolitanism, a more pronounced feeling of safety, places for gathering, and an appealing way to experience the city. Echoing sociologist Elijah Anderson, Philadelphia's sidewalk cafes fell under the "cosmopolitan canopy" of busy, yet bounded quasi-public spaces where people could "relax their guard" against urban elements.[6] In another sense, the proliferation of sidewalk cafes indicated that for a city long considered provincial and tradition-bound, Philadelphia finally was importing (and embracing) a tenet of European public urban culture. Philadelphia's sidewalk cafes blossomed in the vertices of political and economic changes, those transformations of the late 1990s that led the city from disaster (real and imagined) to recovery.

Figure 1. Sidewalk cafe at South Twentieth and Locust Streets, Rittenhouse Square area (June 2009), photograph by author.

Crime rates dropped, jobs were created, tax abatements generated new development, and Center City added nearly twelve thousand new housing units. These improvements led historian Steven Conn to declare in 2006 that, "Philadelphia is now a more exciting, lively, vibrant place than at any time since Jefferson and Franklin were walking the streets."[7]

For Conn to classify postindustrial Philadelphia as "vibrant," he most likely witnessed more than new housing starts and fewer murders; he needed to see people outdoors—interacting and enjoying the city. When measured against waning attendance at parades, the disappearance of "street theater," and among some scholars a sense that public spaces have vanished from American urban landscapes, sidewalk cafes encourage behaviors that are less politicized and more reliant on conspicuous consumption. The activities practiced *within* them (dining, imbibing, conversing, people watching, and commercial transactions) provide for owners, patrons, and passersby a form of urban spectacle, one both profitable and pleasantly contagious.[8] Sociologist Ray Oldenburg states that in Parisian life, sidewalk cafes' "openness lends a legitimacy born of visibility."[9] Despite differences between the sidewalk cafes of Paris and Philadelphia—such as size, design, and patrons' behaviors—their proliferation indicated in both cities a desire to gather and socialize in public view. Finally, sidewalk cafes became devices through which people could experience postindustrial Philadelphia. While its cultural offerings (performing arts venues, universities, museums, and historic sites) contributed to Philadelphia's urbanity, many of these establishments required some degree of cultural aptitude in order to be fully appreciated. Sidewalk cafes cast a wider net. Largely informal—when compared with the nineteenth-century practice of urban promenading, which in Philadelphia commanded formal types of dress and courtly mannerisms—the city's twenty-first-century sidewalk cafes were casual spaces for dining out and people watching. Existing in various neighborhoods and offering different types of cuisine, they were in theory more inclusive places for people to attain an urban experience.[10]

Despite those urban experiences, the limitations of Philadelphia's sidewalk cafes were equally numerous. First, the overwhelming majority of them appeared in affluent Center City areas such as Rittenhouse Square, Washington Square West, Old City, Independence Park, and Queen Village. This geographic specificity indicates the target audience of sidewalk cafes, mainly middle- and upper-middle-class patrons that sought what sociologist Pierre Bourdieu identified as cultural capital. For them, sidewalk cafes represented bastions of the good life, helping transform portions of Center City into a glamour zone. Secondly, as a result, the concentration of sidewalk cafes in Philadelphia's well-to-do neighborhoods generated a cultural force field, one seemingly impenetrable to the protracted problems of infrastructural decay, abandoned properties, and crime that plagued areas peripheral to Center City. Thirdly, in areas weathering the process of gentrification, such as Northern Liberties, Fairmount, and University City, sidewalk cafes represented agents of class conflict and worries over rising property values; in some cases, notably in the city's Far Northeast, early proposals for sidewalk cafes were defeated due to such concerns. Finally, the arduous process of legalizing these cafes in Philadelphia demonstrated ambiguities in and disagreements over the use of public space and the types of commerce allowed in the city's central neighborhoods.

While many people assumed Rouge was the city's first (Stein defended the assumption), Philadelphia's sidewalk cafes had a long-contested history couched in spatial politics. Initially authorized by the city council in May 1979, several factors stalled their growth until the late 1990s.[11] First, Philadelphia's bitter (and long-running) feuds over street vending pitted merchants' associations, health officials, citizens, and the city council against entrepreneurs operating on the city's sidewalks. The comprehensive urban planning proposed for Philadelphia's renewal in the 1950s and 1960s, with its sleek modern fluidity, had no place for street vendors. More, in preparing for the Bicentennial, which transformed portions of Philadelphia into what geographer David Lowenthal termed a "make-believe landscape," bazaar-like sidewalk retail was viewed by many politicians and citizens as detrimental to the city's cosmetic improvement. In these contexts, debates over commercial and aesthetic uses of sidewalks ultimately stalled cafe growth. Second, Philadelphia's restaurantscape changed considerably in the early 1970s as haute, California nouvelle, and ethnic cuisines began edging out automats, luncheonettes, and supper clubs. Commenting on the shift in 1974, food writer Craig Claiborne opined that the city "long was a negligible place to dine." Compared with the palates of New York, Los Angeles, or Paris, Philadelphians were unsophisticated and undemanding of sidewalk cafes.[12]

Finally, instead of placing tables on sidewalks (as stipulated by councilmanic law), during the 1980s Philadelphia restaurateurs erected permanent structures in defiance of building regulations. These structures, many of which were enclosed patios partitioned from the sidewalks, generated friction among the W. Wilson Goode Administration (1983–91), the City Planning Commission (CPC), city council members, neighborhood associations, and restaurateurs. As CPC executive director Barbara Kaplan remarked in 1999, "it took a while for restaurateurs to understand the [sidewalk cafe] law."[13] Until Philadelphia's sidewalk cafe law was amended in the 1990s, all applicants were required to own prohibitively expensive liquor licenses. Issued by the Pennsylvania Liquor Control Board (PLCB), the high cost of licensing discouraged sidewalk cafes for decades. Last, despite moderate quality-of-life improvements in the 1980s, Philadelphia continued to suffer from blight and crime. Those restaurateurs who petitioned for sidewalk cafes were unwilling to directly expose their patrons to the street. As *Inquirer* architecture critic Thomas Hine opined in 1987, "the places at which Philadelphians like to dine outdoors tend to be walled and sheltered and as far from any sidewalk as possible."[14]

When historicizing sidewalk cafe development in Philadelphia, the political tensions surrounding street vending and sidewalk use mark a point of departure. Typically, debates over the legality and placement of urban street vendors were fraught with public health issues, although as Daniel Bluestone, John Gaber, John Cross, and Sharit Bhowmik indicate, such debates (from New York to Mexico City) were usually undergirded by racial and class animosities.[15] In Philadelphia, the so-called "vendor wars" created raw sensibilities over legitimate and proper use of sidewalks. Ultimately, similar dynamics came into play in regard to Philadelphia's sidewalk cafes; as with vendors, many city officials and residents lamented their flimsy appearance, nonconformity with building codes, incongruity with historic architecture, generation of noise and congestion, and the stubbornness of restaurateurs who skirted the proper licensing channels. In these contexts, historic bouts over Philadelphia's street vendors set the stage for later debates over the role(s) and legality of the city's sidewalk cafes.[16]

Philadelphia's street vending hailed from the colonial period, when its port and commercial operations were among the busiest in the world. William Penn's original city plan (1682) specified that High Street (now Market Street) be lined with hucksters and market stalls; this pattern persisted well into the 1850s. Through the nineteenth and into the twentieth centuries, seafood, soups, clothing, jewelry, leather products, candles, and fruit were sold by hucksters who burst into song or blew their truck horns while factory workers and housewives shouted their orders from upper-story windows. Many vendors were immigrants, trade providing their initial entry into the U.S. labor force. Several operated in the same neighborhood for generations. Though lively and theatrical, the vendors were not universally accepted. In 1927, building inspection bureau chief Morris Brooks complained about their spread throughout Center City. Calling their operations unfair competition and "eyesores on our principal streets," Brooks believed their appearance drove down property values and made Philadelphia "look like a jay town."[17] Despite noise and cluttered sidewalks, this urban bazaar was integral to the city's economy and provided citizens with a wealth of chance encounters before the dominance of privatized central business districts (CBDs) and shopping malls.

In the summer of 1940 Philadelphia's street

vendors, particularly those selling food, came under heavier fire. Health director Hubley R. Owen lobbied the city council to regulate the vendors in ways similar to the city's storefront dining establishments. Owen argued that vendors required licenses, sanitary inspections, and should be prohibited from roaming freely. More, he complained that several vendors paid "protection fees" to the police to avoid harassment. Vendors felt Owen's proposal resulted from merchants' complaints about unfair competition and lost profits.[18] But in August, a food poisoning epidemic broke out and was traced back to sandwich vendors operating in the city's northeast section. Framed as a health crisis, the outbreak gave Owen the upper hand. In April 1941, the city council passed an ordinance regulating all food vendors in Philadelphia. Effective July 1, the law required them to obtain licensing, cover their foods adequately, and adhere to strict rules of personal hygiene. Those who failed to comply faced fines between ten dollars and fifty dollars. Although vendors voiced concerns that the new restrictions would harm business, the law proved difficult to enforce. During the early 1950s, the police conducted "drives" in Center City, with many vendors cited and/or arrested for health code violations, not displaying proper permits, or using vulgar language. In most cases, vendors were given warnings. Few were fined. But the word was out: the city of Philadelphia was cracking down. As *Bulletin* columnist Phillip Schaeffer noted, "a germ-conscious city council killed the vendors."[19]

The fight between vendors and the city gained momentum after 1950, when the Philadelphia Redevelopment Authority (PRA) and Greater Philadelphia Movement (GPM) cited them not as health code violators but as obstacles to reviving Center City.[20] By this time, urban planning in the United States had assumed a modernist direction, with the primary goal of reshaping cities to suit the country's growing car culture. From Detroit and Cincinnati to New York and Los Angeles, U.S. cities forsook density and mass transit, instead demolishing slums, building expressways, and removing much of the prewar city. Philadelphia was no exception.[21] Representatives of the Urban

Land Institute (ULI) visited Philadelphia in 1951, finding "a sleepy, unprogressive city" and chiefly recommended redeveloping the square blocks adjacent to city hall.[22] These areas had devolved into a "honky-tonk zone" as suburban migration left voids in downtown real estate filled by adult entertainment venues, seedy bars, and street vendors. When Joseph Clark became mayor in 1952, he pledged to address the business community's concerns about cleaning up the area. Edmund Bacon, who stood at the helm of the CPC, envisioned a "total-design concept" for Philadelphia, a macrorenewal strategy to open up the CBD and clear away vestiges of the prewar city.[23]

Bacon cherished space and fluidity in his Better Philadelphia model, the sense that "bringing light to darkness" would attract people to Center City. A cluttered arrangement of street vendors was simply incongruous with his vision. Denise Scott Brown, one of Bacon's earliest critics, stated that he underestimated suburbanization's appeal. The prewar urban core had, by the mid-1950s, blended into a decentralized "city-region," with development projects (and population growth) in Philadelphia's suburbs radically outpacing those in the city. Scott Brown felt the primary goal of Better Philadelphia should rely less on widened spaces. Rather, Bacon and his architects needed to focus on maintaining economic activity via retail and residents, if Philadelphia was to remain

Figure 2. *From left*: Earle Barber, chairman of the PRA; Edmund Bacon, executive director of CPC; and architect Vincent Kling discuss a scale model for Center City's redevelopment (June 1950). Temple University Libraries, Urban Archives, Philadelphia, Pa.

viable in the postwar years.[24] Bernard Spain, a restaurant and real estate investor in Philadelphia since the late 1960s, explains, "to this day, the CPC still believes in comprehensive design as opposed to smaller-scale development. For some reason, Bacon felt that open space would attract people." In regard to Penn Center, Spain contended, "he [Bacon] ended up being wrong."[25]

The renewal was not only architectural. The newly elected Democrats in city hall sought ways to improve the city's tax base. Due to their history of subverting tax codes, street vendors were targeted. In April 1953, forty-five Center City food vendors and lunch stands (non-roaming

Figure 3. The modernist centerpiece of the new Philadelphia, 2 Penn Center, Fifteenth Street and JFK Boulevard (July 1963). Temple University Libraries, Urban Archives, Philadelphia, Pa.

operations) received notices to vacate within fifteen days. The following day, twenty vendors and stand operators gathered in chief building engineer Samuel Bernhang's office to protest the removal. They complained that for more than thirty years, despite occasional police harassment, they never had been *forced* to move out. Bernhang sympathized with the vendors but explained that he was following orders. Councilman Samuel Rose of west Philadelphia, attending the meeting on the vendors' behalf, stated, "it seems strange that these businesses are illegal now, after all these years. Some of these people have made investments in their businesses."[26] The removal had aesthetic reasons as well. In 1957, *Bulletin* columnist Frank Brookhouser remarked "an ironic aspect to the building of the Penn Center is that right across from this glistening, handsome, modern edifice lies the honky-tonk stretch of Market Street with a conglomeration of gaudy neon-lit penny arcades, pinball palaces, cheap shops, and hot dog and orange drink stands.[27] Arthur Kaufman, head of the Philadelphia Civic Affairs Council (PCAC) further stated in 1958, "it's up to us to protect both the public and the businessmen from an onslaught of pitchmen who would do nothing but clutter up central Philadelphia and in too many instances offer shoddy merchandise for sale." In the end, only newsstands and pretzel vendors were permitted to remain in the CBD.[28]

The development of Penn Center (the centerpiece of Bacon's Better Philadelphia) required the demolition of the "Chinese Wall" rail trestle and the Pennsylvania Railroad's Broad Street Station. With rail lines submerged beneath a warren of concourses and street vendors ordered to disperse, Bacon's project reflected what Anastasia Loukaitou-Sideris and Renia Ehrenfeucht describe as "modernist planning replacing complexity with order."[29] Vendors contributed to that complexity. While many lunch stands disappeared by the mid-1960s, street vending grew considerably in the early 1970s, spreading to university campuses, subway stations, and neighborhoods beyond the CBD. In 1973, the Rizzo administration introduced a bill to city council prohibiting vendors selling anything besides newspapers and pretzels from being less than 300 feet from a storefront establishment selling similar wares. More, they were forbidden to operate in "no parking" zones. The vendors believed they were in the right, earning an honest living and lending the city a "picturesque image."[30] Other parties supported the vendors. The ACLU called the Rizzo bill "unconstitutional harassment," claiming the city was "destroying part of the counterculture." T. T. Chang, executive director of the Chinatown YMCA, called the vendors "the root of the free-enterprise system."[31] Some vendors operated out of their own cars, ready to pack up and move in the face of harassment. But chronically lax enforcement angered the vendors' opponents. The anger grew when the city began planning for the Bicentennial, which many officials viewed as an opportunity to cosmetically improve Philadelphia. In a 1975 *Bulletin* survey regarding the vendor issue, a Philadelphia homemaker commented, "they [vendors] make the sidewalks into a junk shop and with the Bicentennial coming up, what are outsiders going to think?" Greater Philadelphia Chamber of Commerce vice president Henry Reichner delivered more invective: "let no one be misled into believing that the vendor is an individual craftsman or proprietor. The great majority are salesmen of goods manufactured and distributed by others. . . . They're archaic, unpleasant, unsafe, and a costly mess; the vendors must go!"[32]

For decades, rifts over street vending overshadowed the development of sidewalk cafes in Philadelphia. With urban planning that streamlined mobility and directed people inward, commercial transactions (of most kinds) in the public right-of-way appeared too contentious. Comparatively, New York City engaged in similar feuds with its street vendors. At various times, New York settled on strict licensing and zoning regulations, going so far as to reassign vendors into enclosed "pushcart markets." But that city recognized the importance of sidewalk cafes. In 1955 New York had exactly three sidewalk cafes; by the late 1960s, after their appearance was encouraged as beneficial for reducing street crime, there were over one hundred. Though licenses and fees were expensive, New York res-

taurateurs significantly increased their seating capacities.[33] In Philadelphia, the first proposal for the approval of sidewalk cafes did not appear until the late 1970s. In November 1978, at the request of city solicitor Sheldon L. Albert, the council's Licenses and Inspections (L&I)

Figure 4. A typical twentieth-century Philadelphia street-vending landscape, South Seventh and McKean Streets (July 1951). Temple University Libraries, Urban Archives, Philadelphia, Pa.

Figure 5. Center City street vending, Eleventh and Market Streets. George Fencl (foreground, right), of the Philadelphia Police Civil Affairs Unit, checks vendors' tables (July 1976). Temple University Libraries, Urban Archives, Philadelphia, Pa.

Committee postponed consideration of a cafe ordinance. Soured by the acrimonious climate over vending, Albert stated the proposal's language needed "clarification separating sidewalk cafes from street vendors." As it stood, the cafe proposal permitted "restaurants and bars to temporarily place tables on sidewalks in front of their establishments as long as the tables would not interfere with or impede pedestrian travel."[34] The proposal was delayed for several months. Councilman Melvin Greenberg continued sponsoring the bill on behalf of restaurateurs, arguing that unlike the vendors, the cafes would rest against building facades away from both curbs and the center of the sidewalks. Greenberg stated, "the restaurant people own their own building or pay rent. They pay their taxes. The vendors operate on the sidewalk without paying rent to anyone. Besides, the cafes would be alongside the restaurants not out near the curbs." Jack Downey, owner of Downey's Irish Bar, also pushed for the measure; he reasoned that "twenty to thirty other cities in this state permit sidewalk cafes . . . why can't we?" William F. Gillen, executive vice president of the Philadelphia-Delaware Valley Restaurant Association, stated, "outdoor cafes will enhance the image of our city."[35] In the minds of these proponents, sidewalk cafes provided a regulated, taxed, and culturally appealing alternative to street vending. On May 7, 1979, bill number 1262, allowing sidewalk cafes in specific areas of Center City, passed the council ten to one and was signed into law by Mayor Rizzo.[36]

To soothe the foes of sidewalk retail and to minimize conflict over usage of public space, the 1979 sidewalk cafe law was heavily influenced by street vendor-related concerns and set forth provisional guidelines. To open a sidewalk cafe, the city required a licensed and inspected storefront, thereby undermining "pushcart" food vendors; a costly Pennsylvania Liquor Control Board (PLCB) license; submission of a detailed proposal of the cafe to be accepted or rejected by council's Licenses and Inspections (L&I) Committee; an eighty dollar annual fee; and approval from the Philadelphia Department of Streets to ensure the cafe area would not impede pedestrian travel or utility maintenance. Most importantly, all cafes were required to be temporary, easily removed structures. If at any time cafe operators violated the council's terms, they were given thirty days to remove the cafe. Failure to remove the cafe would then lead to demolition by the city, with the operator(s) shouldering the expenses. In theory, the Philadelphia City Council announced that these regulations served to "protect the general public"; in reality, during the 1980s and early 1990s, the city council had a habit of approving bills tailored to restaurateurs' advantages in "sidewalk encroachment cases."[37]

The approval of sidewalk cafes appeared in the wake of the Bicentennial and the "back-to-the-city" movement of the 1970s, both of which brought new residents and restaurants to Philadelphia. Bacon's Society Hill project (on the former site of the Dock Street food market stalls) stood out as an exceptional case of urban rehabilitation with its restored colonials, pocket parks, and the New Market Festival Plaza. Haute cuisine, prepared in restaurants such as La Panetiere, Lautrec, Déjà Vu, and Le Bec Fin, found a niche among the area's most sophisticated palates. Younger, more adventurous diners chose nouvelle or ethnic upstarts such as Frog or the "buy local" pioneers of the White Dog Café and Astral Plane.[38] In tandem, the city's automats disappeared, many supper clubs closed, and hotel dining lost its luster. Philadelphians were moving beyond their culinary desert and seemed poised to accept sidewalk cafes. Yet as a whole, Philadelphia still wrestled with image crises. To meet the challenges of postindustrial economic change, big-ticket proposals to improve the city surfaced in the late 1970s.[39] These included a convention center, expanded museums, new public transit options, a revitalized Broad Street subway concourse, business-class hotels, and the development of the "Avenue of the Arts." Though the CPC, city council, and mayor's office recognized that the city's future relied on enticing residents and attracting suburbanites and tourists, these bodies rarely saw eye-to-eye. Many proposals (Pennsylvania Convention Center, the Gallery Mall, hotels, and the Avenue of the Arts) were realized while others (the subway concourse, a World's Fair, Olympic Games bids, and the infamous Chestnut Street "Transitway") died completely or were left to languish. However, those projects realized failed to resuscitate public space and instead directed people inward.

Given the optimism expressed by sidewalk cafes' earliest proponents and the restaurant growth of the 1970s, surprisingly few restaurateurs took advantage. Arguably, the high cost of a liquor license deterred many would-be operators. Without alcohol sales, most restaurants could not survive. Those who did venture into this new territory (and who owned liquor licenses) defied the spatial regulations of the 1979 law. Downey's, located at Front and South Streets, was the first sidewalk cafe to open under the new law. Yet the Irish restaurant's cafe resembled a giant patio on the sidewalk. This sparked a trend during the 1980s, causing restaurateurs to meet resistance from various city agencies and officials.[40]

One of the first high-profile cases was Apropos. Opened in September 1984, Apropos filled the South Broad Street space vacated by Horn and Hardart, the Philadelphia-based automat chain. Gone now were elderly men drinking coffee from paper cups, eating prepackaged pies, and reading leftover newspapers. With nouvelle sophistication, Apropos's snappily attired patrons sipped espresso, ate fruit tarts with beurre noir, and enjoyed entrees reflective of the "sunny cuisine of the West Coast."[41] In December Apropos opened its sidewalk cafe, which served owner Shimon Bokozva in two ways: he maximized his seating capacity and enticed his patrons with a view of South Broad Street. Less than two years later, tensions flared. City officials argued that the structure did not qualify as a temporary structure. Rather than having easily moved tables, Bokozva built a "greenhouse" that extended seven-and-one-half feet beyond the set boundary between building and curb. He claimed that his cafe, the roof of which was hoisted in good weather, promoted urban renewal by deterring prostitutes from gathering along nearby Locust Street's "Barbary Coast." Yet many city groups did not share Bokozva's optimism; the CPC believed his glass enclosure hindered sidewalk passage, the Philadelphia Law Department stated that it violated building codes and took him to common pleas

Figure 6. One of the city's first "sidewalk cafes" with a patio barrier erected between patrons and the sidewalk. Jack Downey's Restaurant, Front and South Streets (June 2009). Photograph by author.

Figure 7. Apropos's highly controversial "greenhouse" sidewalk cafe from the 1980s as it appeared in 2010, South Broad Street (December 2010). Photograph by author.

court, and the art commission felt it clashed with surrounding architecture. Bokozva stuck to his guns, claiming he'd navigated the maze of cafe regulations, city agencies, and obtained all necessary permits. The CPC was equally steadfast; it claimed Bokozva knew from the beginning that his structure violated the law.[42]

The volleying continued for two years. Bokozva found allies in city council, while the CPC lobbied the Goode administration to declare Apropos's cafe illegal. Coming to Bokozva's aid was first district city councilman James Tayoun. Tayoun, not persuaded by the CPC's position, was well versed in Philadelphia's sidewalk politics. He was a brash, outspoken opponent of street vendors in the 1970s and upon siding with Bokozva, himself faced a municipal court case regarding the sidewalk cafe (also an enclosed patio) at his restaurant, Middle East, in Old City.[43] Tayoun opened the cafe despite the fact that four city agencies rejected the plan. Specifically, the CPC claimed Middle East's permanent concrete base violated the 1979 ordinance. Due to "ethical concerns," Tayoun stated he would not introduce legislation protecting his own sidewalk cafe, but when he learned of the CPC's plan to illegalize Apropos's cafe, he stated "my strongest opposition is to City Planning sitting in an ivory tower telling Philadelphia's little businessmen what they can and cannot do." CPC officials grew agitated during the protracted battle. In recommending legislation to outlaw Apropos's cafe, CPC deputy director David Baldinger announced "I think this is a wonderful story: how one of the best restaurants in town blatantly disregarded the law for five years!" CPC executive director

Barbara Kaplan personally lobbied Mayor Goode to intervene and stated that Apropos's enclosure was "not a sidewalk cafe. It's an addition to a building where we are giving up the public sidewalk for private interests." To further prove her point, Kaplan refused to patronize Apropos.[44]

In November 1988, city council voted thirteen to four in favor of the Apropos's sidewalk cafe. According to the city council journals, those four who voted "nay" did so more to protect "public property than to uphold building codes." Councilman Lucien Blackwell, voting "yea," remarked "this is just a case of the CPC once again wanting not to recommend, but run the city. And if they want to run the city, then they have to be elected to do that." Mayor Goode, who cut his political teeth as a housing and community activist, vetoed the ruling immediately, arguing, "we must protect our public right-of-ways." During the first week of December, the council overrode Goode's veto, with Tayoun calling it a "statement by council that sidewalk cafes are an improvement to the city of Philadelphia." Other city council members argued that sidewalk cafes enhanced Philadelphia's image and made the city safer.[45] The owners of Apropos and Middle East did not install open-air French cafes that Neil Stein argued "make the city safer." But in 1980s Philadelphia, feeling safe was a hard sell. Grisly home invasions in Society Hill, a garbage crisis, street crime, homelessness, and the MOVE debacle cast a dark shadow over the city, making its sidewalks undesirable spaces in which to dine. This climate influenced Bokovza and Tayoun, who decided to shield their patrons.[46]

Apropos closed in 1989 with the new tenant Baci, an Italian restaurant, preserving the greenhouse. As of 2009, the structure remained part of the Italian Bistro restaurant. Viewing the structure today, one imagines dining behind the glass barrier of a professional hockey rink. Bokovza moved on, founding Sushi Samba, a trendy Japanese-Brazilian fusion chain with stores in New York, Miami, and Las Vegas.[47] Middle East restaurant retained its glass and masonry addition after it was made legal in 1991 (without Goode's signature). That same year, Tayoun resigned his council post amid political corruption charges.[48] Middle East closed and the space has since been home to a number of restaurants and bars; the patio's glass was eventually removed. Between 1983 and 1991, nearly thirty restaurants applied for sidewalk cafes. In several cases, Goode exercised his veto power; he repeatedly argued that structural additions obstructed public right-of-way or violated zoning laws. In 1987 alone, Downey's, La Cucina, Bridget Foy's, and Montserrat saw their cafes denied by Goode.[49]

In every case the council overrode Goode, allowing the restaurants to keep their cafes, but the CPC remained adamantly opposed. In the wake of restaurateur Pete Antipas getting the council to back his cafe addition at New City Café (Twentieth and Ludlow Streets), Kaplan claimed, "these aren't 'sidewalk cafes' with tables and chairs. They're buildings on the sidewalk." The CPC argued that cafe owners were getting use of free, untaxed land at the expense of pedestrians. Opposition to the cafes was not solely the province of elected officials. Center City Residents Association (CCRA) board member Judith Eden lamented, "why don't we let all businesses push to the sidewalk and we can walk in the streets?" While Goode usually denied sidewalk cafe permits based on existing zoning laws (commercial operations in residential areas) or the specifics of the 1979 ordinance (temporary versus permanent structures), he never publicly voiced opposition to the idea of cafes; in 1989, Goode explained that he "liked sidewalk cafes," but added that Apropos (and other cafe operators) "do not even meet the basic threshold requirement for sidewalk cafes since they are not outdoor dining areas and provide no opportunity for partaking of sun and air." More, Goode often trumpeted Philadelphia's wealth of restaurants and how they bolstered the urban economy. Praising the sixth annual "Book and the Cook" food festival in 1990, Goode stated "one-third of the exhibitors at the fair are small businesses from Philadelphia. . . . My administration has made major efforts to assist small businesses in any way we can." Surprisingly, there is no mention of sidewalk cafe debates in Goode's autobiography, very likely the result of the fact that his second term was overshadowed by the MOVE tragedy of May 1985.[50]

The 1980s stood as the most contentious period for the development of Philadelphia's sidewalk cafes. Bokozva and Tayoun's patios required entry through their restaurants, offered detached views of the streetscape, and minimized social contact. These spaces shielded patrons from elements (exhaust, panhandlers, noise, or pigeons) and introverted their urban experience. As Marc Cosnard, French cultural attaché in Washington, D.C., explained to the *Daily News* in 1985, a true sidewalk cafe "must be exposed to the sky."[51] While Center City in the late 1980s was a twenty-billion-dollar commercial area with nearly 300,000 jobs for 10,000 companies, these modified "patio cafes" became diamonds in the rough. As Allan Domb, a condominium developer and principal investor in Stephen Starr Restaurants explained, "At the end of the 1980s, the city started to deteriorate. A lot of baby boomers concerned with things such as dirt, crime, and above all, homelessness, moved to the suburbs."[52] Safety figured prominently in the minds of residents, workers, and visitors alike. Gauging the collective sense of the city often evoked negative opinions and apprehension; in 1989 *Inquirer* columnist Mark Bowden noted, "many of the stockbrokers, secretaries, and financial specialists . . . believe the streets are filled with lunatics."[53] City hall—just three blocks north of Apropos—was routinely broken into by the homeless, who slept in the hallways and defecated on floors. Though the Barbary Coast prostitutes moved on, high murder rates, bureaucratic gridlock, homelessness, and panhandling continued to tarnish Philadelphia. It would not be until the late 1990s, when Rendellian optimism improved public perceptions of the city, that restaurateurs felt comfortable developing true, "exposed-to-the-sky" sidewalk cafes.

The 1990s represented a pivotal decade for Philadelphia and a cultural moment for its sidewalk cafes. With its economy hobbled by deindustrialization, its job base shifted from manufacturing to service industries. A consumerist reinvention of the city followed, producing refurbished historic sites, new hotels, pricey retail chains, and hip restaurants.[54] Between 1992 and 2007, fine-dining restaurants in Center City alone increased threefold to just over 200. And from 1993 to 1998 the regional economy added 11,000 jobs, with one out of every six in the restaurant industry. In 1993, *Money* ranked the city eleventh on its "Finest Restaurant Towns" list; only three years prior, the same survey had labeled Philadelphia "undiscovered." Congruous with national trends, increased patronage of restaurants in Philadelphia reflected what historian Hal Rothman described as consumers' desires turning from goods to experiences. More precisely, *Gastronomica* editor Darra Goldstein argued, "where we once placed our faith in so-called durable goods—furniture and appliances—we are now purchasing evanescent things." In postindustrial Philadelphia, restaurant growth played a key role in this consumer shift; after decades of privatized development and suburbanization, people wanting to experience the city indulged in its sophisticated restaurants. In complementary fashion, eager restaurateurs set up tables on the sidewalk. Remarking on sidewalk cafe growth, Domb stated, "people like to eat and drink outside, *to be seen*. They want activity. They don't want to just sit in their houses and not see anybody."[55]

Many observers of Philadelphia's recent past credit mayor Ed Rendell (1991–99), with restoring the faded metropolis's image. Typical of many moderate Democrats during the 1990s, Rendell espoused a pro-growth agenda that included ten-year tax abatements and other policies to spur development. With a bootstraps-managerial style and a sense of urgency, Rendell embarked on a mission to make the city appealing. He was, according to Le Bec Fin owner and chef George Perrier, "a businessman. He made people *believe* in the city."[56] To achieve his goal, Rendell attacked Philadelphia's chronic inefficiency. Upon entering office, he tapped his corporate connections (over forty CEOs, managers, and executives) and created the Private Sector Task Force. Designed to streamline the city's slovenly management, the force set out to improve various functions, from operating fleet vehicles and computerizing vital services, to privatizing the airport and scrutinizing employee benefits. The spirit of reform demonstrated by Rendell's task force was so wide-ranging it was dubbed "urban perestroika."[57] For restaurants, the task force was a godsend. Potential restaurateurs looking to open shop in Philadelphia, Perrier recalls, "could now pick up the phone and have all of their licenses and permits in twenty-four hours. Twenty-four hours!" Before Rendell, said Perrier, "Philadelphia was the hardest town in the country" in which to open a restaurant.[58] The streamlining extended to sidewalk cafes, Rendell legalizing them throughout the city by executive order in 1995. Prior to 1995, such cafes were allowed only in precisely defined central areas.[59] In 1999, Stephen Starr considered a sidewalk cafe for Buddakan, his successful pan-Asian restaurant in Old City. Regarding the licensing process, Starr commented, "it used to be a real hassle. In the past year or two, Rendell has made it much looser."[60]

While Goode and Rendell headed adjacent mayoral administrations, effectively bridging Philadelphia's economic transition, their politics regarding sidewalk cafes' legality differed sharply. Goode, when measured against Rendell, stood as the last mayor of Philadelphia's era of bureaucratic slog, a time of "gross mismanagement" and enmity-filled tensions among city agencies, labor unions, law enforcement, business owners, and citizens. Whether he was truly to blame, Goode led Philadelphia during one of the city's most unflattering (and deadly) episodes of mismanagement and neglect, the MOVE tragedy of 1985. In attempts to weed out MOVE members from a row house in West Philadelphia during an exchange of gunfire, the city police department dropped a "satchel" bomb onto the home's roof. Once ignited, the fire quickly spread to adjacent homes. The city fire department, refusing to act until the bullets stopped, waited more than an hour before extinguishing the flames. Several MOVE members perished in the blaze and an entire square block of homes was incinerated. The event polarized Philadelphia and Goode was portrayed as complicit in the tragedy. Though Goode vehemently denied authorizing the bombing, the inferno sealed his political fate.

As Rendell's biographer stated of Goode, "the city, like a living creature, began to devour him." By the end of Goode's second term, his campaign promises to attack the city's bloated budget and slovenly politics were unrealized; Philadelphia ranked dead last on *City and State*'s list of fifty fiscally sound large cities.[61]

Ed Rendell inherited this unsavory image of Philadelphia. Crime, fiscal disaster, and the city's relevance were all challenges for the new mayor. Rendell was turned on to sidewalk cafes as a rehabilitative tool in 1992, when his fledgling administration instituted a city hall cleanup. The mayor showed his commitment by scrubbing a bathroom on his hands and knees for the cameras. When Rendell and his staff moved into the nearly one-hundred-year-old building, it had sunk into what Buzz Bissinger termed a "mockery of the majesty of government."[62] The pigeon droppings were knee deep, rats were as large as beavers, and false fire alarms rang so often that no one bothered to exit. Yet for Rendell, scrubbing grime from the city's most splendid edifice was just the start. The mayor asked public property commissioner Joe Martz what else might be done to spruce up city hall and its plazas. When deputy mayor Joe Torsella proposed the idea of a sidewalk cafe, Rendell, an avid food lover, expressed delight and asked Martz to conduct a feasibility study. Following the study, the city solicited bids for city hall's first-ever sidewalk cafe. The sole bidders were Rose Parotta and Eileen Dowd, both former managers of Apropos. On July 17, 1992, the Politico Cafe opened for business on Dilworth Plaza. Hibiscus plants and palm trees were imported for the occasion. The Savoy Jazz Trio was on hand to liven up the event. Parotta and Dowd offered sandwiches, vegetarian dishes, and Italian "street food" on paper plates. As per the Rendell administration's request, Politico faced northwest, affording patrons views of the Ben Franklin Parkway and the art museum. Martz indicated the important precedent being set by the first outdoor concession ever allowed on city hall's grounds, stating Politico "will be the measure of our success. Success for us will be if people start coming in and filling the seats."[63] The cafe operated July through October. Rendell's staff and other city planners hoped it would "ignite excitement" and generate a "Champs Elysees ambiance."[64]

Emulating Paris was a Philadelphia tradition. From the colonial period, Philadelphia planners had had an infatuation with things Parisian. French Second Empire and Beaux-Arts architecture abounded in Center City. Signs along South Eighteenth Street just north of Rittenhouse Square proclaimed the area the "French Quarter"; the designation resulted mainly in Philadelphia having more French restaurants per capita than any other U.S. city.[65] The design of the Ben Franklin Parkway borrowed directly from the Champs-Elysees. Planned by transplanted French architect Paul Philippe Cret to mirror the Parisian thoroughfare with vibrant cafes and street culture, the Parkway was in the early 1990s an auto-traffic arterial without a single sidewalk cafe. In 1993 the city hosted the Philadelphia-Paris Forum, which brought three of Paris's top planners to the Bellevue Hotel to reveal the secrets of their city's success. While Philadelphia's twentieth-century urban planning took inspiration from Le Corbusier (whose notion of "speed equaling success" influenced Bacon) and Francois Mitterrand's *Les Grands Projets* redevelopment of Paris in the 1970s, David Slovic, a forum organizer, remarked that great cities were defined by their civic spaces and the amenities that surrounded them. Philadelphia, Slovic said, "should copy that most Parisian of amenities, the [sidewalk] café."[66]

That same year, and under pressure from council members, the 1979 sidewalk cafe ordinance was amended for the first time. Not only was the PLCB licensing requirement abandoned but also the permissible boundaries of sidewalk cafes were extended. Championed by first district councilman Joseph Vignola and fourth district councilman Michael Nutter, sidewalk cafes were now permitted in the city's gentrifying Manayunk neighborhood.[67] Once a gritty textile district on the city's northwest edge, Manayunk in the early 1990s was reborn as a pedestrian-oriented retail corridor. Art galleries, clothing boutiques, furniture stores, and bars took root along Main Street. Allen Newman, Derek Davis, and other restaurateurs came as well, bringing sophisticated cuisine and sidewalk cafes. This combination of amenities was geared to attract the "right kind of people," namely Main Line residents who now could cross underneath the Schuylkill Expressway (I-76) and indulge themselves in an urban village of greater convenience than Center City.[68] By 1999, the neighborhood was thriving and its sidewalk cafes were integral to that success. Newman, whose Arroyo Grill and Sonoma restaurants both featured sidewalk cafes, remarked that despite the narrowness of Main Street, "people sit there and they drink and dine, regardless of the fact that they're next to the street and there's vehicles going by."[69] Clearly, the appeal of sidewalk cafes had extended beyond Center City, proving their ability to generate a desirable urban setting. And Rendell, supportive of almost any idea that made venturing into Philadelphia more desirable, recognized the value in sacrificing sidewalk space to create something inviting; in 1995, the mayor legalized cafes throughout the entire city.

Rendell's championing of sidewalk cafes set a new tone for the relationship between formerly warring entities. The enmity over the cafes between the politically powerless CPC, the mayor's office, and the city council eventually lessened. And while the council's lobbying for and Newman's opening of sidewalk cafes aided Manayunk's second coming, in the history of Philadelphia's sidewalk cafe culture, few figures have been more influential than Neil Stein. At sixty-seven, he remained Philadelphia's big kid, forever young in designer jeans, leather jacket, New Balance sneakers, and Porsche roadster. With well-known episodes of drug use, cash skimming, and tax evasion behind him, in 2009 he operated a consulting business called One on One and remained one of the city's authorities for investors seeking restaurant advice.[70] He owned and/or operated some of the most notable restaurants in Philadelphia after the early 1970s. In 1973, he opened the Fish Market, a small grocery/restaurant in a nineteenth century building one block north of Rittenhouse Square. "I was young. I got up every morning at 4 a.m., went

to the food market, bought all the food, all the fish, brought it back, and unloaded the truck. We had eighteen seats and my wife was up front selling cheese; I was in the center by the fish case." From these humble origins, Stein went on to found Marabella's at the Academy House (later opening additional locations), the popular Rock Lobster on the Delaware River waterfront, and in 1994, Walnut Street's celebrated Striped Bass. Along with Perrier's Le Bec Fin and the avant-garde Susanna Foo, Striped Bass elevated the block to new heights. Toward the end of the 1990s, Walnut Street emerged as the city's answer to Rodeo Drive, a destination for high-end retail and top-notch restaurants. In March 1997, Visa Credit Issuers called the block "one of the ten best urban shopping streets in the nation."[71]

Rouge became one of Stein's most influential concepts. Before its opening, Rittenhouse Square Park had always attracted people and events in daytime. At night, the silence on the square was almost deafening. In the early 1990s, area residents confronted muggings, panhandling, "vent people" sleeping in the park, and burglaries. Two blocks away, Perrier had a $25,000 painting stolen from Le Bec Fin's lobby. With alarming frequency, neighborhood businesses installed steel "riot gates" to pull down over their storefronts, fortifying them from the streets after dark.[72] Stein, then living on Rittenhouse Square, recognized from his frequent travels to New York and Paris those sidewalk cafes brought people out at night and increased safety. "It was so much fun walking down Madison Avenue, in SoHo, or in Paris to see people in spring, summer, and fall sitting outside under umbrellas, where the conversation was good, where safety was good." While vacationing in St. Barts in 1997, Stein's friend Susan Wasserman told him the wine store on the east side of the square was closing. Wasserman, a commercial realtor in Philadelphia, had recently lured New York's Le Colonial restaurant (French-Vietnamese fusion) to open a location in one of her other Rittenhouse properties. It was then that Stein had an epiphany. "Regarding that wine store, I said 'this is it. . . . a little French-American bistro with an outdoor café on Rittenhouse Square would just be fantastic.'" Stein left the beach and immediately flew back to Philadelphia.[73]

After returning home, Stein spent hours in the park, glaring at the vacant space and visualizing his concept. Of the wine store he said, "I think that the biggest issue was the space. I didn't want to take it without doing an outdoor café. It wasn't Rittenhouse Square to me; it was a piazza. And, there was no way to do volume without using the outside." He collaborated with interior designer Marguerite "Meg" Rogers, who also designed the Striped Bass's space. They envisioned a 1920s-style European bistro, with silk-curtained walls, distressed mirrors, egg-shaped tables, velvet banquettes, and leather chairs. Rouge became a slice of Paris imported to Rittenhouse Square, with *Inquirer* restaurant critic Craig LaBan calling it a "jewel box salon." Stein hired French-trained chef Peter Dunmire (formerly of Deux Cheminées and Brasserie Perrier) to oversee the kitchen. The "Rouge burger" (a sixteen-dollar entrée) quickly became the city's most popular hamburger and Dunmire's steak frites and tuna tartare two of Rouge's best-selling dishes. Philadelphia's power brokers and hipsters flocked to Rouge in droves. Tourists and suburbanites quickly followed, making it the social attraction of Rittenhouse Square. The outdoor seating generated such demand that Stein eventually placed two rows of tables on the sidewalk, one at the curb and one against the façade. Because Rendell had legalized sidewalk cafes three years prior (and himself became a Rouge regular), Stein initially had no troubles over his sidewalk cafe.[74] But less than two years later, Rouge's success came under fire.

While many hailed the congenial atmosphere Rouge created, other Philadelphians grew irritated. In previous decades, Rittenhouse Square was the subject of various debates about its public usage, from wartime soldier drills and the building of underground garages to the removal of hippies and canine feces.[75] In the summer of 2000, one Rittenhouse Square resident explained, "I think it's [sidewalk cafe growth] wildly overdone. I don't object to the concept; I'm objecting to the overuse and abuse." L&I Committee members were particularly incensed by Rouge's curbside tables, which—similar to the structural addi-

Figure 8. Neil Stein's Rouge, Rittenhouse Square East, South Eighteenth and Chancellor Streets (June 2009). Photograph by author.

tions of the 1980s—violated the original ordinance. Between 1998 and 2000, the committee had issued permits for more than forty new sidewalk cafes, Rouge among them. While Stein maintained that he always instructed his employees to ensure fluid passage along the sidewalk, Dominic Verdi, the L&I deputy commissioner, stated that half of Rouge's eighteen sidewalk tables were illegal. Because L&I was granting more cafe permits than ever, Verdi's subordinates, who traversed the city to make sure cafes were in compliance, were spread thin. About Rouge, Verdi stated "I've received about ten complaints this summer."[76] The complaints came not from planning agencies or mayors, but from long time Rittenhouse residents who, in defending their neighborhood, worried about crowded sidewalks and the swelling crowds that Rouge attracted after dark. Pertaining to his neighbors, Stein said, "the complaints I got in the first few years were from older citizens who lived on the Square for a long time. They said 'there's too much noise on the square at eleven o'clock at night. It's not the way it used to be.' I used to fight back and say 'it's safer.'"[77]

For its first decade of business, Rouge occupied the center of the universe for well-heeled and well-connected Philadelphians, many of whom "couldn't even remember what Rittenhouse was like" before its 1998 debut.[78] The restaurant symbolized not only Stein's entrepreneurial moxie but also fueled the transformation of Rittenhouse Square from a residential neighborhood into Philadelphia's premier shopping and gathering spot. Stein realized that people desired much more than a meal; they wanted a stage; they wanted to be seen. Rouge delivered on its promise by providing the ideal urban spectacle. Though not the first sidewalk cafe to grace Philadelphia, Rouge undeniably became the most influential. It seemed any opposition it generated regarding noise or crowded sidewalks could not overcome public enthusiasm for the space. In April 1999, the *Philadelphia Daily News* announced, "it's taken this town a while to catch on, but at last, restaurants [throughout the city] are leaping on the streetside bandwagon." Stein himself continued riding the wave, opening Bleu, a sister restaurant to Rouge, on Rittenhouse Square in the summer of 2000. The mayor at the time, John Street, attended the opening to show his support for sidewalk cafes. In the new millennium sidewalk cafes cropped up throughout the city, making clear that a desire for public socializing, withering fears about the city, and an easing of political gridlock fueled the growth. As first district city councilman Frank DiCicco stated, "as a culture, we've really withdrawn and pulled ourselves indoors. Sidewalk cafes change the entire environment and they're a major component to the revitalization of Center City."[79] Rouge continued to attract crowds; during a summery weekend in October 2009 the restaurant realized its highest Saturday gross on record.[80]

In July 2009, the Central Philadelphia Development Corporation in conjunction with the Center City District (CCD) published its eighth-annual sidewalk cafe report, claiming that they "multiply the possibility of chance encounters and enhance the friendliness of Center City." The report concluded that between July 2001 and July 2009, the number of sidewalk cafes in Center City increased from 69 to 249. While the

proof of their success was in the numbers (both in gross receipts and their mounting appearance around town), Philadelphia's sidewalk cafes were not without drawbacks. Given their density on certain blocks, unobstructed foot passage indeed proved difficult. Along stretches of Walnut Street (west of Broad), Market Street in Old City (between Second and Third Streets), and on Rittenhouse Square East, the high concentration of outdoor tables often forced pedestrians to walk in the streets.

More, as much as Rendell's measures improved Philadelphia, the maligned urban features of homelessness and panhandling did not go away completely, but for sidewalk cafes to be successful, minimizing both was crucial. In 1998, the Philadelphia City Council passed an ordinance restricting both homelessness and panhandling. Led by then-councilman John Street, the ordinance's key provisions expressly banned persons from lying on sidewalks or panhandling within eight feet of any building entrance. Though homeless advocacy groups protested the proposal as "labeling homelessness a crime," the ordinance passed council fourteen to three.[81] It is no coincidence that sidewalk cafes grew spectacularly after the ordinance's passage. As Neil Smith claims, such legislation (in Philadelphia and elsewhere) emanated from the "revanchist" tone that many U.S. cities assumed in the 1990s.[82]

Whether contextualized as "revanchist," "gentrification," or what historian Jason Hackworth describes as "urban neocolonization," the coming of sidewalk cafes in Philadelphia undeniably signaled social and economic change. As Hackworth further illustrates, sidewalk cafes rode with the "third wave" of gentrification that swept through U.S. cities in the late 1990s. This wave, unlike those of the 1970s and 1980s, was "more state-facilitated and less resisted," spreading to marginal areas that were bypassed in previous phases.[83] In Northern Liberties, a former factory district that first witnessed "pioneer" residents in the form of artists and other creative types in the 1990s, large-scale developments flooded the area in the early 2000s. In 2009, Northern Liberties boasted of its replicated Roman piazza on the site of the defunct Schmidt's Brewery, a community

Figure 9. Old City's sidewalk cafes, Market Street between Second and Third Streets. With large numbers of cafes on certain streets, navigating sidewalks can be difficult for pedestrians (June 2009). Photograph by author.

anchor complete with apartments, retail stores, and numerous sidewalk cafes. In these contexts, Philadelphia's sidewalk cafes appealed mainly to a middle- and upper-class—yuppie—sensibility desirous of certain amenities (or what urban historian Ann Breen terms "hipness"), while simultaneously creating physical and psychological barriers for the former blue-collar or working-class residents who once called those neighborhoods home.[84] For some, the very appearance of a sidewalk cafe indicated an impending rise of rents. But as Richard LeGates and Chester Hartman demonstrate, the "outmovers" of places such as Northern Liberties or nearby Fishtown (a formerly working class area undergoing a shift at present) are predominantly white—although increasingly nonwhite—within the third wave.[85] In this context, the spread of sidewalk cafes in Philadelphia could be viewed as culturally selective; one would be hard-pressed to find vibrant sidewalk cafes in statistically low-income or dangerous areas such as Olney, Strawberry Mansion, and Gray's Ferry, or in the decidedly un-hip neighborhoods of Feltonville, Walnut Hill, or Mantua.

Sidewalk cafes, while providing spaces in which to gather, are not truly public spaces. They are privately owned-and-controlled hybrid zones that spill onto what is perceived as public space. For instance, many sidewalk cafes do not allow people to occupy tables if they are not paying customers. Most establishments remove their tables after closing, storing them inside, or piling them on one another with chained locks to prevent theft. Within the urban landscape, these are not spaces for whimsical moments of respite but spaces for commercial transactions. Additionally, the tables positioned outside Rouge—or the host of other restaurants—do not permit public amusement, solicitation, or ideological posturing; it's a rare occasion to witness intense political debates or street performances occurring at a Philadelphia sidewalk cafe. More, as sidewalk cafes reflect preferences for relaxation and leisure, most patrons prefer not to experience a mixture of dining and unwanted or unsightly urban features. Lastly, while legal hassles have diminished in the last ten years, sidewalk cafes continue to incite debates about the overlapping of public and private realms. Chris Scarduzio, chef

Figure 10. Sidewalk cafes at the Piazza at Schmidt's in Northern Liberties, a mixed-use residential and commercial complex inspired by Rome's Piazza Navona (June 2009). Photograph by author.

de cuisine and part-owner of Table 31 (currently Philadelphia's largest sidewalk cafe), recalls his experiences with the sidewalk cafe at Brasserie Perrier: "although I think these cafes are part of cultural movement in the restaurant industry as a whole, Philadelphia was ignorant about their value for a long time. I had one major complaint about Brasserie [the cafe]." To complement the restaurant's atmosphere, Scarduzio had played jazz over Brasserie's stereo system. "It echoed out onto the street and there was one politician (who Scarduzio insisted remain anonymous) that just brought me . . . almost to my knees. I almost had to shut the café down."[86] Scarduzio removed the stereo speakers that faced the sidewalk.

In postindustrial Philadelphia, the growth of sidewalk cafes was nothing short of miraculous. What began as a Center City phenomenon fraught with political and legal complexities eventually spread beyond its perimeter in scattered fashion. By 2009, sidewalk cafes could be found throughout Philadelphia at coffee shops, pizzerias, pubs, gelato bars, French bistros, taquerias, and even alongside food trucks moored to the city's college campuses. The CCD gauged that pedestrians in Center City encountered a sidewalk cafe every 155 feet and/or 75 seconds.[87] It seemed that restaurant operators (no matter their cuisine or price points) could throw a table and chairs on the sidewalk and generate a welcoming atmosphere. The spirit was contagious. In tandem with the expanding Pennsylvania Convention Center, the Pennsylvania Academy of the Fine Arts in 2008 proposed closing Cherry Street between North Broad and Fifteenth Streets to vehicular traffic and allowing for an outdoor plaza with sidewalk cafes. It seemed that in several central neighborhoods, sidewalk cafes had been instrumental in the revitalization of Philadelphia. For a city that had long struggled through deindustrialization, suburbanization, and crime, sidewalk cafes emerged as a vital part of the urban form and as stages upon which to display the good life.

NOTES

1. *Esquire* hailed Stein's Striped Bass as the "best new restaurant of the year" in 1994. Jenice M. Armstrong, "Saloon passes Stein's Scrutiny," *Philadelphia Daily News*, January 2, 1998, 31; Craig LaBan, "Superb Bistro Fare in a Scene Worthy of Fellini," *Philadelphia Inquirer*, August 16, 1998, SO1. Scholars have offered numerous explanations for the origins of "bistro" in the French lexicon. See Andrew F. Smith, ed., *The Oxford Companion to American Food and Drink* (New York: Oxford University Press, 2007), 53–54.

2. Judy West, "Food Red Hot," *Philadelphia Weekly*, May 20, 1998, 119.

3. Interview with Neil Stein conducted by the author, November 10, 2009.

4. Craig LaBan, "To the Sidewalks: The City Is Warming to the Café Life," *Philadelphia Inquirer*, April 11, 1999, B1.

5. April White, ed., *Philadelphia Magazine's Ultimate Restaurant Guide* (Philadelphia: Temple University Press, 2004), 35; Peter Van Allen, "Color Neil Stein 'Bleu,'" *Philadelphia Business Journal*, March 5, 2004, 3; in his examination of lower-income neighborhoods, Alexander Von Hoffman argues that in the absence of federal support, successful urban renewal since the early 1990s has occurred at the localized level through the combined efforts of citizens, clergy, entrepreneurs, wealthy benefactors, and private institutions. Alexander Von Hoffman, *House by House, Block by Block: The Rebirth of America's Urban Neighborhoods* (New York: Oxford University Press, 2003).

6. Elijah Anderson, "The Cosmopolitan Canopy," *Annals of the American Academy of Political and Social Science* 595 (2004): 14–31, 15, 28.

7. Steven Conn, *Metropolitan Philadelphia: Living with the Presence of the Past* (Philadelphia: University of Pennsylvania Press, 2006), 21.

8. The notion of sidewalk cafes as "urban spectacle" borrows from Anne Friedberg's social contextualization of arcades in post-Haussmann Paris. Anne Friedberg, *Window Shopping: Cinema and the Postmodern* (Berkeley: University of California Press, 1993), 68–70; for analyses of street theater and public behaviors in Philadelphia, see Susan Davis, *Parades and Power: Street Theater in Nineteenth-Century Philadelphia* (Philadelphia: Temple University Press, 1986), 5.

9. Ray Oldenburg, *The Great Good Place: Cafes, Coffee Shops, Bookstores, Bars, Hair Salons, and Other Hangouts at the Heart of a Community* (New York: Paragon House, 1989), 149.

10. In an 1826 comparison between the cafe and

the "box in the theatre" of London, Leigh Hunt remarked that the theatre box represented a kind of confinement while the "old coffeehouse" (cafe) represented a "more humane openness of intercourse." While this statement referred to the disappearance of coffeehouses in imperial London, it highlights the difference between cultural aptitude and casual socialization. Markman Ellis, *The Coffeehouse: A Cultural History* (London: Weidenfeld and Nicolson, 2004), 208; Mona Domosh, "Those Gorgeous Incongruities: Polite Politics and Public Space on the Streets of New York City," *Annals of the Association of American Geographers* 88 no. 2 (1998): 209–26.

11. Despite their benefits, in the first ten years of their being legal, only seventeen sidewalk cafes appeared in Center City. Long before the city council ordinance, Da Vinci Ristorante (located at 2007 Walnut Street) had sidewalk tables. But in a 1965 restaurant review, Nancy Love stated "nobody ever sits at the sidewalk tables out front. They merely prepare you for the cozy feeling inside." Nancy Love, *Guide to Philadelphia* (Philadelphia: Greater Philadelphia Magazine, 1965), 206.

12. David Lowenthal, "The Bicentennial Landscape: A Mirror Held up to the Past," *Geographical Review* 67 (1977): 253–67; For more on the development of haute and nouvelle cuisines in the United States, see John Mariani, *The Four Seasons: A History of America's Premier Restaurant* (New York: Crown, 1994); David Kamp, *The United States of Arugula: How We Became a Gourmet Nation* (New York: Broadway Books, 2006); Thomas McNamee, *Alice Waters and Chez Panisse* (New York: Penguin Press, 2007); Craig Claiborne, "The Chef Could Only Beam and Tell His Class, 'Une Merveille!'" *New York Times*, March 21, 1974, 48.

13. Erin Einhorn, "Dining Out[side]: Taking It to the Streets, Outdoor Dining Is Springing to Life throughout the City," *Philadelphia Daily News*, April 30, 1999, 5.

14. The PLCB formed at the end of Prohibition in 1933. By the early 1980s, Governor Richard Thornburgh's administration had devoted considerable energy to greater decontrol of alcohol sales in hopes of dismantling the PLCB. Thornburgh felt the system was "outdated, corrupt, and poorly managed." Frederick Cusick, "This Time, Liquor-Reform Plan May Pack More Punch," *Philadelphia Inquirer*, December 4, 1983, D1; Mark Wagenveld, "Rounding up Cen-

ter City Prostitutes," *Philadelphia Inquirer*, September 25, 1983, B2; Thomas Hine, "The Central Issue Is the Size of Philadelphia's Center," *Philadelphia Inquirer*, July 17, 1983, A5; Thomas Hine, "Sidewalk Syndrome: If It's Not Cafes, It's Construction," *Philadelphia Inquirer*, November 8, 1987, G16.

15. Daniel Bluestone, "The Pushcart Evil: Peddlers, Merchants, and New York City's Streets, 1890–1940," *Journal of Urban History* 18 (November 1991): 68–92; John Gaber, "Manhattan's 14th Street Vendors' Market: Informal Street Peddlers' Complementary Relationship with New York City's Economy," *Urban Anthropology* 23 (Winter 1994): 1–36; John C. Cross, *Informal Politics: Street Vendors and the State in Mexico City* (Palo Alto: Stanford University Press, 1998); Sharit Bhowmik, ed., *Street Vendors in the Global Urban Economy* (New York: Routledge, 2010).

16. Edward Colimore, "On Foot, It's No Cakewalk in the City," *Philadelphia Inquirer*, January 10, 1988, A1.

17. Richard J. Beamish, "Lunch Wagon Drive to Be Called Off," *Philadelphia Evening Bulletin*, May 9, 1927, 4.

18. Morley Cassidy, "Hokey-Pokey, Pretzels, Pepper Pot: Picturesque Army on Way Out," *Philadelphia Evening Bulletin*, July 18, 1940, B2.

19. Philip Schaeffer, "Soft Pretzel Street Vendors All Ready for Busiest Season," *Philadelphia Evening Bulletin*, November 12, 1950, 12.

20. The Philadelphia Redevelopment Authority was created by federal statute in 1945. Using government funding, the PRA acquired land and/or demolished buildings being put to "undesirable uses." See Russell Weigley, ed., *Philadelphia: A 300-Year History* (New York: Norton, 1982), 670; The Greater Philadelphia Movement, established in 1949, was a public–private interest alliance aimed at expanding the city's service sector as its manufacturing base began to decline. Carmen Teresa Whalen, "Citizens and Workers: African Americans and Puerto Ricans in Philadelphia's Regional Economy since WWII," in *African-American Urban History since World War II*, ed. Kenneth L. Kusmer and Joe W. Trotter (Chicago: University of Chicago Press, 2009), 106.

21. Though Philadelphia engaged in slum clearances, the amount was less than those conducted in New York, New Haven, or Boston. For a comparative explanation of Philadelphia's postwar overhaul, see Scott Knowles, ed., *Imagining Philadelphia: Edmund*

Bacon and the City of the Future (Philadelphia: University of Pennsylvania Press, 2009).

22. For a recent revision of postwar urban planning and its legacies in the United States, see Hilary Ballon and Kenneth T. Jackson, ed., *Robert Moses and the Modern City: The Transformation of New York* (New York: Norton, 2007); Leo Adde, *Nine Cities: The Anatomy of Downtown Renewal* (Washington D.C.: Urban Land Institute, 1969), 15–43.

23. Bacon was especially insistent about removing the food vendors and stalls from the Dock Street Market (adjacent to Old City) in hopes of redeveloping the area as "Society Hill." The vendors and stalls were removed in 1959 and relocated to the Food Distribution Center in South Philadelphia, clearing the way for the I. M. Pei-designed Society Hill Towers and colonial refurbishment. Joseph Guess, "Society Hill Developers Sign Contracts," *Philadelphia Evening Bulletin,* January 9, 1959, F4; "Two Councilmen Balk at Razing in Society Hill," *Philadelphia Evening Bulletin,* January 28, 1959. Bacon called contemporary urban planners "space blind," arguing they were more concerned with mass. See Edmund Bacon, *The Design of Cities* (New York: Viking Press, 1967), 13–17.

24. For perspectives on Philadelphia's "honky-tonk zone," see Robert W. Bailey, "Sexual Identity and Police Practices in Philadelphia," in *Gay Politics, Urban Politics: Identity and Economics in the Urban Setting,* ed. Robert W. Bailey (New York: Columbia University Press, 1999), 251–52. The Better Philadelphia exhibition was a downscaled model of Bacon's renewal plan, unveiled at Gimbel's Department Store in 1947. Historians have likened Better Philadelphia to Norman Bel Geddes's Futurama exhibit at the 1939 World's Fair in New York. Doug Hassebroek, "Edmund Bacon: Savior of the Streams," *Perspecta* 30 (1995): 84–92; Denise Scott Brown, "Form, Design, and the City," *Journal of the American Planning Association* 28 (November 1962): 293–99.

25. Interview with Bernard Spain conducted by the author, October 13, 2009.

26. Many of the lunch stands (non-roaming operations) were dilapidated structures of wood and corrugated metal that were in non-compliance with Philadelphia's building codes. Some of these lunch stands had been in operation since the 1920s. "Operators of Lunch Stands Protest City Order to Move," *Philadel-* *phia Evening Bulletin,* April 14, 1953, F4; and Temple University Urban Archives, Philadelphia, photo gallery, "Street Vendors" folder.

27. Frank Brookhouser, *Our Philadelphia* (Garden City: Doubleday, 1957), 11.

28. "Merchants Battle City Bill to Drop Bans on Peddlers," *Philadelphia Evening Bulletin,* July 13, 1958, B3; Guian McKee, "Blue Sky Boys, Professional Citizens, and Knights in Shining Money: Philadelphia's Penn Center Project and the Constraints of Private Development," *Journal of Planning History* 6 (February 2007): 48–80. In March 1960, the Philadelphia City Council voted sixteen to one to allow newsstands to remain in the CBD, citing them as a "public commodity" and the "only way that people have of finding out what's going on in the world." Pretzel vendors were allowed to remain, for they sold foodstuffs uniquely representative of Philadelphia's heritage. David Runkel, "Council Panel Curbs a Proposal for Center City Sidewalk Cafes," *Philadelphia Evening Bulletin,* November 1, 1978, A1.

29. The "Chinese Wall" was a masonry rail trestle that bisected Center City between Penn Square and the Schuylkill River. Aside from being difficult to cross at street level, the constant movement of elevated trains made the Chinese Wall a source of derision. Anastasia Loukaitou-Sideris and Renia Ehrenfeucht, *Sidewalks: Conflict and Negotiation over Public Space* (Cambridge, Mass.: MIT Press, 2009), 4.

30. Marc Schogol, "Uneasy Ceasefire Exists in Merchant–Vendor War," *Philadelphia Evening Bulletin,* July 16, 1974, A2.

31. L. Stuart Ditzen, "ACLU Assails Bill to Restrict Street Vendors," *Philadelphia Evening Bulletin,* May 8, 1973, A8; T. T. Chang, "There Is Room for the Vendors," *Philadelphia Evening Bulletin,* February 6, 1975, A10.

32. Henry Reichner, "Vendors Mar the City's Image," *Philadelphia Evening Bulletin,* November 6, 1975, A11.

33. Oldenburg, *The Great Good Place,* 150; Bluestone, "The Pushcart Evil," 68–92; Bernard Rudofsky, *Streets for People: A Primer for Americans* (Garden City: Doubleday, 1959), 313; Diane Cardwell, "Lured by a Hint of Spring, Diners Flock Outdoors," *New York Times,* March 9, 2010, A19.

34. "Section 9–208 Sidewalk Cafes," *Ordinances 1979* (Philadelphia City Archives), 416–20.

35. David Runkel, "Council Panel Curbs a Proposal for Center City Sidewalk Cafes," *Philadelphia Evening Bulletin,* November 1, 1978, B1.

36. "Section 9–208 Sidewalk Cafes," *Ordinances 1979* (Philadelphia City Archives), 416–20.

37. Ginny Wiegand, "Downtown, a Sidewalk Battle Revisited," *Philadelphia Inquirer,* June 18, 1993, B1.

38. For more on the notion of adventure and ethnic cuisine, see John Mariani, *Eating Out: Fearless Dining in Ethnic Restaurants* (New York: Quill, 1985).

39. Larry Ford argues that postmodern urban planning focused less on promoting the growth of office space (of which Philadelphia had a glut in the 1980s) and more on developing sports stadiums, waterfront parks, convention centers, and cultural centers. Larry Ford, *America's New Downtowns: Revitalization or Reinvention* (Baltimore: Johns Hopkins University Press, 2003), 146–48.

40. "Future of Center City: It Has Regional Role," *Philadelphia Inquirer,* March 5, 1985, A1. While Downey's opened its patio addition in 1980, it was not officially approved via the city council until 1988. *Journal of the Council of the City of Philadelphia,* vol. 2, July 1, 1988–December 31, 1988, 1844–45.

41. Gerald Etter, "At the Site of Horn and Hardart, the Latest from the West Coast," *Philadelphia Inquirer,* September 14, 1984, F1. For more on the demise of the Horn and Hardart Co., see David Freeland, *Automats, Taxi Dances, and Vaudeville: Excavating Manhattan's Lost Places of Leisure,* (New York: New York University Press, 2009), 169–86.

42. Roger Cohn, "Temporary Café Isn't, City Says, and Tells Restaurant to Remove It," *Philadelphia Inquirer,* April 17, 1986, B14; Ben Harvey, "Business Meets Brotherly Love," *Advocate,* May 2009, 44–47.

43. The majority of city council members voted against street vending in the 1970s. For example, in September 1978, the council delivered a vote of fifteen to one outlawing street vending in Society Hill. "Bill # 1363," *Journal of the Council of the City of Philadelphia,* vol. 2, July 1, 1978–December 31, 1978, 1844–45.

44. Vernon Loeb, "Council Comes to Aid Illegal Additions," *Philadelphia Inquirer,* July 21, 1988, B2; Edward N. Eisen, "Streets Warn Police: Hands off Vendors," *Philadelphia Evening Bulletin,* July 8, 1980, A7; Howard Schneider, "City Taking Tayoun to the Wall,"

Philadelphia Daily News, July 7, 1987, 16; Thomas Ferrick, "Restaurants Get a Reprieve from Council," *Philadelphia Inquirer,* November 18, 1988, B1.

45. *Journal of the Council of the City of Philadelphia,* vol. 2, July 1, 1988–December 31, 1988, 1111; Vanessa Williams, "Council Flexes Muscle, Overrides Veto on Sidewalk Café," *Philadelphia Inquirer,* December 9, 1988, B8.

46. Craig LaBan, "To the Sidewalks: The City Is Warming to the Café Life," *Philadelphia Inquirer,* April 11, 1999, B1.

47. Elissa Elan, "Having Words with Shimon Bokovza: Owner and Founder, Sushi Samba," *Nation's Restaurant News,* January 12, 2009, 22.

48. Tayoun served a forty-month sentence in federal prison in the early 1990s after pleading guilty to racketeering, mail-fraud, and tax-evasion charges. Emilie Lounsberry, "Vincent J. Fumo Will Be Sentenced Today," *Philadelphia Inquirer,* July 14, 2009, A1.

49. *Journal of the Council of the City of Philadelphia,* vol. 1, January 1, 1987–June 30, 1987, 1363–65.

50. Mark McDonald, "City's Becoming a Sidewalk Café Society," *Philadelphia Daily News,* December 19, 1991, 18; Vanessa Williams, "Won't Quit on Apropos, Goode Says," *Philadelphia Inquirer,* January 6, 1989, B3; Ginny Wiegand, "Battle for Café Addition Nears End," *Philadelphia Inquirer,* December 19, 1991, B1; "The Book and the Cook Fair, Featuring the Fare of PA," *Philadelphia Tribune,* March 20, 1990, 2C; W. Wilson Goode, *In Goode Faith* (Valley Forge: Judson Press, 1992).

51. Stuart Bykofsky, "Dine and Drink as the World Strolls By," *Philadelphia Daily News,* May 10, 1985, 12.

52. Interview with Allan Domb conducted by the author, November 2, 2009.

53. Mark Bowden and Hank Klibanoff, "Nighttime in Center City, Where Two Worlds Collide," *Philadelphia Inquirer,* October 27, 1989, A1.

54. For more on the "consumerist reinvention" of Philadelphia, see David Grazian, *On the Make: The Hustle of Urban Nightlife* (Chicago: University of Chicago Press, 2008), 9; Joel Kotkin, *The Next Hundred Million: America in 2050* (New York: Penguin Press, 2010), 59–61.

55. Bob Fernandez, "Restaurants Are Fattening Region's Economy," *Philadelphia Inquirer,* July 26, 1998, A1; Joseph Coyle and Amanda Walmac, "America's

Finest Restaurant Towns," *Money* 22 (July 1993): 120–30; Hal K. Rothman, *Neon Metropolis: How Las Vegas Started the 21st Century* (New York: Routledge, 2002); Darra Goldstein, "The Way We Live Now," *Gastronomica* 4 (Spring 2004): 1–2; Tom Belden, "Viewing What the Convention Center Has Delivered," *Philadelphia Inquirer*, December 19, 2007, B1. Jane Jacobs argues that the primary benefits of sidewalks are the safety and "casual social life" they encourage. See Jane Jacobs, *The Death and Life of Great Cities* (New York: Vintage, 1961), 55; from the author's interview with Allan Domb, November 2, 2009.

56. Interview of George Perrier conducted by the author; Monday, October 26, 2009.

57. "Hope in Philadelphia," *Wall Street Journal*, January 8, 1992, A10; Buzz Bissinger, *A Prayer for the City* (New York: Random House, 1997), 122; Ben Yagoda, "Ed Rendell: The Philadelphian's Formidable Energy Has Earned Him a Reputation as a Miracle Worker," *New York Times*, May 22, 1994, SM26.

58. "Executive Advice: Can Corporate Types Make Sense of City Hall?" *Philadelphia Inquirer*, March 30, 1992, A10; In respect to the difficulty of opening restaurants in Philadelphia, Perrier was referring mainly to the Liquor Control Board (LCB), which for many years imposed "blue laws" and high taxes on Philadelphia businesses. Typically, the bulk of a restaurant's profits come from alcohol sales. Interview with George Perrier conducted by the author; Monday, October 26, 2009. In 1957, former mayor Richardson Dilworth relaxed (but did not eliminate) the blue laws to attract visitors and conventions. For more on "blue laws" in Philadelphia (or "Sunday legislation"), see David Laband, *Blue Laws: The History, Economics, and Politics of Sunday Closing Laws*, (Lexington, Mass.: Lexington Books, 1987), 123–24. In 1965, Nancy Love lamented that Pennsylvania's blue laws "don't stimulate the growth of eating places and night spots." More, she stated, "segments of the Philadelphia population prefer dining and entertaining at home." Love, *Guide to Philadelphia*, 198.

59. The 1979 Sidewalk Café Ordinance allowed cafes only from the Delaware to the Schuylkill Rivers and between South and Vine Streets. "Ordinances 1979," *Philadelphia City Archives: City Council Journals*, 416–20; Section 9–208, "Sidewalk cafes."

60. John McCalla, "Curbing Diners' Appetites," *Philadelphia Business Journal*, March 26, 1999, 6.

61. Jim Davis, "People See New Day with Goode," *Philadelphia Tribune*, January 3, 1984, 1; Bissinger, *A Prayer for the City*, 23.

62. Bissinger, *A Prayer for the City*, 10.

63. Doreen Carvajal, "Outside City Hall, the Chomps Elysees Where Cars Once Parked," *Philadelphia Inquirer*, July 14, 1992, B1.

64. Dave Davies, "Call It a Food Court: Sidewalk Café Set outside City Hall," *Philadelphia Daily News*, July 14, 1992, 7; Doreen Carvajal, "Serving Up Protests at City Hall Café," *Philadelphia Inquirer*, July 17, 1992, B2.

65. Joseph L. Borkson, *Philadelphia: An American Paris* (Philadelphia: Camino Books, 2002), 84.

66. David Brownlee, *Building the City Beautiful: The Benjamin Franklin Parkway and the Philadelphia Museum of Art* (Philadelphia: The Philadelphia Museum of Art, 1989); for more on Paris's twentieth-century urban planning, see Colin Jones, *Paris: Biography of a City* (New York: Viking Press, 2004); Inga Saffron, "Le Grand Philly with the Convention Center and Avenue of the Arts," *Philadelphia Inquirer*, November 12, 1993, A5; Paris's cafe numbers were staggering: its first opened in 1643. By 1800, Paris contained 700, in 1967 13,977, and in 1989, a slight decrease to 12,500. Noel Fitch, *Paris Café: The Select Crowd* (New York: Soft Skull Press, 2007), 12; and John Gunther, *Twelve Cities*, (New York: Harper and Row, 1969), 70.

67. *Journal of the Council of the City of Philadelphia*, vol. 2, July 1, 1993–December 31, 1993, 1641–45; Doreen Carvajal, "Restaurateurs Go to Council to Ease Sidewalk Café Laws," *Philadelphia Inquirer*, June 17, 1993, B1.

68. Loukaitou-Sideris and Ehrenfeucht, *Sidewalks*, 52.

69. Einhorn, "Dining Out[side]," *Philadelphia Daily News*, 5.

70. In 2005, Stein plead guilty to filing false tax returns for 1999, 2000, and 2001. More, he had directed employees to skim cash from his restaurants at the rate of $200 per day and to funnel the money directly to him. He displays candor in reference to his past drug problems, although he has never faced drug charges. Michael Hinkelman, "Feds: 'Tax Cheat' Stein Should Get Jail," *Philadelphia Daily News*, January 18, 2006, A1.

71. Nathan Gorenstein, "Rittenhouse Row on Visa Short List," *Philadelphia Inquirer*, March 10, 1997, B2.

72. "Community Rights How to Restore Civilization in Center City," *Philadelphia Inquirer,* February 4, 1990, B1; Sheila Simmons, "They're Not Nuts about Walnut Street," *Philadelphia Daily News,* March 1, 1990, B4.

73. Interview with Neil Stein conducted by the author, November 10, 2009.

74. Author's interview with Stein; Craig LaBan, "Superb Bistro Fare in a Scene Worthy of Fellini," *Philadelphia Inquirer,* August 16, 1998, SO1.

75. For a history of Rittenhouse Square's public use and its role in public space debates, see Charles J. Cohen, *Rittenhouse Square: Past and Present* (Philadelphia: Privately Printed, 1922); and Nancy M. Heinzen, *The Perfect Square: A History of Rittenhouse Square* (Philadelphia: Temple University Press, 2009).

76. Linda K. Harris, "Are They Culture or Clutter? Sidewalk Cafes Provide Atmosphere—The Real Kind—But Also Debate," *Philadelphia Inquirer,* September 2, 2000, A12.

77. As told to the author in interview on November 10, 2009.

78. Christine Speer, "Bistro Confidential," *Philadelphia Magazine,* April 2009, 56; Jessica Pressler, "Rouge," *Philadelphia Magazine,* September 2006, 71.

79. Linda Loyd, "Convention Center Expansion Spurs Development," *Philadelphia Inquirer,* June 11, 2008, B1; Harris, "Are They Culture or Clutter?" *Philadelphia Inquirer,* September 2, 2000, A10.

80. Stein requested that the actual amount of sales remain confidential. As told to the author in interview on November 10, 2009.

81. Noel Weyrich, "Mean Sweeps or Clean Sweeps?" *Philadelphia Weekly,* June 17, 1998, 15.

82. Neil Smith uses the term "revanchist," loosely meaning "revenge," to describe a fortifying of urban public spaces against elements of crime, vandalism, and illegal occupation. See Neil Smith, *The New Urban Frontier: Gentrification and the Revanchist City* (New York: Routledge, 1996), 44–47.

83. Jason Hackworth, *The Neoliberal City: Governance, Ideology, and Development in American Urbanism* (Ithaca: Cornell University Press, 2007); for greater explanation of "third wave" gentrification, see Loretta Lees et al., ed., *Gentrification* (New York: Routledge, 2008), 178–79.

84. Ann Breen considers "hipness" ("something you know when you see it") as integral to definitions of urbanity. See Breen and Dick Rigby, *In Town Living: A Different American Dream* (Westport, Conn.: Praeger, 2004), 4.

85. Richard Legates and Chester Hartman, "The Anatomy of Displacement in the United States," in *Gentrification of the City,* ed. Neil Smith and Peter Williams, 178–200 (Boston: Allen & Unwin, 1986).

86. Interview with Chris Scarduzio conducted by the author, November 11, 2009.

87. "Center City Reports Sidewalk Cafes," *Central Philadelphia Development Corporation,* July 2009. http://www.centercityphila.org/pressroom/prelease070709.php, accessed December 1, 2009.

SARA McDOWELL AND CATHERINE SWITZER

Violence and the Vernacular

Conflict, Commemoration, and Rebuilding

in the Urban Context

The Bogside, Crossmaglen, the Falls, the Shankill, and Andersonstown. In the mental maps of those who had never been to Ireland, these places had tiny crossed swords after their names. People thought them deathfields—remote, televised knacker's yards.
— McLiam Wilson, *Eureka Street* (1997)

The Northern Ireland Troubles transformed everyday landscapes into places akin to battlefields. The above excerpt from McLiam Wilson's novel *Eureka Street* captures something of how external observers perceived particular areas in the region. Yet even as the violence took place, these same areas were the venue for thousands of everyday lives. The overarching aim of this paper is to sketch the journey of an everyday vernacular landscape through a time of conflict to its more recent history in that conflict's aftermath. Vernacular landscapes exist, argues Stangl, to provide a "complex array of spatial forms to support everyday life and the world, with lived experience and representation in a supporting role."[1] Clearly, in times of armed conflict, violence becomes part of everyday life and plays out across everyday landscapes. However, in postconflict situations the issue of representation can be crucial, making the vernacular a venue for conflict of another kind.

Using the example of the Bogside in Derry as our case study, we explore how violence and the postconflict process of commemoration have interacted with a specific urban landscape.[2] The segregated nature of residential space in Northern Ireland's urban centers makes this a useful approach to take in relation to the region's commemorative culture; as Dawson observes, "local variability . . . mean[s] that careful attention must be paid to the locatedness of cultural memories formed in the course of the war."[3] Wherever it takes place, commemoration is often a partisan practice, replete with "memories which are publicly articulated" and "those which have been privatized, fragmented, or repressed."[4] This is particularly true in Northern Ireland, where the fragmented nature of the memorial landscape reflects a deeply divided society. Although some five hundred physical memorials to the thirty-five hundred victims of the Troubles exist throughout Northern Ireland, very few commemorate the dead collectively. Instead they are erected by a variety of organizations, such as paramilitary groups and units within the police and armed forces, each with the intention of commemorating their own dead. Efforts to commemorate all Troubles victims, regardless of their backgrounds or the circumstances surrounding their deaths, have been fraught with controversy.

The Bogside is one of the most well-known districts of Northern Ireland, made famous—or infamous—in music and on film.[5] On the eve of the Troubles, the Bogside was one of the most economically deprived wards in the city, with high unemployment levels and housing shortages stemming from decades of state and local government discrimination.[6] Home to a tightly knit Catholic nationalist community, bound by close family ties and a commonality of background, class, and religious affiliation, it possessed high levels of social capital. In the late 1960s and early

1970s, the area played a key role in the nationalist challenge to the Northern Ireland state when a combination of residents, civil rights activists, and Republican paramilitaries turned the Bogside into a virtual no-go area for state security forces for the best part of three years.[7] Around this time the Bogside was the scene of some of the most infamous violence of the Troubles, witnessing the deaths of civilians, members of the state security forces, and Republican paramilitaries. It was thrust into the global spotlight following the events of January 30, 1972, better known as Bloody Sunday, when members of the Parachute Regiment opened fire on an anti-internment rally organized by the Northern Ireland Civil Rights Association. Fourteen civilians died and a further thirteen were injured.[8] The events of that day rose to prominence again after the creation of the Bloody Sunday Inquiry in 1998 to investigate what had happened. The Inquiry, under Lord Saville, finally published its report in June 2010. In contrast to the original 1973 investigation under Lord Widgery, the Saville Inquiry exonerated those killed of any wrongdoing and found that the actions of the British army that day had been, as British Prime Minister David Cameron put it, "unjustified and unjustifiable."[9]

Throughout its existence, the Bogside has been home to thousands of people, constituting the vernacular spaces of their everyday lives even as it provided a venue for the deaths of civilians, paramilitaries and members of the security forces during the Troubles. In recent years, it has also become an intensively memorialized landscape, in which traditional monuments and other forms of memorial, including wall murals, are located in the everyday spaces of the people who live there.[10] This paper begins by introducing the theoretical framework, discussing briefly the functions of cities and the challenges they face during conflict. With a focus on the Bogside, we then go on to show how actors in the Northern Ireland conflict utilized the urban landscape to engage in warfare. The third section of the paper examines the postconflict context and the return to a peaceful society, discussing how the contested practices and processes of commemoration and memory politics often come into conflict with the ongoing reshaping and reimagining of the Bogside's urban geography.

Violence, the Urban Landscape, and the Bogside

> To envisage the city . . . as something that is just there, a backdrop to life, is to misapprehend the way in which lived experience always unfolds in reciprocal engagement with the urban landscape.[11]

De Certeau's seminal work *The Practice of Everyday Life* invites us to conceptualize the city as a place controlled and resisted.[12] Exploring the diverse ways in which cities are negotiated, he identifies two key actors: strategists and tacticians. Strategists, he suggests, impose order—they are responsible for infrastructural governance including the planning, construction, and direction of urban space. Tacticians are the city's residents. They refute and resist this order, both consciously and subconsciously, by utilizing space in a variety of ways that often conflict with the strategists' intended purpose. During violent conflict, urban spaces in the city assume heightened importance and take on functions beyond those intended by both strategists and tacticians. Streets become battlefields, while buildings house snipers and bombs.[13] Combatants are tacticians, moving through and negotiating a battlefield designed and constructed by noncombatant strategists. Urban battlefields have a specific set of characteristics. Seen in military terms, the layout of urban areas "creates a highly physically structured but fragmented series of compartmentalized battlefields," which influence how combatants experience the conflict there. As Ashworth puts it, the "continuous high level of alertness demanded by close actions, the physical discomfort and the insecurity of isolated small-unit operations without fixed lines, secure flanks, or protected rear all contribute to the rapid onset of battle fatigue."[14] Elements of urban architecture and design therefore become intrinsic to the conflict, offering or closing down opportunities to attack opponents, reclassifying space into open or dead ground, and turning items of street furniture into potential sites of improvised cover.

For combatants, the intended target is the "other," yet as Hills observes, military urban operations take place against, within, and through civilian movements.[15] Likewise, the movements of residents' everyday lives take place against, within, and through those undertaken by the military. Clearly, for those living in these urban areas, this creates a serious challenge to ideas of the home as "a place to withdraw to, a place of rest, and a place where one has a large degree of control over what happens," even if, as Reid notes, in Northern Ireland the "privacy of the home has been repeatedly compromised" from both within and without.[16] The nature of the conflict in Northern Ireland meant that many acts of violence took place within vernacular landscapes, even as uninvolved bystanders went about their day-to-day lives. The landmark publication *Lost Lives,* which tells the stories of more than thirty-five hundred people who died during the Troubles, provides a litany of instances in which people were intentionally killed in the most everyday of places: a bus station, a train, a shopping center, a pub, office buildings, a classroom, the street.[17]

Where the specific example of the Bogside is concerned, the area's urban geography had important ramifications for the way in which the conflict unfolded there. Taking its name from the bog from which it emerged in the 1600s, the Bogside is located on the West Bank of the city just below its seventeenth-century walls. Built between 1614 and 1618 during the Ulster Plantation, the walls helped consolidate the Protestant colonial settlement of Londonderry and played a vital role in its resistance to siege in 1689.[18] Much of the original structures still stand and the walls have witnessed events "where military encounters were won and lost but where psychological victories are still being sought."[19] The walls overlook the Bogside and acted as both a physical and symbolic interface between the state and residents during the Troubles. In practical terms they provided the British Army with an almost panoramic view of the Bogside neighborhood below (Figure 1).

During the 1960s, the geography of the Bogside changed radically as the area was redeveloped. The Bogside was part of the city's South Ward, where levels of overcrowding were the highest of any urban area in Ireland.[20] The high population density was largely a result of the city's complex electoral geography, which demanded that the Catholic vote be crowded into the South Ward if the Protestant Unionists who dominated the city's local government were to retain their majority. By the early sixties over half the city's population lived in the South Ward.[21] Much of the housing stock was in a very dilapidated state, and redevelopment not only involved replacing buildings in the crowded Bogside but also moving much of its population to newly built housing estates on the edge of the city. While the architectural style and layout of these developments were influenced heavily by modernist urban planning, the changes were made necessary by the controversy surrounding housing allocation. Beginning in 1963, the Northern Ireland Housing Trust demolished sections of existing housing, including a number of terraced streets (themselves a product of a previous era of industrial urbanism), and replaced them with new buildings. Most prominent among these was the Rossville Flats complex, erected on the site of a former cattle market.[22] The clean lines of modernism replaced much of the more haphazard gathering of older buildings but initially, as Shea puts it, "relief far outweighed regret" for most Bogside residents, who were pleased that the housing issue was finally being addressed. As time went on, many opinions changed as the full implications of the massive population movement for interpersonal relationships become clear. Some 15,000 people had left the area by 1974, halving its population density but breaking up extended families and pre-existing religious, social, and community ties.[23]

This redevelopment process was in full flow when the Troubles erupted in the late 1960s. In the Bogside, newly built properties overlooked large open areas still waiting to be redeveloped. A number of streets made up of terraced housing still stood, albeit largely empty and derelict.[24] Aerial photographs taken at the time show a

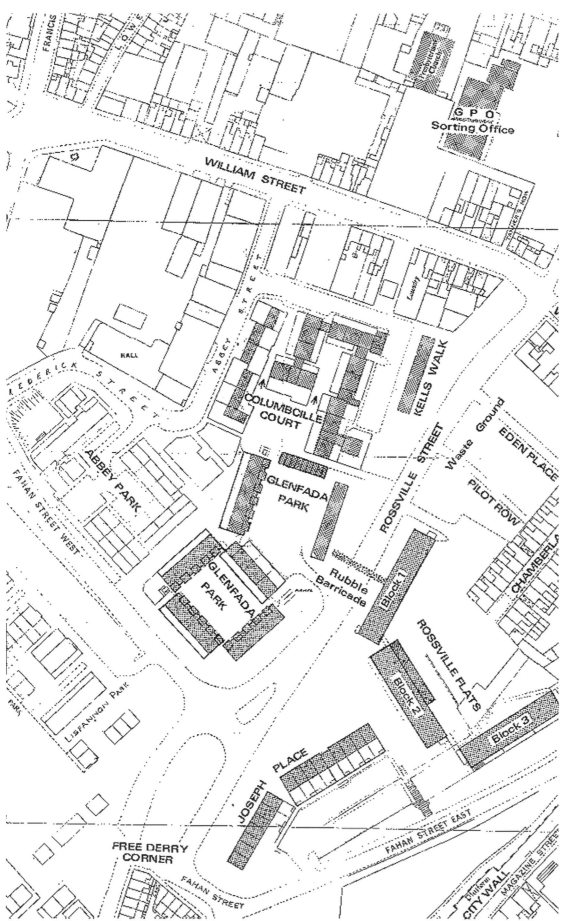

Figure 1. Map of the Bogside area of Derry, circa 1972. Extracted from the Widgery Report, Appendix C, Plan of Londonderry. Crown copyright material is reproduced with the permission of the Controller of HMSO and the Queen's Printer for Scotland.

mixture of old terraces and newly built properties, including the Rossville Flats, alongside extensive areas of open ground strewn with rubble and other detritus (Figures 2, 3, and 4).[25]

Civilians, activists and paramilitaries in the neighborhood used the landscapes around them to engage in both armed and symbolic warfare against members of the state security forces. In the case of the barricade placed across Rossville Street, the landscape literally became a part of the protest, since the rubble used to construct it was sourced from the area's demolished houses. The barricade also incorporated an oil drum and wooden trestles that could be moved to allow vehicles to pass through.[26] Skinner likens

this engagement with the everyday fabric to an aestheticization of violence, arguing that there was almost a resourcefulness in the creation of protest vehicles. Milk crates and bottles became petrol bombs and the lids of garbage cans were banged loudly by women to warn the community of a police or army presence.[27]

The urban landscape also became a means for symbolic resistance. In 1969 resident John "Caker" Casey painted the slogan "You are now entering Free Derry" on the gable end of a row of terraced houses. Jarman notes that this painting represented the first engagement with public space by nationalists in Northern Ireland and as such was highly controversial.[28] Since 1954, the Flags and Emblems Act had banned such displays wherever they were likely to cause offense. For the authorities this categorization of space effectively meant anywhere in Northern Ireland. The symbolic currency of Free Derry Corner (as it became known locally) as a symbol of resistance quickly gathered value and despite its defiant message it survived against the odds at a time when virtually all other nationalist/Republican markings were not tolerated.[29]

Dawson has written of how "these competing imaginative geographies of control and resistance [transformed] the material territory into a cultural landscape formed on the pattern of the conflicted past," but it is important to note that this was not just a geography of the imagination. The complex urban geography of the area had a crucial influence on the shape of the violent events that occurred within it.[30]

Open spaces are one of the characteristics of European urban planning at this time, but Shea argues that, in the case of the Bogside, the "tidying" of the area's layout according to broadly modernist thinking functioned to assist the military authorities in observing and controlling the area: "strategies for the maintenance of public order and the quelling of terrorism became increasingly visible in the emergent environmental design that accompanied urban renewal."[31] The removal of alleys, the layout of cul-de-sacs, large open spaces, and positioning of public buildings all functioned, she contends, to "maintain order, create fast and easy access for military vehicles to

Figure 2. Eden Place, off Rossville Street, circa 1969. Copyright Eamon Melaugh (cain.ulster .ac.uk/melaugh).

enter previously dense and erratically organized urban neighborhoods, increase possibilities for surveillance, decrease opportunities for civil disturbances, and limit escape routes out of housing estates."[32]

Whatever the validity of these contentions (and Shea provides no evidence of intent on the part of the authorities), "schemes of top-down control are frequently partial and piecemeal," and this was certainly the case where redevelopment in the Bogside was concerned.[33] Rioters and paramilitaries familiar with the area could build their escape routes "around an intimate knowledge of backyards and alleyways."[34]

For the British army on the other hand, the geography was frequently a hindrance rather than an opportunity. Giving evidence to the Saville Inquiry, Colonel Roy Jackson, who commanded the 1st Battalion of the Royal Anglian Regiment in the city, explained how:

> The topography of Londonderry, particularly with its high city walls and buildings in the Bogside ranging from the high Rossville Flats to older streets and new purpose-built houses, meant it was almost impossible to establish immediately where explosions occurred or from where shots were fired, unless the smoke of the explosion or the flash from the weapon on firing could be seen. Noise reverberated in the usual confrontation areas and we stressed the problem of the "Derry sound" to all soldiers who would need to make those all important split second decisions on patrol or when deployed in Londonderry. Whenever new soldiers joined us we made sure they were familiar with this problem.[35]

The cluttered geography of urban landscapes, replete with escape routes, potential ambush points, and lack of security and clear lines of sight, made them ideal for the guerrilla-style tactics employed by the IRA (Figure 6). Colonel Jackson included this in his evidence when he described how the microgeography immediately surrounding the Rossville Flats made it a particularly difficult area for the military: "There was a tremendous honeycomb of walkways and passageways between the three blocks, in which

people could move around very quickly. It was, because of its design, a gunman's paradise."[36]

As a commanding officer, Jackson viewed the landscape of the Bogside from a largely strategic perspective, but the soldiers under his command experienced it in a more intimate and immediate way. For soldiers who entered the Bogside, its unfamiliar urban environment was mentally categorized into points of cover and areas of exposure accompanied by the assessment of personal risk. Submitting evidence to the Saville Inquiry, Soldier C described being on the balcony of the small block of flats at Kells Walk on Bloody Sunday:

> I vaguely remember running up some stairs with a hand rail on the right and bricks on the left. I recall looking for somewhere safe to shelter and

Figure 3. IRA "checkpoint" in Lecky Road, circa 1971. Copyright Eamon Melaugh (cain.ulster .ac.uk/melaugh).

Figure 4. Rioting on Rossville Street, circa 1970. A rubble barricade is clearly visible blocking the road. Copyright Eamon Melaugh (cain .ulster.ac.uk/melaugh).

Figure 5. Rioters in Rossville Street, circa 1970. The layout of the newly constructed housing shaped the violence that took place in the Bogside area. Copyright Eamon Melaugh (cain.ulster .ac.uk/melaugh).

Figure 6. British Army checkpoint in William Street, circa 1969. Copyright Eamon Melaugh (cain.ulster .ac.uk/melaugh).

covering another soldier on a "one over one" basis as we moved south along the balcony on the western side of the building . . . using the doorways as cover.[37]

Soldier C's comments on his thoughts after hearing gunfire nearby reveal this mental division of space:

> This was not a riot but close quarters warfare and very dangerous . . . My adrenaline was flowing and I was alert for people who were trying to kill me; I was doing what I was trained to do. I was alert, but I was concerned that I was vulnerable to gunfire direct from the front (south-west) of my position. I was not concerned about gunfire direct from my

right (west) because there were sheds along the balcony which afforded me protection.[38]

For residents, however, the landscape was more than a collection of points of cover and exposure; it was the setting for their everyday lives. People used the phone box at the foot of the Rossville Flats to contact relatives or make social arrangements, they bought sweets and newspapers in the nearby shop, and they walked through the Rossville Street area to go shopping or visit the city center. In short, these places were the venue for all the small acts and movements that make up everyday life. The contrast with the military perception of the same space could hardly be more stark. Giving evidence on the events of Bloody Sunday one resident, Mrs. Anderson, for example, told how:

> When everyone started running, this woman's door was open so we got into it, and the soldiers came running up like mad men, in the house next door a little girl was being carried in because she was hit by a saracen [an armoured vehicle used by the British Army]. They had just got into this house when they all had to lay on the floor as bullets were flying everywhere.[39]

Joe Friel told the Inquiry how he saw: "soldiers about five or six feet into Glenfada [Park] . . . The soldier in front was moving at no great pace and firing. He had his gun in front of him . . . The other soldiers were not firing their weapons. There were other individuals dotted around the car park." Friel was shot by the soldier and subsequently carried to a nearby house: "I was carried into the house feet first . . . I was laid on the floor in the front room. I was continuing to throw up blood and I remember apologising for throwing up on the carpet."[40] In a similar vein, another resident, Frank Carlin:

> ran across the car park [at Rossville Flats] and through the gap between Blocks 1 and 2 of the Rossville Flats. I kept running until I reached the telephone box at the southern gable end of Block 1. I sheltered against the gable end together with a group of other people . . . Barney McGuigan was

sheltering at the telephone box with me when he took a handkerchief in his left hand and stepped away from the telephone box towards Rossville Street [to help two men who had been shot] . . . He had only taken a couple of steps out from the telephone box . . . when he fell to the ground. He had been shot in the head. His head was a terrible mess.[41]

The Troubles created numerous similar sites linked to traumatic personal memories, but as Dawson observes, these "sites of atrocity are—or were—real geographical places . . . where everyday life was located before, and continued after."[42]

Postconflict Normalization

In the years since the events of Bloody Sunday, the urban landscape referred to by both the residents and soldiers in the above excerpts has changed beyond recognition. Time, the peace process, and economic regeneration have all contributed to the area's shifting topography. Writing about places associated with Bloody Sunday, Pringle and Jacobson observed in 2001:

> The flats on Rossville Street where five young men were gunned down around a rubble barricade have been demolished. William Street, where the first shots wounded a man and boy near the Nook bar, has been rebuilt with neat maisonettes where the burnt-out buildings once stood. The scruffy Victorian terrace at Free Derry Corner . . . where the twenty-four-year-old Bernadette Devlin urged the civil rights marchers to stand their ground against the advancing paratroopers, is now a wide avenue with a grassy intersection.[43]

Since the signing of the Good Friday/Belfast Agreement in 1998, there has been a marked attempt by the state to promote the demilitarization of Northern Ireland's militarized landscape, divesting urban streetscapes of their defensive armour and introducing a great degree of normality into Northern Irish society.[44] This process of "normalization" has removed checkpoints, some military barracks, and, in the case of the Bogside, involved the removal in 2005 of an army watchtower perched above the community. Alongside

this demilitarization, urban regeneration has led to a substantial restructuring of aesthetics by planners and officials. The Rossville Street Flats that overlooked the area were demolished in the late 1980s and replaced by two story buildings, while other properties were renovated and roads improved in the early years of the Peace Process.

Such substantial change in the urban landscape had serious implications for the gathering of evidence for the Bloody Sunday Inquiry, which took place under Lord Saville between 1998 and 2010. Understanding the urban terrain and the nuances of the landscape as it was in 1972 proved crucially important to uncovering what happened that day. Saville and his team examined hundreds of photographs and maps, considering them alongside thousands of witness statements in an attempt to recreate that particular geography.[45] Such has been the extent of change in the Bogside that virtual reality software was specially designed for the Inquiry.[46] Senior developer for the Northern Ireland Council for Curriculum, Examinations, and Assessment, Malachy McDaid, stated, "Our brief was to rebuild the city as it was . . . and create a memory jogger."[47] The pioneering software allowed witnesses to move around 360 degrees within a virtual panorama in an effort to jog blurred memories and provide a clearer picture of the day's events. Reconstructing the Bogside of 1972 also posed problems for directors of two dramatizations of the events of Bloody Sunday for British television. Scenes from Paul Greengrass's *Bloody Sunday* and Jimmy McGovern's *Sunday* were filmed in housing estates in Ballymun, Dublin, and inner-city Manchester (Figure 7).

The changes to the Bogside's geography have also become implicated in the processes of remembering and forgetting. Etching the past onto urban space through memorialization is in many ways dependent on what Gough terms "topographical legibility," but the constant change and movement within urban space renders this process difficult. Memorials on former battlefields are sited within the complex, ongoing and interwoven processes of preservation and change and, as Gough has noted, memorialization demands "compromise and the judicious use of the power

Figure 7. Filming the 2002 dramatization of Bloody Sunday in Manchester. Courtesy Gaslight Productions, http://www.sunday-film .net/Process.htm.

of suggestion" to be successful.[48] Temporally bounded violent events, however significant or traumatic, often leave no trace of their having happened; and even when they do, such traces are highly vulnerable to the change inherent in an urban context. Commemorative monuments and memorials aim to record particular events and places in both time and—in the case of the Bogside—often also in space, on the sites where the events occurred. To a certain extent this process is reliant on the surrounding landscape maintaining some resemblance to the landscape in which the events being commemorated happened, to provide a context. A return to the "normality" of an everyday vernacular landscape poses a danger for any attempt to preserve the events of the Troubles in the landscape. "Normality" therefore poses serious challenges to commemoration's effort to provide fixed points, as do the inevitable changes in the urban landscape that take place over time. In many ways the process of normalization in Northern Ireland "has the effect of eradicating evidence of the Troubles . . . and thus effectively writing the conflict out of [the] history of urban places."[49] When a landscape has changed significantly, the markers placed within it are crucial to the viewers' understanding of the events that occurred there.

A number of monuments of various forms have been placed within the urban landscape of the Bogside, ranging from fairly conventional stone memorials to plaques and wall murals. Up until the peace process, memory work in the Bogside—with the exception of the Bloody Sunday monument—was restricted to disparate, sporadic, and ephemeral mural painting. The vast majority of the physical, permanent memorials date from after the signing of the 1998 Belfast Agreement, characteristic of memory work more generally throughout Northern Ireland. The Agreement consolidated the presence of Sinn Féin, the political wing of the IRA, in the political arena. This period was marred by uncertainty as the fledging government attempted to restore normality and instill a sense of unity. Tasked with moving society forward, the Belfast Agreement made little attempt to reflect or deal with the past. This was left to a variety of different stakeholders, each with different priorities and agendas. The memorial landscape in the Bogside has been created, negotiated, and maintained by a range of actors including the families of the dead, paramilitary organizations, former prisoner groups, politicians, public bodies, and the community.

Clearly we can only discuss a selection of the Bogside's memorials here, and as such we focus on the civil rights monument in Rossville Street, the memorial to Sammy Devenny in William Street, the wall at Free Derry Corner and the series of Republican memorials placed in front of it, and the murals of the Bogside

Artists—all of which are in Rossville Street (Figures 8 and 9).[50]

For the families of the Bloody Sunday dead, demarcating the spaces where fatal shootings took place amid the Bogside's shifting topography

Figure 8. Bloody Sunday memorial, Rossville Street, 2010. The demolition of the Rossville Flats completely changed the context of this memorial. Photograph by Catherine Switzer.

became crucially important. As early as 1974, the event was marked by the erection of an obelisk dedicated to the memory of those "murdered by British paratroopers on Bloody Sunday." Initially the memorial was located in the car park of the Rossville Flats, but their demolition in the 1980s completely changed the context and the memorial is now surrounded by a small memorial garden, complete with plants, a bench, and a specially designed fence. In 2001 a new plaque explaining the events of that day and including a map depicting the now-vanished landscape of 1972 was added to the memorial garden close to the former site of the Rossville Flats.

The wider socioeconomic and political changes taking place during the 1990s contributed to the increasing currency of Bloody Sunday memory, and families worked hard to preserve the original material sites.[51] Through a form of "active remembering," the families ensured that despite the shifting topography, visitors to the Bogside could narrate the events (and visualize their versions and interpretations) of that day.[52] Large bill-

boards displaying old photographs now help clarify the geography for outsiders. Without these markers the landscape of Bloody Sunday appears distant and hard to visualize. In Glenfada Park a protracted effort secured the building, complete with bullet holes, where six of the dead were shot.[53] In 2006, the building became the Museum of Free Derry, marking one of the first community-based museums in Northern Ireland to deal with the conflict—albeit in a single-identity perspective in which no attempt is made, as Elizabeth Crooke notes, "to gratify alternative interpretations, viewpoints, or audiences."[54] Drawing on a new social history approach, the Museum of Free Derry aims to present the "community's story from the community perspective."[55] Every year an annual commemorative march retracing the movements of the original march takes place, at the same time describing "the pathways and the fissures of a continuously changing political and geographic landscape."[56] While the Saville Inquiry provided much of the impetus to protect the original urban fabric, growing tourist interest in sites of conflict has undoubtedly contributed to the resolve to narrate the Bogside's history.[57] Conway suggests that these "mnemonic spaces do not speak to different publics but rather represent different occasions for retelling the vernacular nationalist memory of the event."[58]

The struggle to "actively remember" is also pertinent in the commemoration of Sammy Devenny, the first victim of the Troubles in the Bogside. Devenny died in July 1969, three months after being beaten by police officers who were giving chase to a group of youths, following the outbreak of violence during a civil rights march (Figure 10).[59] The family home in William Street was destroyed in a fire a month after Devenny's death, was subsequently demolished, and is now part of a car park.[60] However, since the thirtieth anniversary of Devenny's death in 1999, the site has been marked by a memorial plaque, which stands somewhat awkwardly among the concrete bollards that mark the edge of the car park. The absence of the family home

effectively removes the events that occurred there—well remembered by those Bogside residents old enough to have witnessed them—from the landscape. The new memorial site attempts to commemorate Devenny's death, but the awkwardness of the car park setting testifies to the difficulty of giving past events permanent form in the changing urban landscape. As Ladd has argued in the very different context of Berlin, "the presence of a plaque raises but does not settle questions about how a place of death should function in a living city."[61] The Devenny family laid flowers at the plaque on the fortieth anniversary and, although they do not usually use it as a place of remembrance, they are very aware of it in the landscape. "It's between the bollards, it's a wee black stand with the plaque on it," said Devenny's son, Jim, in 2009. "But you see the tours going round and I drive past and I've never ever seen anybody standing at it. It's strange, you know, considering my father was supposed to be the first person to die in the Troubles in Derry."[62]

Figure 10. Memorial to Sammy Devenny, William Street, 2010. Photograph by Catherine Switzer.

Figure 11. Free Derry Corner, Rossville Street, 2010. Photograph by Catherine Switzer.

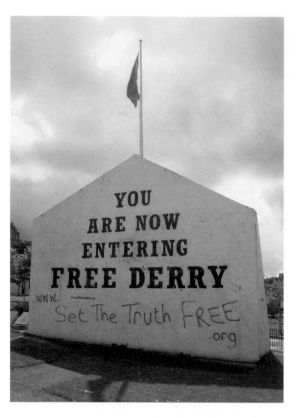

If Devenny's house constitutes the marking of an absence in a changed context, the far better-known Free Derry Corner is the conscious preservation of an element of the Bogside's urban landscape long after its original context was removed (Figure 11). Once painted on the gable end of a row of terraced houses, the Free Derry wall stood at the junction of Lecky Road and Fahan Street and was associated with both the Free Derry Era that gave rise to it and the events of Bloody Sunday that occurred within view of it. By the mid-1970s, the terraced houses stood derelict and isolated after the demolition of all the surrounding buildings, while their location in the planned route of a four-lane road left them in imminent danger of following suit.[63] Residents protested that the site held a historical significance, and after some discussion the preservation of the wall was secured.[64] Today it stands completely dislocated from the terraces it was once part of, alone in a grassy area surrounded by the 1970s roads. The terraced houses are gone,

Figure 12. *Operation Motorman,* mural, Rossville Street, 2010. One of ten murals painted in Rossville Street by the Bogside Artists group. Photograph by Catherine Switzer.

replaced by a wider road and slightly altered road layout. It is worth noting that these roads have been built around the free-standing wall, which remains in the same location.

The attempt to retain traces of past events in the area also stands at the center of the well-known series of murals that have been painted on the gable ends of properties along Rossville Street. This project began in 1994, when three men calling themselves the Bogside Artists began painting the murals to chronicle the community's experiences of the Troubles. Between 1994 and 2005 the Artists painted a series of ten murals in the area, each assiduously selected to depict particular points in time. Most of the murals, many of which were adapted from photographs, are place specific to the Bogside, while the remainder represent a broadly Republican past. The Bogside-specific murals depict Bloody Sunday, the Battle of the Bogside, and Operation Motorman, while others portray the role of women throughout the Troubles, Republican hunger strikes, and children killed by plastic bullets (Figures 12 and 13). Yet here again, the attempt to bring past events into the present environment is at odds with the urban landscape as a place where people live their day-to-day lives. The properties on which the murals are painted are the responsibility of the Northern Ireland Housing Executive, a government body that runs public housing across Northern Ireland. Flags and emblems generally have been a thorny issue for the housing executive in the post-Agreement era, but in the Bogside the executive has had to deal with a clash between its efforts to improve the existing housing and the Bogside Artists attempts to preserve the past in the landscape. One of these clashes took place in the early 1990s, when the housing executive proposed to pebble dash the exterior walls of many of its properties in the Rossville Street area. This action would have spelled the end for the artists' work, and as a result they began to mobilize community support for their project. "We went around all the people in the Bogside, we went into bookies, houses, bars, and gathered a few-thousand signatures," said Tommy Kelly, one of the artists. "The debate went to Belfast and word came back that not only would they not paint the murals out but they would render the gable walls the rest of the way down Rossville Street for us to continue to tell the story."[65]

A second clash occurred in 2005, and again showed the difficulty of preserving the past within a living urban landscape. This round of renovations included the installation of several access ramps, allowing residents with impaired mobility or using wheelchairs or prams to access the upper of the two stories. In doing so they interfered with the ways in which two of the murals could be viewed. Despite protestations, the ramps remain, effectively cutting several murals in half. These examples point to the ongoing

Figure 13. *The Saturday Matinee*, mural, Rossville Street, 2010. The view of the mural is now partially blocked by a pedestrian access ramp. Photograph by Catherine Switzer.

difficulty in commemorating the past in an evolving urban present that must adhere to the everyday functions of a community.

The Politics of Memory

The controversies over commemoration in Northern Ireland do not solely revolve around its ramifications for the physical environment. Commemoration in many ways has become a metaphorical battleground as a result of the linkages it attempts to create between the present and a particular version of the past, and the ways in which it "places" that past in the landscape. Commemoration can therefore effectively continue the conflict by other means.[66] It is also virtually always a struggle over power and territory. Territorial claims remain vitally important in post-conflict Northern Ireland, where the geography of urban areas is sharply demarcated into areas seen as dominated by one community. The commemoration of different pasts in these largely single-identity areas can therefore be seen as a particular point of difference between the two main communities "not only in terms of identity formation, but also in the physical geography of the urban and memorial landscape."[67]

Commemoration involves telling particular stories about the past, which in Northern Ireland often revolve around representations of victimhood. As Bairner and Shirlow note, "In each community, the commemoration of suffering and violation is activated via the instrument of telling. Telling of the 'Collective Self's' suffering at the hands of the 'collective other' is a conventional feature of living in both communities."[68] These kinds of representations therefore clearly privilege certain versions of the past over others. Particular stories are told while others are silenced.

As is the case with many of Northern Ireland's neighborhoods, commemoration within the Bogside communicates a single historical narrative. In this instance that narrative focuses on broadly Republican understandings of the past. The area generally, and in particular the important Rossville Street site close to Free Derry Corner, is now home to a variety of monuments and memorials erected by groups within the Republican move-

ment. Most visible among these are the series of monuments erected on the grassy area directly in front of Free Derry Corner. In May 2001, a monument was erected here by the Derry Republican Graves Committee who construct and maintain many IRA monuments in the city. It honours ten Republican hunger strikers who died in 1981 while agitating for the right to be treated as political prisoners rather than criminals. The Bogside monument was part of a broader campaign to raise the profile of the event locally, nationally, and internationally.[69] Its Irish language inscriptions translate as "they died for Irish freedom . . . their names are among the heroes of the Irish people." Adjacent to the monument are two plaques dedicated to other Republicans who died on hunger strike in different parts of Ireland throughout the last century. Another monument situated in the "cradle of Derry's history" was erected by the same organization.[70] It was unveiled by former IRA volunteer and Sinn Féin representative Raymond McCartney a couple of feet away in 2003, and it commemorates eighteen IRA volunteers who, as the memorial puts it, "died in places where circumstances do not permit the erection of a commemorative plaque." Although the Rossville Street area clearly has immense symbolic significance for nationalists and Republicans generally, these memorials add further layers to the area as a site of nationalist and Republican suffering. They attempt to construct a lineage of Republican suffering at the hands of the state, encouraging the local community to accept their history as one of victimization and oppression (Figure 14).[71]

It is worth bearing in mind that the community within the Bogside is not monolithic, and that the Republican narrative does not represent the views of all residents. Mainstream Republicanism, as represented by Sinn Féin and the IRA, is only one voice within the broader nationalist community, albeit the dominant voice at the time of writing. On the one hand, moderate nationalism still has a place within the Bogside—two of the area's four local government councillors are members of the Social Democratic and Labour Party—but on the other, dissident Republicans also have a growing presence. The

Figure 14. Hunger striker memorial, Rossville Street, 2010. This memorial is one of several that attempt to construct the idea of a Republican past. Photograph by Catherine Switzer.

fragmenting of Republicanism is illustrated by the fact that four separate events were held in the city to mark the anniversary of the 1916 Easter Rising: the largest event was organized by Sinn Féin, while the Irish Republican Socialist Party, Republican Sinn Féin, and the thirty-two County Sovereignty Movement all held separate commemorations.[72]

It is interesting to note, in light of the previous discussion of place-based commemoration, that many of the Republicans commemorated on the memorials close to Free Derry Corner did not die in the Bogside. Indeed, many had no connection at all with the city of Derry. The fact that they are commemorated in the Bogside underlines the extent to which this memorial site functions as a Republican space, the connection between site and memorial manipulated by what Conway terms "memory choreographers" to enforce a Republicanism-inflected connection and resonance.[73] This reflects Graham and Whelan's argument that, in Northern Ireland, "It is difficult to escape the conclusion that the burgeoning landscape of commemoration represents an orchestrated process in which paramilitary organisations and their political parties are consciously creating these sites and their memorial practices as one means of perpetuating identity politics and territorial control."[74]

Intrinsically linked to this process of the creation of a Republican past is the parallel process of silencing alternative pasts. In the case of the Bogside, one silenced past concerns the deaths of at least sixteen soldiers of the British army in the area. These deaths include that of Ranger William Best, himself a Derryman, who died in an execution-style killing close to the Bogside Inn in 1972. These deaths are arguably considerably more place specific to the Bogside than many of the deaths commemorated on the various Republican memorials, but none has received any kind of acknowledgement in the landscape. We have argued elsewhere that such unmarked sites of violence constitute "lost spaces," since the lack of permanent markers in the landscape means that the stories, which might be attached, are rendered silent and are effectively lost.[75]

In general, the commemoration of the security forces in Northern Ireland has been problematic, with much of commemorative activity undertaken within the confines of security force premises. In public space, security forces commemoration "is far less prevalent or visible . . . than is that of the paramilitary organisations . . . It also occurs only in places considered unionist."[76] Clearly, the construction of the Bogside as a Republican place does not permit any references to the deaths of British soldiers, who are presented as the enemy. British soldiers can only be present in the area's representations of the past as perpetrators of violence, never as its victims. The Bogside is indisputably a place where the British army has been the perpetrator of violence—the events of Bloody Sunday alone stand as evidence of that—but a series of other occasions on which its soldiers were on the receiving end of brutally violent acts are not part of the story told by the area's memorial landscape. The stories of the soldiers who died on the streets of the Bogside cannot be acknowledged there not only as a result of the army's actions on Bloody Sunday but also because they hold the potential to disrupt the Republican construction of the area as Republican and because they challenge the definitions of victim and perpetrator that the area's Republican memorials attempt to naturalize.

The silencing of these narratives is important for a new wave of actors who were not directly involved in the conflict or who have no direct memory of it. Among the new generations of spectators are an increasing number of tourists visiting Derry from across the world. Indeed, the future of the Bogside is likely to be influenced by its incorporation into the contemporary history theme of recent tourism-development plans. The city's Tourism Development Strategy for 2009–12 identifies the Bogside as one of a number of "unique historic attractions" that the city has to offer and looks for ways to develop this (Figure 15). "The Bogside has proved itself as a significant tourist draw," observes the Strategy. "Existing products include the Museum of Free Derry, The Bogside Murals and People's Gallery, and Tours and Trails."[77] These "attractions" appear to be well received by visitors. On the travel website Tripadvisor, the Museum of Free Derry is described as "a moving, thought-provoking experience" by one visitor, while a walking tour of the murals is a "must do." The influence of tourism is only likely to increase with the announcement that Derry will be the United Kingdom City of Culture in 2013. Yet, where the place of memorials in the landscape is concerned, the Tourism

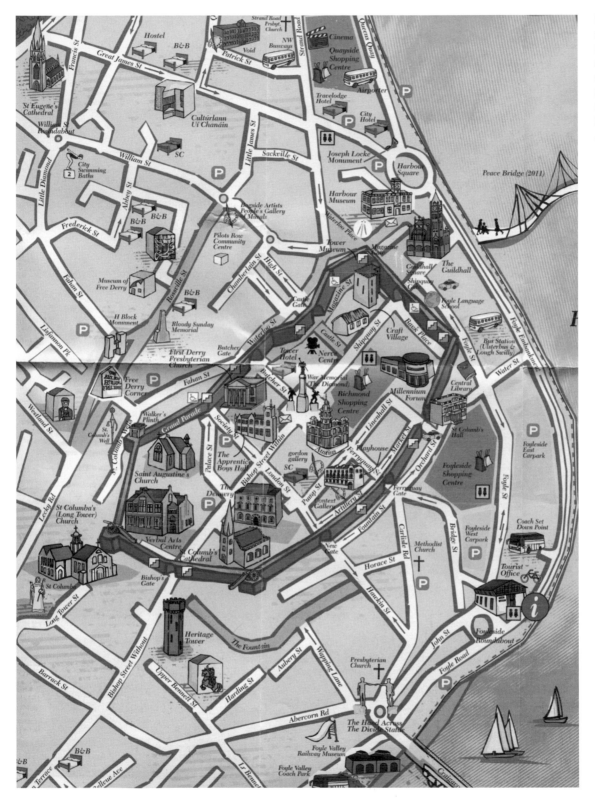

Figure 15. Derry visitors map, showing several Bogside monuments and murals as tourist attractions. Courtesy Derry Visitor & Convention Bureau, http://www.derryvisitor.com/.

Development Strategy unintentionally acknowledges the vital role of physical monuments in making past events comprehensible in a changed urban landscape when it argues that "contemporary History is most frequently based on three elements: a tour highlighting landmarks linked to the story; opportunities to engage with local members of the community and localised interpretative centres."[78] Such tours are also available elsewhere in Northern Ireland, most notably in Belfast, but as we have observed, an approach that focuses on existing landmarks can only reinforce the pre-existing presences and absences in the version of the past being presented. The Republican narrative presented by most of the Bogside's memorials ensures that visitors will perceive the area's history as one of purely nationalist/Republican suffering, while the stories of other victims of violence are rendered both silent and invisible.

Conclusion

The Bogside provides an example of a place that experienced what Gilligan has called "a disaster": "Disasters are moments when the social fabric is torn. When lives are turned upside down—when expectations about how life works are confounded; when routines are disrupted; everything is thrown into turmoil. . . . The Bogside in Derry/Londonderry was the epicentre of that eruption."[79] This paper has attempted to explore the ramifications of that "disaster" for the urban landscape in which it unfolded. As we have seen, violence and its legacy have had a profound effect on the streetscape of the Bogside. The presence of memorials commemorating some of those violent events ensures that the legacy of the past has become an integral part of the present, preventing a return to complete "normality."

Till suggests that monuments erected on sites of violence, are "open wounds" that ask the viewer to "confront this past (and this pain), to keep the wound open in the present, to continue the work of memory."[80] In the Bogside, memories of Bloody Sunday and the Republican struggle have been successfully reified; concretized in an urban space. These are the open wounds the area presents to residents and visitors alike.

Conversely, the sites where soldiers and members of the local security forces died remain unmarked. The absence of any markers on these sites illustrates how commemoration "includes not only the organisation of memory but the organisation of silences as well."[81]

The purpose of any physical monument is to keep the memory of the event or person being commemorated alive. Yet monuments placed within the vernacular landscape very quickly become part of it, rendering them almost invisible because they are seen every day. However, passivity toward the past is something that the families of the Bloody Sunday dead and the Republicans have resisted, maintaining the open wounds to keep past events in the public eye. For the families, the Civil Rights memorial and the Bloody Sunday march were an important part of the calling for justice for their relatives; for mainstream Republicanism the memorials in Rossville Street are an important way of grounding present-day political activities in a Republican past. These Republican memorials also illustrate another facet of commemoration in vernacular places. While vernacular surroundings can render memorials less visible, the context also helps memorials accrue "to themselves the naturalizing power of time and place. . . . The transformation from new to matter-of-fact suggests that the memorial's message enjoys a measure of orthodoxy. This orthodoxy is a form of power—the power of the norm—as a particular interpretation of the past becomes granted, assumed."[82] The memorials help to construct and naturalize the area's past as Republican; they stand as "focal points of a complex dialogue between past and present, between historical events, producers of monuments, and successive generations of spectators who inquire into the significance of the past on the basis of historical artefacts."[83]

Despite the strong influence this naturalization process potentially has on future "memories," the fact remains that "collective memory and commemoration are, after all, dynamic processes."[84] The political context within which commemoration in the Bogside takes place has changed radically over the last few decades, and at the time of writing is yet again in flux. The vast majority of the Bogside's memorials were erected within the last fifteen years. Likewise, the murals of the Bogside Artists all date from this crucial postceasefire period. This was a period in which Sinn Féin committed itself to the political process and the memorials served as a physical reminder that the movement had not forgotten its past. However, no new memorials have been erected in the Bogside in recent years, reflecting the political clout of mainstream Republicanism and its presence in places like the Bogside, and also symptomatic of the relatively stable political climate in Northern Ireland.

The context of Bloody Sunday commemoration too, has changed. Following the publication of the Saville Report in June 2010, the Bloody Sunday commemorative march—held each January retracing the route of the 1972 march—no longer needs to call for justice. In January 2011 the families of the Bloody Sunday dead announced that the thirty-ninth anniversary march will be the last. The Bogside will no longer serve as the venue for this particular performance of memory, a testament to the reactive and dynamic nature of memory itself.

NOTES

We are grateful to Martin Melaugh for permission to use his father's photographs as illustrations, to Dr. Bryonie Reid, and to Gaslight Productions. We would also like to thank the two anonymous reviewers for their constructive comments.

1. Paul Stangl, "The Vernacular and the Monumental: Memory and Landscape in Post-War Berlin," *Geojournal* 73, no. 3 (November 2008): 245–53.

2. The name of the city is a point of political contestation, with "Londonderry" predominantly used by Unionists and "Derry" by Nationalists. Although acknowledging this contestation, we employ the name "Derry" in this paper for both brevity and clarity.

3. Graham Dawson, *Making Peace with the Past? Memory, Trauma, and the Irish Troubles* (Manchester: Manchester University Press, 2007), 28.

4. T. G. Ashplant, Graham Dawson and Trevor Roper, *Commemorating War: The Politics of Memory* (New Brunswick: Transaction Publishers, 2000), 16.

5. The events of Bloody Sunday inspired "Sunday, Bloody Sunday," one of U2's best-known songs, while

John Lennon also recorded a song of the same name for his album "Some Time in New York City." Two dramatized versions of the events of that day were screened on British television in 2002, one directed by Paul Greengrass, the other created by screenwriter Jimmy McGovern.

6. Guy King, "Murals in the Bogside," *The Local Historian* 33, no. 4 (2006): 226–42.

7. Eamon McCann, *War and an Irish Town* (London: Pluto Press, 1993).

8. Raymond McLean, *The Road to Bloody Sunday* (Dublin: Poolbeg, 1983); Eamonn McCann and Maureen Shiels, ed., *Bloody Sunday in Derry: What Really Happened* (Dingle: Brandon Books, 1992); Peter Pringle and Philip Jacobson, *Those Are Real Bullets, Aren't They: Bloody Sunday, Derry, 30 January 1972* (London: Fourth Estate, 2000); Don Mullan and John Scally, *Eyewitness Bloody Sunday* (Dublin: Wolfhound Press, 2001); Brian Conway, "1972: Local Conditions, Global Environment, and Transnational Discourses in Memory," *Memory Studies* 1 (2009): 187–209.

9. "Bloody Sunday Report: David Cameron Apologises for Unjustifiable Shootings," *The Guardian*, June 15, 2010, 2.

10. Graham Dawson, "Trauma, Place, and the Politics of Memory: Bloody Sunday, Derry, 1972–2004," *History Workshop Journal* 59, no. 1, (Spring 2005): 221–50, Sara McDowell, "Renegotiating the Past in Post-Conflict Northern Ireland: Consolidating a Republican Place for a Republican Past," in *Public Places, Public Pasts*, ed. Gregory Ashworth, Peter Groote, and Tialda Haartsen, 49–60 (Utrecht: Royal Dutch Geographical Society, 2007).

11. Thomas Hall, "Hurt and the City: Landscapes of Urban Violence," *Social Anthropology* 16, no. 1 (2008): 72.

12. Michel De Certeau, *The Practice of Everyday Life* (Berkeley: University of California Press, 1984), 38.

13. Stephen Graham, "The Urban 'Battlespace'," *Theory, Culture, and Society* 26, no. 7–8 (December 2009): 278–88.

14. G. J. Ashworth, *War and the City* (London: Routledge, 1991), 121.

15. Alice Hills, "Continuity and Discontinuity: The Grammar of Urban Military Operations," in *Cities, War, and Terrorism*, ed. Stephen Graham (Oxford: Malden, 2004), 235.

16. Lewis Holloway and Phil Hubbard, *People and*

Place: The Extraordinary Geographies of Everyday Life (Harlow: Pearson, 2001), 90; Bryonie Reid, "'Rearranging the Ground': Public and Private Space in Belfast, Northern Ireland," *Gender, Place and Culture* 15, no. 5 (2008): 493.

17. David McKittrick, Seamus Kelters, Brian Feeney, and Chris Thornton, *Lost Lives: The Stories of the Men, Women, and Children Who Died as a Result of the Northern Ireland Troubles* (Edinburgh: Mainstream, 2005).

18. The city's name has been a source of contestation since the Plantation period. The name Doire (the Gaelic translation of Derry) predated the Plantation. With the growth of the Catholic population throughout the eighteenth and nineteenth centuries, "London" became frequently omitted.

19. http://www.derryswalls.com/ (Accessed July 15, 2010).

20. Margo Shea, "'Once Again It Happens': Collective Remembrance and Irish Identity in Catholic Derry, Northern Ireland, 1896–2008" (PhD diss.: University of Massachusetts Amherst, 2010), 299.

21. Shea, "'Once Again It Happens,'" 295.

22. Shea, "'Once Again It Happens,'" 303, 372.

23. Shea, "'Once Again It Happens,'" 375.

24. For photographic evidence of Derry at this time, see Eamon Melaugh's photographs on the CAIN website, accessed July 16, 2010, http://cain.ulst.ac.uk/melaugh/portfolio1/index.html

25. *Report of the Bloody Sunday Inquiry,* vol. 2, chap. 11, accessed July 16, 2010, http://report.bloody-sunday-inquiry.org/volume02/chapter011/.

26. *Report of the Bloody Sunday Inquiry,* vol. 5, chap. 68, accessed July 16, 2010, http://report.bloody-sunday-inquiry.org/volume05/chapter068/.

27. Jonathan Skinner, "The 'PB' and the Aestheticization of Violence in Northern Ireland," *Ethnography* 9, no. 3 (September 2008): 403–14.

28. Neil Jarman, "Painting Landscapes: The Place of Murals in the Symbolic Construction of Urban Space," in *Symbols in Northern Ireland,* ed. Neil Jarman (Belfast: Institute of Irish Studies, Queens University Belfast, 1998), 88.

29. McDowell, "Renegotiating the Past in Post-Conflict Northern Ireland," 50.

30. Dawson, "Trauma, Place, and the Politics of Memory," 160.

31. Shea, "'Once Again It Happens,'" 374.

32. Shea, "'Once Again It Happens,'" 374–75.

33. Mikael Hard and Thomas J. Misa, "Modernising European Cities: Technological Uniformity and Cultural Distinction," in *Urban Machinery: Inside Modern European Cities,* ed. Mikael Hard and Thomas J. Misa (Cambridge, Mass.: MIT Press, 2008), 17.

34. Shea, "'Once Again It Happens,'" 339.

35. *Report of the Bloody Sunday Inquiry,* Evidence of Colonel Roy Jackson, accessed July 16, 2010, http://report.bloody-sunday-inquiry.org/evidence/CJ/CJ_0002.pdf.

36. *Report of the Bloody Sunday Inquiry,* Evidence of Colonel Roy Jackson, accessed July 16, 2010, http://report.bloody-sunday-inquiry.org/evidence/CJ/CJ_0002.pdf.

37. *Report of the Bloody Sunday Inquiry,* Evidence of Soldier C, accessed July 16, 2010, http://report.bloody-sunday-inquiry.org/evidence/B/B44.pdf.

38. *Report of the Bloody Sunday Inquiry,* Evidence of Soldier C, accessed July 16, 2010, http://report.bloody-sunday-inquiry.org/evidence/B/B44.pdf.

39. *Report of the Bloody Sunday Inquiry,* Evidence of Mrs Anderson, accessed July 16, 2010, http://report.bloody-sunday-inquiry.org/evidence/AZ/AZ_0007.pdf.

40. *Report of the Bloody Sunday Inquiry,* Evidence of Joe Friel, accessed July 16, 2010, http://report.bloody-sunday-inquiry.org/evidence/AF/AF_0034.pdf.

41. *Report of the Bloody Sunday Inquiry,* Evidence of Frank Carlin, accessed July 16, 2010, http://report.bloody-sunday-inquiry.org/evidence/AC/AC_0033.pdf.

42. Dawson, "Trauma, Place, and the Politics of Memory," 161.

43. Pringle and Jacobson, *Those Are Real Bullets,* 1.

44. Catherine Switzer and Sara McDowell, "Redrawing Cognitive Maps of Conflict: Lost Spaces and Forgetting in the Centre of Belfast," *Memory Studies* 2 (2009): 337–53.

45. Paul Bew, "The Role of the Historical Advisor and the Bloody Sunday Tribunal," *Historical Research* 78, no. 199 (February 2005): 113–27.

46. David Mather, "Extended Memory: Early Calculating Engines and Historical Computer Simulations," *Leonardo* 39, no. 3 (June 2006): 237–43.

47. BBC News, "Creating a Virtual Bloody Sunday," accessed July 6, 2010, http://news.bbc.co.uk/1/hi/sci/tech/1791596.stm.

48. Paul Gough, "Sites in the Imagination: The Beaumont Hamel Newfoundland Memorial on the Somme," *Cultural Geographies* 11, no. 3 (July 2004): 251.

49. Switzer and McDowell, "Redrawing Cognitive Maps of Conflict," 343.

50. For other memorials in the Bogside and in Northern Ireland generally, see "Physical Memorials to the Conflict in Northern Ireland," accessed July 16, 2010, http://cain.ulst.ac.uk/victims/memorials/search.html.

51. Conway, "1972: Local Conditions, Global Environment, and Transnational Discourses," 187–209.

52. Brian Conway, "Active Remembering, Selective Forgetting, and Collective Identity: The Case of Bloody Sunday," *Identity* 3, no. 4 (October 2003): 305–23.

53. Museum of Free Derry, Location, accessed July 15, 2010, http://www.museumoffreederry.org/location.html.

54. Elizabeth Crooke, "The Politics of Community Heritage: Motivations, Authority, and Control," *International Journal of Heritage Studies* 16, no. 1–2 (January 2010): 26.

55. Museum of Free Derry, Introduction, accessed January 19, 2011, www.museumoffreederry.org/introduction.html.

56. Tom Herron and John Lynch, "Like 'Ghosts Who'd Walked Abroad': Faces of the Bloody Sunday Dead," *Visual Culture in Britain* 7, no. 1 (Summer 2006): 76.

57. Sara McDowell, "Selling Conflict Heritage through Tourism in Northern Ireland," *International Journal of Heritage Studies* 14, no. 5 (September 2008): 405–21.

58. Brian Conway, "Rethinking Difficult Pasts: 1972 as a Case Study," *Cultural Sociology* 3, no. 3 (November 2009): 369.

59. McKittrick et al., *Lost Lives*, 32.

60. BBC Radio Foyle Interview with the Devenny family, April 2009, BBC Radio Foyle, accessed January 11, 2011, http://www.bbc.co.uk/northernireland/radiofoyle/features/devenny.shtml.

61. Brian Ladd, *The Ghosts of Berlin: Confronting German History in the Urban Landscape* (Chicago: University of Chicago Press, 1997), 153.

62. BBC Radio Foyle Interview with the Devenny family, April 2009.

63. Shea, "'Once Again It Happens,'" 385–86.

64. Shea, "'Once Again It Happens,'" 388–89.

65. "The Bogside Artists," *Derry Journal*, August 17, 2009, 13.

66. McDowell, "Selling Conflict Heritage," 414.

67. Switzer and McDowell, "Redrawing Cognitive Maps of Conflict," 340.

68. Alan Bairner and Peter Shirlow, "When Leisure Turns to Fear: Fear, Mobility, and Ethno-Sectarianism in Belfast," *Leisure Studies* 22 (July 2003): 209.

69. Sara McDowell, "Commemorating Dead 'Men': Gendering the Past and Present in Post-Conflict Societies," *Gender, Place and Culture* 15 no. 4 (August 2008): 337.

70. "Derry Volunteer's Memorial Unveiled," *An Phoblacht*, October 16, 2003, 16.

71. Paul Arthur, "Reading Violence: Ireland," in *The Legitimization of Violence*, ed. David Apter (London: Macmillan, 1997), 43.

72. "Easter Commemorations," *Derry Journal*, March 30, 2010, 4.

73. Conway, "Rethinking Difficult Pasts," 396.

74. Brian Graham and Yvonne Whelan, "The Legacies of the Dead: Commemorating the Troubles in Northern Ireland," *Environment and Planning D: Society and Space* 25, no. 3 (2007): 489.

75. Switzer and McDowell, "Redrawing Cognitive Maps of Conflict," 343.

76. Catherine Switzer and Brian Graham, "'From Thorn to Thorn': Commemorating the Royal Ulster Constabulary in Northern Ireland," *Social & Cultural Geography* 10, no. 2 (March 2009): 159.

77. Derry City Council, *Focus on the Future: Tourism Development Strategy 2009–2012*, 27.

78. Derry City Council, *Focus on the Future*, 27.

79. C. Gilligan, "Community Responses to Disaster in Northern Ireland: 1969 as a Case Study," in *Community Movements and Local Organisations*, ed. R. A. Cnann and C. Milofsky (London: Springer, 2007), 311.

80. Karen E. Till, *The New Berlin: Memory, Politics, Place* (Minneapolis: University of Minnesota Press, 2005), 99.

81. Sarah Bennett Farmer, *Martyred Village: Commemorating the 1944 Massacre at Oradour-sur-Glane* (Berkeley: University of California Press, 1999), 208.

82. Owen J. Dwyer and Derek H Alderman, *Civil Rights Memorials and the Geography of Memory* (Athens: University of Georgia Press, 2008), 13.

83. Peter Carrier, *Holocaust Monuments and National Memory Cultures in France and Germany Since 1989* (New York: Berghahn Books, 2006), 7.

84. Vered Vinitzky-Seroussi, *Yitzhak Rabin's Assassination and the Dilemmas of Commemoration* (Albany, N.Y.: SUNY Press, 2009), 178.

Reviews

Michael P. Conzen, editor
The Making of the American Landscape,
second edition

New York: Routledge, 2010.

568 pages. Numerous black-and-white illustrations.

ISBN 978-0-415-95006-0, $155.00 (HB)

ISBN 978-0-415-95007-7, $79.95 (PB)

Review by Chris Wilson

Since its publication in 1990, *The Making of the American Landscape* has remained the best single-volume introduction to the country's cultural landscape mosaic. The original edition began life as a twelve-part series in the *Geographical Magazine* in 1979–80 edited by Michael P. Cozen, who subsequently solicited additional essays to round out the eighteen-chapter first edition of this book. The revisions made by the author and publisher for this second edition seek to extend the useful life of the volume. How well they succeed is the pivotal question.

To update the book's coverage, one of the original chapters has been dropped, three essays have been replaced by new contributions on the same topics, and three new chapters have been added. The texts of the fourteen remaining original chapters remain essentially unaltered, modified only with some subsequent scholarship in their endnotes. Wherever possible, color photographs have replaced the previous black-and-white images, and color has been added to the existing maps and plans.

Most of the authors are members of the Association of American Geographers, and the considerable strength and cohesion of these essays stem from their shared methodology. This approach to historical, cultural geography begins, of course, with a grounding in the regional conditions of climate, topography, and natural resources. Pre-industrial cultural traditions are seen as emerging (or being transplanted from Europe) in cultural hearths, and over time diffusing through migration into larger cultural domains. By the mid-nineteenth century, the technological, economic, social, and political forces of modernization increasingly produce shared national landscape patterns.

An overview of the natural environments of the United States (chapter 1) sets the context for discussions of Native (2), Spanish (3), and French (4) landscape traditions, as well as the largely English imprints in New England and the Mid-Atlantic (5) and the South (6), which emerged as the primary strains of the national, American culture. The township survey grid (7), forest clearance and logging practices (8), the settlement of the Great Plains (9), and irrigation of the arid West (10) each shaped large expanses of the county. Amid a strongly commercial and officially secular culture, many groups have nevertheless inscribed their ethnic subcultures (11) and religious beliefs (12) on the landscape.

The development of industry (13), the rise of cities (14), the growing importance of government (15), and the emergence of a civil society first chronicled by Alexis de Tocqueville (16) represent major currents of modernization. The landscapes of the rich, writes Conzen in the Introduction, "sit like islands amid an ocean of ordinary residential and recreational landscapes" (17)—landscapes shaped over the last century first by the automobile (18) and more recently by megacorporations through large-scale consumer environments (19). A concluding chapter speculates on the possible continuing landscape impacts of core American preferences for individuality, mobility, and consumerism (20).

The art of writing overview essays such as these hinges on the ability to provide a balanced, concise synthesis of an often large body of scholarship, and on presenting the big picture without lapsing into overgeneralizations. The best of these essays, and in fact the majority of them, open with overviews of major environmental, cultural, technological, and other factors (academic discourse of interest primarily to scholars is placed in the endnotes). Each deftly summarizes the tangible imprints of these forces on the landscape by characterizing their recurrent components and patterns of spatial organization.

A graphic hierarchy organizes the various spatial scales of a topic: from a map of the regional or national spread of a particular landscape culture; to a map or generic diagram of organization at the township or metropolitan scale; and, finally, to a finer-grained plan of a representative farm, village, or suburban subdivision. Comparative diagrams showing a landscape type in different periods—of successive kinds of logging camps, plantations, or shopping malls, for instance—provide a powerful visual distillation of an author's written analysis.

The vast majority of the authors succeed admirably on these points while making arguments that are clear and sometimes classic. Peirce Lewis asserts in "Americanizing English Landscape Habits," for instance, that settlers migrating west past the Appalachian Mountains in the nineteenth century drew selectively from developments in Pennsylvania (enormous, German-inspired barns; gridiron town plans) and New England (the township as the unit of social and political organization; a preference for wooden, free-standing houses). The federally imposed rectangular township survey grid fused these two regional strands.

Michael Williams likewise makes a compelling case in "Clearing the Forests" that vast landscape transformations were wrought by the frontier phase of ad hoc forest clearing to create fields, a process that also provided homesteaders with building materials and firewood. Beginning in the early 1800s, industrialized logging companies also began to refine methods as their territories shifted first from New England to New York, then from the Great Lakes states to the South, and finally on to the Pacific Northwest.

William Wyckoff's chapter, "Imposing Landscapes of Private Power and Wealth," reminds us of English cultural affinities. He describes the affectations of the top one-half of one percent of the population and their conflicting desires for spatial exclusivity and ostentatious display. He captures the phenomenon at the national scale with a map naming key elite communities (well-known upper-crust urban neighborhoods, suburban communities, and favored resorts), and on a metropolitan scale with a generic diagram of the relative locations of downtown private clubs, old high-status neighborhoods, elite shopping districts, high-rise luxury condominiums, suburban estates, tony subdivisions, private schools, and country clubs. (The prevailing middle-class landscapes of railroad towns and suburbs each receive strong chapters, but discussion of the landscapes of the poor and working class are fragmentary.)

Reviews of the first edition of *The Making of the American Landscape* lauded many of these same virtues while also calling attention to significant overlooked topics and the occasional weak chapter.[1] Conzen masterfully addresses one of these areas himself in "Developing Large-Scale Consumer Landscapes." His tour of the increasingly large-scale consumer environments produced by megacorporations—shopping malls (and their supporting distribution networks), sports arenas, convention centers, megachurches, and gambling casinos—is the best, most substantive addition to this edition. In his strong new chapter "Organizing Religious Landscapes," Wilbur Zelinsky speculates on the secondary position of religion in the landscape relative to commerce and government.

Other topics previously pointed out as neglected continue to be absent or lightly covered in this second edition, however. The unaltered chapter on Hispanic landscapes remains unbalanced in its almost exclusive emphasis on California (where the Mexican population annexed to the United States in the 1830s and 1840s was smaller than in Texas and New Mexico); it also continues to relegate the Laws of the Indies town planning ordinances to a passing mention in an illustration caption. The widely noted jump in Hispanic population in recent U.S. censuses—first in the inner cities and then in suburbs and small towns across the country—receives even less attention. The Mexican imprint, for instance, is characterized in a new chapter on ethnic landscapes as consisting of "public plazas, neighborhood cantinas, and colorful wall murals" (247). A synopsis of Richard Nostrand's classic New Mexico/Colorado regional geography, *The Hispano Homeland,* might have balanced the historical account, while Daniel Arreola's excellent monographs and edited volume *Hispanic Spaces, Latino Places* could have provided ample material to do justice to the contemporary scene.[2]

More surprising is the almost total omission of gender as a category of analysis, a flaw noted by one reviewer of the first edition.[3] Despite the outpouring of scholarship in women's and gender studies over the past generation, key publications by George Chauncey, Setha Low, Dolores Hayden, Linda McDowell, Doreen Massey, and Virginia Scharff are missing from the bibliography. The work of these and other scholars—who show how the nineteenth-century parlor, the department store, the urban bathhouse, the child car seat, and even the human body are important landscape sites—suggests various ways that the analysis of gender might have enriched this edition.[4]

Amid a half-dozen laudatory cover blurbs, one learns that "earlier essays have been substantively revised and new essays added to present critical new perspectives." This is what one would expect from the second edi-

tion of a landmark book first published twenty years ago. But unfortunately this is largely not the case (with the notable exception of Conzen's own new chapter). The incorporation of subsequent scholarship is spotty, and even its listing in the bibliography is uneven. The book's breadth is impressive, but the holes in its coverage remain significant.

So, if this is not the thoroughgoing revision that one might wish, is it still a useful book? Despite my criticisms, it remains an excellent introduction to the subject. The publisher undoubtedly envisions it as a textbook for a college course in the cultural landscape or human geography of the United States. I would likely select it for such a course but would supplement it with readings by the above-mentioned scholars and excerpts from D. W. Meinig's magisterial four-volume *The Shaping of America: A Geographical Perspective on 500 Years of History, 1492–2000.*[5] That said, the insufficient revisions of this second edition open the door for someone to author a new synthesis on the subject, one more comprehensive in its coverage and systematic in its inclusion of recent scholarship and methodologies.

NOTES

1. Reviews of the first edition of *The Making of The American Landscape* (1990): Peter Boag, *Forest and Conservation History* 35 (October 1991): 198; Richard L. Nostrand, *Annals of the Association of American Geographers,* 82, no. 1 (March 1992): 156–57; Hugh Price, *Transactions of the Institute of British Geographers,* New Series, 17, no. 1 (1992): 374–75.

2. Richard L. Nostrand, *The Hispano Homeland* (Norman: University of Oklahoma Press, 1992); Daniel D. Areolla and James R. Curtis, *The Mexican Border Cities: Landscape Anatomy and Place Personality* (Tucson : University of Arizona Press, 1993); Daniel D. Areolla, *Tejano South Texas: a Mexican American Cultural Province* (Austin: University of Texas Press, 2002); Daniel D. Areolla, ed., *Hispanic Spaces, Latino Places: Community and Cultural Diversity in Contemporary America* (Austin: University of Texas Press, 2004). Indeed, *Border Cities,* and

Hispanic Spaces, both key sources, are not even included in the bibliography of this second edition.

3. Boag review, 198.

4. Among the multiple works by each of these authors, I cite one for each: George Chauncey, *Gay New York: Gender, Urban Culture, and the Makings of the Gay Male World, 1890–1940* (New York: Basic Books, 1994); Setha M. Low, *On the Plaza: The Politics of Public Space and Culture* (Austin: University of Texas Press, 2000); Dolores Hayden, *The Power of Place: Urban Landscapes as Public History* (Cambridge, Mass.: MIT Press, 1995); Doreen Massey, *Space, Place, and Gender* (Minneapolis: University of Minnesota Press, 1994); Linda McDowell, *Gender, Identity, and Place: Understanding Feminist Geographies* (Minneapolis: University of Minnesota Press, 1999); Virginia Scharff, ed., *Seeing Nature Through Gender* (Lawrence: University Press of Kansas, 2003).

5. D. W. Meinig, *The Shaping of America: A Geographical Perspective on 500 years of History*, 4 vols. (New Haven, Conn.: Yale University Press, 1986, 1993, 1998, 2004). John R. Stilgoe, *Common Landscape of America, 1580 to 1845* (New Haven, Conn.: Yale University Press, 1982), would also bear close consideration as a primary textbook, limited for this purpose primarily by its time frame.

Peter Guillery, editor
Built from Below: British Architecture and the Vernacular

London: Routledge, 2011.
214 pages; 80 black-and-white plus 8 color illustrations.
ISBN 978-0-415-56532-5, $155.00 (HB)
ISBN 978-0-415-56533-2, $53.95 (PB)

Review by Carl Lounsbury

When I attended my first spring conference of the Vernacular Architecture Group in Essex, England, in 1984, I decided to investigate the flint-walled medieval parish church in the small village where several dwellings were open for our inspection. After a couple of days of touring, I had seen one too many for-

mer open-hall houses with smoke-blackened trusses and so unlatched the ancient porch door and walked inside the church. Alone among many treasures, I gazed up at the exposed roof frame, which, to me at that stage of my education in English framing, appeared as early and certainly more complete than any that I had seen in the nearby dwellings. Afterward, I mentioned the church roof to one of the veteran members of the VAG who looked slightly askance at what I had done. Surely, he mused, here was an American who needed to be informed about the ways of the group before he committed another fieldwork faux pas. The VAG didn't do medieval churches, which was the purview of other groups. The academic boundaries were tightly drawn. In the English lexicon, vernacular architecture denoted early farmhouses and associated buildings and rarely tiptoed over into the eighteenth century, the Georgian era commonly perceived to mark the end of regional building practices.

The concept of vernacular studies in Britain has changed considerably since that time as it has expanded beyond the field of domestic architecture of a certain social class and period to encompass a broader approach to looking at buildings of every age, form, and function. Parish churches are no longer studiously avoided. This more catholic perspective closely matches the intellectual underpinnings of the Vernacular Architecture Forum in America, which from its inception wished to avoid floundering in trying to define the margins between vernacular and polite or to distinguish between popular and folk forms and building practices. Among a host of rising voices, Peter Guillery has been a champion of the reconceptualization of vernacular studies in Britain, urging scholars to reconsider the old categories and narrative framework of British architectural history. How might that story be reconfigured if issues of style, building types, and technology were subjected to new theoretical frameworks that made old barriers irrelevant? Though the VAG has yet to schedule a visit to a twentieth-century council

estate in one of its spring conferences, there are an increasing number of British historians perfectly willing to consider the impact of local attitudes on modernist principles in the design of public housing.

Built from Below: British Architecture and the Vernacular illustrates this new direction in vernacular scholarship. The ten articles in this book edited by Guillery extend the concept of British vernacular architecture beyond its traditional boundaries to embrace structures such as medieval churches, seventeenth- and eighteenth-century villas, hospitals designed by Quakers, arts and crafts houses inspired by the traditional architecture of the Lake District, speculative "Tudoresque" suburban dwellings built between the world wars, and postwar mass housing. Arranged in chronological order, topics vary from an exploration of the use of compass geometry in laying out the twelfth-century nave of Ely Cathedral to contemporary design sources for "workhomes"—a tin-eared neologism that describes buildings containing domiciles and places of work under the same roof. Although most of the articles focus on buildings in England rather than Britain as a whole, one study makes a brief transatlantic foray to Jamestown, Virginia, where its author makes the case for geometrical design in the plan of one of the early timber-framed rowhouses, unfortunately misidentified as the governor's house.

This collection of papers derives from a 2008 conference sponsored jointly by the Vernacular Architecture Group and the Society of Architectural Historians of Great Britain. The conference's purpose was to explore ways of thinking about relationships between vernacular studies and architectural scholarship. It was an effort to challenge standard academic orthodoxies and bridge disciplines in order to provoke debate and provide templates for a more comprehensive approach to Britain's architectural past. One of the underlying premises that grew out of the conference and informs many of the works in this anthology is the need to explore the ways in which building design emerges not just from the individual agency of architects but also from the collective traditions of society. As Guillery observes in his Introduction, "canonical buildings and elite architecture such as medieval cathedrals, Baroque churches, Palladian villas, or modernist icons" should be "provincialized," not in order to "denigrate or ignore them, but to engage them" in a wider social and cultural context (6). The published proceedings interpreted this charge in ways that reflect the different disciplines of their authors, which include a timber framer, a curator, a planner, architects, and architectural historians. The architects generally analyze the vernacular as a source of design, whereas the historians are more interested in traditional forms as expressions of social history. As with any diverse compilation, some of the papers are outstanding contributions to scholarship, others show sparks of promising research with some provocative insights, and a few provoke without promise.

Two of the essays admirably demonstrate the benefits of Guillery's call for provincialization—taking well-known building types and evaluating them in terms of the impact of local conditions and cultural forces on their development. In his study of "Pre-Reformation Parish Churches," Paul Barnwell rejects the notion that parochial structures were simply reduced versions of England's great cathedrals and abbeys. He argues that they served very different purposes and that the design and function of parish churches should be examined on their own terms. Their development from small two-celled structures to more complex plans derived from a set of pragmatic responses in the twelfth and thirteenth centuries to changes in the nature of religious practices. For example, at the beginning of the twelfth century, most chancels in parish churches were generally dark, small, square compartments. However, by the end of the first quarter of the thirteenth century they were much longer, taller, better lit, and set off by a screen. Barnwell locates the impetus for these architectural changes in the liturgy and the experience of worship.

With the acceptance of transubstantiation as official doctrine in 1215, the nature of the mass took on a more dramatic role whereby the sanctity of the priest's elevation of the host was increasingly emphasized. As the impact of this idea spread across the country, the place where such a miracle occurred required a more worthy, a more numinous setting, which led to the extensive rebuilding of chancels.

Stylistic features allow Barnwell to trace the speed and spread of these alterations over time. His interpretation derives from reading the impact of the liturgical changes in the physical fabric itself instead of finding them in written sources, which are as silent as they are scarce. Nowhere does he find instructions or faculties from diocesan authorities initiating such alterations to conform to the new doctrines; there were no national or diocesan models to follow. He also addresses the emergence of aisles in terms of space set aside for the veneration of the saints, especially the Virgin, and the evolving beliefs in the doctrine of purgatory. With the rise of the latter, there was a growing need for secondary altars for conducting the ever-increasing number of requiem masses. Barnwell offers very tantalizing hypotheses for the dynamics of architectural change in medieval parish churches that need to be pursued in great detail.

Elizabeth McKellar's "The Villa: Ideal Type or Vernacular Variant" is another nicely articulated argument that exemplifies the benefits of recontexualizing well-trodden research ground. Rather than follow James Ackerman's definition of the Renaissance villa as an innovative model conceived in the classical style whose English ideal appeared in the eighteenth century, McKellar argues that this stylistic perspective has missed the larger social issue relating to the emergence of suburban housing among the English middle class a full century earlier. She contends that the villa is not a study of classical design principles expressed in cuboid white boxes in the Thames valley west of London, but part of a process of redefining the relationship of work and home in the growth of middle-class housing built on

the fringe of cities as early as the beginning of the seventeenth century.

In looking at Greenwich, McKellar discovers that the villa was not a "top-down emulative process in terms of style or form" (67). In contrast to Inigo Jones's Queen's House, the villas that grew up around it drew upon a range of metropolitan sources and forms as diverse as multigabled, artisan mannerist brick houses and neo-Gothic fancies designed by John Vanbrugh for his extended family, which, she contends, had nearly all the attributes of a modern gated community. As a socially distinct building type, the villa as an out-of-town retreat took on many forms and flourished in places such as Greenwich decades before neo-Palladianism became fashionable. McKellar's work reveals the shortcoming of the stylistic straitjacket that has confined the study of this form in standard architectural histories of early modern Britain.

Despite the unevenness of the contributions, this volume and recent works by other scholars show the promise of a more protean approach to the study of British vernacular architecture. It frees VAG research from the stultifying antiquarianism that has been one of the hallmarks of its cautious empirical analysis of fabric. Applied to building types and periods once considered outside the pale, this kind of scholarship may do much to demolish the academic hedgerows that have partitioned the British architectural landscape for too long.

Susan Kern
The Jeffersons at Shadwell

New Haven, Conn.: Yale University Press, 2010.
384 pages. 56 black-and-white illustrations.
ISBN 978-0-300-15390-3, $30.00 (HB)

Review by Barbara J. Heath

Historians have long been at odds over Thomas Jefferson's childhood and youth at

Shadwell, his family home on the Rivanna River in Albemarle County, Virginia. They have agreed on the patrician lineage of Jefferson's mother, Jane, but have downplayed her relationship with her eldest son, characterizing it as contentious or cold. Although his father Peter is credited with a warmer, and larger, role in Thomas's life, the elder Jefferson's lesser-known origins and accomplishments cast him alternately as a frontiersman, a man of moderate success, or a man lacking in education and ignorant of the conventions of polite society (4–5). Which of this seemingly mismatched pair held most sway in molding the character of their son, Thomas? Archaeological excavations undertaken in the 1940s and 1950s by Fiske Kimball and Roland Robbins attempted to address the question of Thomas Jefferson's origins through an assessment of the material conditions of his upbringing. They uncovered the footprints of numerous outbuildings at Shadwell but claimed that there was no firm evidence of a house suitable for members of the mid-eighteenth-century Virginia elite. For some historians, the architectural remains of Shadwell placed the young Jefferson more comfortably among backwoodsmen than plantation patriarchs, while for others, his Randolph ancestry and native genius were enough to overcome the limitations of his paternity and the modest, or missing, remains of his home.

In *The Jeffersons at Shadwell*, awarded the Abbott Lowell Cummings prize by the Vernacular Architecture Forum in 2011, Susan Kern disentangles these contradictory historical and material threads and reweaves them into a powerful and convincing new narrative. Through the reexamination of a diversity of existing historical sources and the analysis of more recent archaeological findings, she situates the Jeffersons both materially and socially in the center of a close-knit family and a complex web of relationships with slaves, friends, neighbors, business associates, and visitors. These connections confirm the Jeffersons' standing among the Virginia elite and illuminate key aspects of their son's

initiation into the plantocracy. Indeed, Kern's careful reading of the evidence suggests that Peter and Jane were instrumental in introducing and spreading the ideas and behaviors central to eighteenth-century notions of gentility—and the materials necessary to enact them—to their children, their slaves, and more broadly to the citizens of Albemarle County. Thus, she has written not only an innovative biography of the Jefferson family but has outlined a model for understanding the creation, maintenance, and spread of polite society in colonial Virginia as well.

Kern's work at Shadwell demonstrates the value of incorporating the material world into biographical studies and provides a methodological framework for how it can be done. Drawing inspiration from Dell Upton and Rhys Isaac, she adopts a somewhat phenomenological approach, helping us to imagine the feel of china teacups against our lips in the dining room or the weight of a folio resting on a table in the office, as she explains how the introduction of fashionable goods and ideas helped to define the Jeffersons and transform their neighborhood. The approach of social historians like Laurel Thatcher Ulrich can also be seen in her work, as she carefully mines diverse historical sources to meticulously reconstruct the social, political, and economic contexts of the Jeffersons' world.

Kern sets out her approach in the Introduction, stating that "this is not a study of material culture; it is a history of people written from the things they used and the things they did." She then notes that, while "artifacts enable the historian to animate the site and enliven the now past landscape," the "documents ground the discussion to a particular time and place" (6, 8). This is a fair statement. Kern imaginatively interprets terse notations in account books, legal documents, slave rolls, and family Bible entries along with more standard sources like family letters and Jefferson biographies to carefully reconstruct the Shadwell community and connect it with the broader world. Her use of artifacts and archaeological features, while largely persuasive, is at times more illustrative than active.

Based on her multifaceted training as an architectural historian, archaeologist, and historian, Kern brings a keen understanding of the social construction of space in the eighteenth century to bear on her interpretations of the everyday. She effectively translates material features—cellars, cooking and storage pits, postholes, and planting holes—and the written descriptions that accompany them to reconstruct colonial spaces, drawing from them the outlines of the mansion house, the adjacent kitchen and quarters, and the enclosing fences. Together, these structures and enclosures materialize concepts of order, symmetry, hierarchy, and power.

Kern starts with the mansion. By combining Peter Jefferson's accounts and probate inventory with an augmented archaeological record, she is able to make sense of previously discovered foundations and more recently unearthed postholes. The result, although conjectural, is convincing: a story-and-a-half, 32-foot-by-50-foot dwelling with a hall or dining room, parlor, office, and chamber below, two heated bedchambers above, and a south-facing porch. This, clearly, was no frontier cabin. She then guides her readers room by room through the dwelling, introducing us to the hierarchy of its spaces, richly appointed with fashionable furnishings, and the didactic roles that they were designed to play. Kern applies this process to good effect in the landscape as well. Peter Jefferson's curtilage, a ten-acre square centered on the mansion, also directed family, slaves, and visitors along routes that reinforced their positions within the social and economic hierarchy of his plantation. Although she does not mention it, his son Thomas revived the ten-acre square as a key element of his retirement landscape at Poplar Forest nearly seventy years later.

Having situated the Jeffersons materially, Kern proceeds to connect them to a web of people—enslaved and free—that reinforced their position within society. She starts with the material conditions of the enslaved community, contrasting aspects of daily life experienced by residents of the home quarter and the field quarter. Drawing a wider circle, she uses the documentary record to reconstruct the demography of the quarters and, where possible, delineate kin networks, while employing artifacts to provide a window into daily life. The outlines of this discussion are familiar to students of plantation slavery, and the artifact discussion in particular seems to be fairly standard fare. However, there is much useful information for those interested in the specific timing of community development and in the multigenerational relationships between owners and enslaved. Indeed, one enslaved family that Thomas Jefferson sent to accompany his grandson to Florida in the 1820s traces its roots to Jane Jefferson's wet nurse Sall, and likely Peter Jefferson's manservant Sawney, at Shadwell. The cultural rules governing intergenerational transfer of slaves among the elite are poorly understood, and studies like this provide crucial evidence for discerning them.

In reinforcing her central argument for the Jeffersons as agents of gentility, Kern makes the important point that some enslaved residents of the home quarter were better versed in the practices associated with elite behavior—the use and care of fine fabrics, expensive ceramics and silverware, fine furniture, and modern cooking devices—than most free Virginians. Although they did not benefit privately from the knowledge associated with the use of these fashionable objects, domestic slaves were instrumental in maintaining exacting standards within the household and in teaching the Jefferson children how to use and treat these objects appropriately. Thus, cooks, housemaids, butlers, and other domestics became important purveyors of the rules and standards that accompanied the markers of polite society.

In the remainder of the book, Kern explores the Jeffersons' strategies for ensuring the success of their children. Peter was responsible for forging and maintaining alliances with the outside world, while Jane solidified relationships within the family. Peter cultivated close friendships with members of the clergy, doctors, and other educated professionals, and forged social, economic, and

legal alliances with successful planters. He served as a county office-holder, performed valuable services for the colony as surveyor, and invested, with his peers, in land ventures. These connections and roles served the family for more than economic gain; they maintained its position within the social hierarchy in the short term and laid the foundation for beneficial marriages for the children in the future. When Peter died in 1757, he enlisted other members of the gentry to administer his estate. Their role went beyond keeping accounts and ensuring proper payments, to include taking charge of the education of his sons and guiding them toward their proper place in gentry society.

Jane's role was equally important—she gave birth to, raised, and educated a large family, trained enslaved men and women to maintain the standards that she set for her household and to educate her children and grandchildren about them, recorded and preserved the family history, and strengthened the ties between her adult children and their kin through letter writing and family visits. Shadwell remained the geographical center of the family, and Jane was buried there upon her death in 1776.

In *The Jeffersons at Shadwell*, Kern reconstructs the Jeffersons' social and material world. She makes a convincing argument for their elite status, putting to rest the myth of the backwoodsman and providing a strong counterargument to the myth of the cold relationship between mother and son. In its place she musters strong evidence that, following Peter's death, the family remained close-knit, mutually supportive, and genuinely fond of one another. Despite their physical location in the backcountry, Peter and Jane Jefferson were active, self-conscious participants in a network of gentry throughout the colony; they built and furnished a home, educated their children, amassed and trained their slaves, and participated in county affairs to advertise and maintain their position near the top of the social and economic hierarchy. They committed significant resources to ensure that their way of life was perpetuated. Kern ends the

book with the paradox of Thomas Jefferson's legacy. The product of this culture, Jefferson nevertheless helped to dismantle the slave society in which he was raised through his ideas of the rights of man.

Warren R. Hofstra and Karl Raitz, editors
The Great Valley Road of Virginia:
Shenandoah Landscapes from Prehistory
to the Present
Charlottesville: University of Virginia Press, 2010.
320 pages. 119 black-and-white illustrations.
ISBN 978-0-8139-2885-2, $50.00 (HB)
ISBN 978-0-8139-3190-6, $25.00 (PB)

Review by John Hankey

This is an ambitious book. It offers a roughly 180-mile stretch of the Great Valley Road in Virginia as "a metaphorical route into the history of the Shenandoah Valley and the forces of historic change that give its landscape structure, meaning, and significance" (10). While it doesn't achieve a grand synthesis, it nevertheless offers deeply insightful commentary, and in general, the essays are first-rate.

The Great Valley Road of Virginia's eight chapters originated as papers delivered at Shenandoah University in 2004. The two-day meeting, entitled "The Valley Road of Virginia: History and Landscape," brought professionals and lay people into conversation. Scholars tried to make sense of histories and interpretations. Government and cultural resource management personnel negotiated what was ideal and what was feasible. There were people who attended out of general interest, and others with particular agendas.

It is important to consider the origins of a book like this one. The conference represented decades of engagement with the Shenandoah Valley, its roles as a place of transit and settlement, and the ways we might approach "place" and "landscape" at practical and abstract levels. And like the conference from which it derives, this book rewards those who actively participate. Don't expect a single narrative, the synthesis of a monograph, or a comprehensive overview. Expect to join a sophisticated conversation, and do not be surprised if a certain level of familiarity or expertise is expected of the reader.

One of the most vexing challenges of a project like this is determining how it should convey the kinds of natural familiarity and detailed local knowledge brought to the conference by participants. More broadly, authors must ask what kinds of context and location a book like this owes readers who lack expert local native understanding. These are not trivial points. After all, the physical complexity and characteristics of the Valley bedeviled the Union Army during the Civil War even though it had the benefit of scouts and cartographers. While this book features many images and some maps, the relative insufficiency of effective visual and contextual aids makes it a somewhat tougher go than it might otherwise have been.

The premise of the original conference (and of the book) is straightforward: The Great Valley Road of Virginia was, and continues to be, the trunk of a major Eastern thoroughfare linking the Atlantic Seaboard at Philadelphia and Baltimore with a series of gateways to the Ohio Valley and the Upper South. The Great Valley is a natural highway and has long been the site of evolving negotiations between the people who use the valley, those who understand its larger strategic implications, and those who settle it.

The book's primary challenge in approaching the Valley Road from a variety of critical perspectives is to make the Shenandoah Valley coherent, or at least effective, as a region of study and analysis. The road becomes the organizing principle for understanding the valley, its landscapes, and its cultural resources. Ultimately, the authors can't quite settle on uniform definitions of the valley, the road, or what it is that holds everything together. Landscape, as a central organizing principle, is somewhat unevenly observed.

The book presents the Great Valley Road as part of a larger network of paths, roads, canals, railroads, trade, and population shifts unfolding over several centuries. Yet the railroad is usually dismissed as a disruptive, almost alien intrusion; in point of fact the people traversing and living in the valley regarded it as merely another—and often, superior—kind of Valley Road. One might argue that the railroad offered a distinctive form of industrial landscape and a more useful counterpoint to the Valley Road than the authors considered. Thus the book would have benefitted from more care in setting up conceptual frames and specific contexts.

Partly this has to do with the issues inherent in using a road (or the idea of a road in many iterations over a span of centuries) to help frame a variety of places, landscapes, and cultural artifacts. Is it about the road itself? Or is it about the mobility that a road offers? It works the other way, too. The valley's landscapes, people, and activities shaped, and recreated, the road over time. A project like this necessarily becomes self-reflexive, and in any case has a great many moving parts.

Chapter 1 offers a rather complex explanation of the geography and geology of the valley, especially of how the underlying physical realities presented subtle—but often crucial—sets of opportunities to early settlers. The chapter's overall point is important: "The Shenandoah Valley's physical attributes—climate, streams and rivers, bedrock and karst caverns, soils and bordering ridges—have helped define its cultural character and economy for more than two centuries" (52). Chapters 2 ("Before the Great Road: Indian Travelers on the Great Warriors' Path"), 3 ("The Colonial Road"), 4 ("An Early Road to the Old West, 1780–1837"), and 6 ("The Best Thoroughfare in the South) compose the historical core of the book. They establish a narrative and physical framework for the corridor as a kind of historical "actor" in its own right. The road itself becomes a landscape that, to a degree, is naturally and culturally determined.

These chapters explore the physical, political, and ideological realities of a mundane task: providing a reliable, predictable, and effective pathway for a wide variety of travelers. Some wayfarers were interested in reaching a far destination—perhaps via the Cumberland Gap, at the southern end of the Great Virginia Road, or maybe the Cotton South or the Ohio Valley. Others had business in the valley or were home seekers and found some part of the valley to their liking. They came to regard the Valley Road as the local conduit to remote markets. The wheat of one season in the valley might be the flour in the pantry of a London household a year later. The road was also the overlapping local artery for everything from regional trade to networks of kinship and microeconomics. A road like this can be a powerful organizing principle if handled deftly.

Chapters 5, 7, and 8 are also presented in generally chronological order but differ in approach and insight; they are threads of different conversations. Chapter 5 is a visual culture analysis of Civil War–era maps and illustrations and the ways they affected the course of the war in the valley. The argument is fascinating, but one wishes for better quality illustrations. Chapter 7 is an engaging exercise in regional urban history and offers a useful Eastern counterpart to the more prevalent Midwestern and Western frontier salients. The last chapter bookends the first by explicitly describing U.S. Route 11 (chosen as the "fully evolved version" of the Great Valley Road; the parallel Interstate 81 is essentially ignored) in terms of "A Modern Geography of Culture and Connection." The essay offers a survey and synthesis of building types and road-associated material culture.

This is a rewarding book. A collection of conference papers is necessarily a series of individual essays organized around a premise. The risk comes in the subtle distinction between publishing conference proceedings (which explicitly acknowledge the nature of the project) and offering a volume that aspires to an innovative synthesis of history, visual culture, physical sciences, cultural studies, and a "vernacular" sensibility. As the academic publishing landscape becomes more dire, and Web-based alternatives become more attractive, we—collectively—need to be frank about what is possible and appropriate. After the conference in 2004, these papers obviously seemed like a fine candidates for a book. If the same conference had been held in 2010, they may instead have been understood as excellent "new media" possibilities. Internet publishing is to this book what the railroad was to the Valley Road just after the Civil War—a disruptive, and potentially more efficient, technological solution.

Indeed, the University of Virginia's own path-breaking Web site "Valley of the Shadow" is conspicuously absent from this book. That site (one of the earliest, and most successful, Internet-based history projects) offers a broad and sophisticated resource for two "Great Valley" counties in the mid-1800s: Franklin County in Pennsylvania and Augusta County, which lies squarely in the middle of the defined "Great Valley of Virginia." This book, and that site, are very different projects that ought to be looked at together.

While the conceptual reach of *The Great Valley Road of Virginia* may sometimes exceed its actual grasp, there is a wealth of scholarship and useful insight here. Engage it on its own terms, and it will reward the reader greatly.

Jeremy Foster
Washed with Sun: Landscape and the Making of White South Africa

Pittsburgh: University of Pittsburgh Press, 2008.

424 pages. 108 black-and-white illustrations plus 40 color illustrations.

ISBN 9780822943327, $65.00 (HB)

ISBN 9780822959588, $27.95 (PB)

Review by Rebecca Ginsburg

South Africa's history is much deeper and wider than its apartheid past. From the Dutch imposition of a way station at the Cape that served trading ships en route to the East Indies in the seventeenth century, to the growth of an English-speaking settler community in the early nineteenth century, to the uniting of various African nations under Shaka's rule in the mid-nineteenth century, processes in the region produced currents that resonated throughout southern Africa and beyond. Nonetheless, it is common to find such events, rich and complex in their own right, treated by historians as mere background for the eventual implementation of apartheid. Such is the drive to make sense of the introduction in the mid-twentieth century of the country's notorious and noxious racial policies and to find clues for its appeal among South African whites in their past.

The urge is understandable, of course. One of the accomplishments of Jeremy Foster's smart and thoughtful book is that it satisfies readers' desires to understand the historical roots of apartheid, while not succumbing to the urge to treat the years leading up to apartheid as if they did nothing but lead up to apartheid. Foster has other goals than to set the stage for apartheid, and they are ambitious. First, he argues that the early South African character—that is, the values, attitudes, and sense of self and community that came to distinguish the white inhabitants of what would become South Africa—was formed in large part through settlers' bodily engagement with the distinctive South African landscape. He is concerned especially with the period from 1900 to 1930, the years of national formation that followed the Anglo-Boer War and included Union in 1910 and, although Foster does not much touch on it, the increasingly brutal removal of Africans from the land through means legal and extralegal.

Foster's second and ultimately more important accomplishment is to make a case for the value of studying, as he does here, the corporeal, material nature of landscape experience and comprehension. The intended recipients of his appeal are, I gather, scholars of landscape, design, and allied fields. In truth, though, *Washed with Sun* does such a powerful job of demonstrating how historical investigation is enriched and enlivened through consideration of the physical settings and geographies in which historical characters had to navigate and stake their claims that I hope it will receive broader attention. This book deserves a wide audience, especially among historians of South Africa and scholars whose work examines racial construction and identity.

Scholars of whiteness, in particular, will find much here to chew on. Foster's primary interest is in representations of the South African landscape. He's concerned less with their production than their reception. What do the battlefield drawings of Colonel Robert Baden-Powell, the lyrical descriptions of the Transvaal of writer John Buchan, the landscape paintings of Afrikaner Jan Hendrick Pierneef, and the landscape photographs of the South African Railways and Harbours Corporation have in common? At the most obvious level, all depicted and promoted a reading of the South African landscape that was celebratory, uncomplicated, and romantic. More critically, they supported what Foster calls "metropolitan imaginings," notions held by sectors of the British public about the ruggedness and purity of life in the colonies that provided one basis of support for investment in them. For those living in South Africa, on the other hand, the images simultaneously portrayed content and engaged aesthetic sensibilities that, as Foster writes, "helped nationalist white South Africans imagine themselves as part of a new society that grew out of its landscape" (139). They advocated, albeit implicitly, the necessity of a white nation within the dark continent, a nation that would practice stewardship over exotic peoples and lands. In naturalizing the white presence and, in time, absolute white political and economic control of South Africa, they proved potent forces in the development of apartheid.

One of Foster's most compelling examples relates to a genre of photography that became popular in the 1920s: black-and-white images, commissioned by the South African Railways and Harbours Corporation and reproduced in its numerous publications, that portrayed supposedly empty, unimproved lands in the interior of the subcontinent. Often the photographs were taken from the windows of moving trains, all the better to encourage would-be travelers to purchase tickets that would allow them to seek adventure and truth in wild, remote places. They were mostly of the wide-open expanses of the Transvaal, the Eastern Cape, and the Orange Free State. The simplest and most obvious reading of these images is that depictions of empty lands encouraged whites to consider themselves unproblematic occupiers of the subcontinent, which in fact had long been home to African peoples. Indeed, Foster does justice to that interpretation—but then continues to push his analysis. "Images of the 'empty' unimproved veld [the elevated interior] not only represented space waiting to be filled—by physical settlement... they also inaugurated a new imagined history for the territory they depicted" (230).

This imagined history was, in fact, less a history than a sense of a shared future. In particular, these photographs contributed to a growing sense among whites that to be South African was to feel a certain way about the land. The attitude was one of bodily and spiritual connection to the wide-open spaces and crisp air, a connection made possible by virtue of personal habitation of and acquaintance with the plains. There were explicit references in popular media to what Foster calls "a form of habitus, a sort of bodily alertness" that supposedly came from and was dependent upon the unmediated connection to the land that untamed South Africa afforded whites (232).

A contemporary writer, capturing this spirit, referred romantically to the psychology of inhabiting the lonely veld. Foster recasts that "psychology" as a neurosis. Whites, he argues, were subject to stark anxieties about their roles on the frontier and their destiny as a nation, which were mixed up with conflicted notions of race and cultural character. The small groups of administrators who ran

the railway were sensitive to whites' intense search for a sense of belonging. Foster does not push this too far. He does not claim that railroad photographs in themselves allowed whites to overcome their dread by creating a shared white identity based on a particular, imagined relationship to the land. He does claim, however, that the photos mediated the emergence of such an identity among English-speakers and Afrikaners alike. Images that encouraged viewers to "keep in play an elusive sense of incompleteness and potential" permitted the new (white) South African citizen "to imagine the train journey as a trajectory that subjectively aligned [him] with the nation's territory and its historical destiny as a 'frontier of civilization'" (235). Railway photographs encouraged whites to stake uncomplicated claims to the interior, not only by stirring in them a civic, moral responsibility to improve an empty canvas but also because they stroked whites' vanities about themselves and their capacity to commune with the natural environment of the subcontinent.

Foster's introductory chapters set out his personal interest in integrating ideas about bodily imagination into our understanding of landscape apprehension, provide some historical background to South Africa's period of nationhood, and establish a "theoretical and methodological excursus" that, while an unfortunate interruption to the momentum of his story, is a smart discussion of the implications of understanding landscapes as lived-upon networks of spaces. (The latter chapter earns a place in the syllabus of my doctoral-level course in architectural and landscape history methods.) Foster then moves chapter by chapter through an examination of various genres of South African landscape representation. The Railway's photographs form one chapter; in another, "Prospect, Materiality, and the Horizons of Potentiality on Parktown Ridge," he explores many of the same themes, but in the context of Johannesburg's upper-crust suburban neighborhoods.

The explanation usually given for the siting

of these grand houses on the northern edge of town is that the location afforded refuge from the noise and dirt of the gold mines that ringed the southern end as well as providing closer proximity to Pretoria, the cultural center of the region. Foster does not discount these reasons but presents as well additional ones based on the phenomenological experience of inhabiting the Ridge. We can best understand the design and orientation of the elite Ridge neighborhoods, he argues, by considering the significance of the view that they opened up to their residents. At the turn of the century, the houses faced and had unobstructed views of the uninhabited, featureless veld that faded in the far distance into the Magaliesberg Mountains. This was a view distinctively unlike those to which English eyes were accustomed. In the old country, signs of past and present human habitation such as fences, half-hidden roofs, lanes, and fields spoke to centuries of human presence, even in rural areas. This new South African vista of emptiness and nothingness, as the settlers read it, was less scary than exhilarating, for it carried a meaning that affirmed and fortified the viewer.

On an individual level, the view encouraged private reverie and a powerful sense of respite from the ills of urban life that contemporary elites sought to mediate. On a cultural level, the view offered up by any individual property was understood to participate in the vista shared by all the homes that stood along the edge of the ridge. It was "as impossible for those who lived in them to be unaware of each other as it was for them to be unaware of the view to the north" (152). The houses, conceived of almost as sentries or battlements connected to one another in a gesture of collective defense, provided their owners a sense of taking their stand defiantly upon the outermost edge of the horizon, looking down and out in an attitude of control. Whites who questioned their place in the subcontinent and looked "to the landscape for clues to their own identity" had their doubts resolved when, colonial rhetoric no doubt echoing in their minds, they gazed upon the archaic and primordial horizon that stretched in front of them, beckoning for care (153).

As he does throughout the book, Foster does not stop here but pushes his analysis further. Far beyond whites' vision, but within their ken, lay the Mediterranean, the fount of Western civilization. The northward orientation of the line of homes on the Ridge directed whites' attention at some level to the world of the Greeks and the Romans to which they considered themselves direct inheritors: "It was, after all, the Mediterranean classical world that provided the intellectual warrant for New Imperialism" (157). Like the ancients, elite whites viewed themselves as bringers of civilization to a benighted people. The situation of their homes and gardens, directing residents' attention northward, reinforced a disposition to align one's self and one's people with the Mediterranean world and the imperialist, paternalistic values for which it stood.

Too much? At first I found myself rejecting some of the furthest reaches of Foster's claims on the grounds that he was overinterpreting. I admired his intellectual energy but thought that he pushed too far without sufficient evidence—nay, without, really, any evidence at all to support his assertions. The early twentieth-century matronly madams of Parktown Ridge conceiving of themselves as heirs to the legacy of Roman colonialism? No way. But I could not let go of the powerful image of the string of mansions perched on the precipice between civilization—the hustle and bustle, excitement and danger of the mine works that lent distinctive character to early Johannesburg—and the empty plain, holding a danger of its own, absent domestication in the right hands. Even the design of the houses, as Foster points out, supports this interpretation, for the primary architect of Parktown, Herbert Baker, abandoned the Cape designs that he had been enamored with in his earlier career in favor of tiled roofs, loggias, walled terraces, and arcades that evoked Mediterranean styles and sensibilities.

In addition to being swayed by Foster's prose and his images—and he achieves clear writing and good use of illustrations (including the wonderful and necessary color reproductions) throughout his book—I found myself persuaded eventually by my body's memory of what it has been like for me, since the 1980s, to wander the Ridge. The "great spaces washed by sun," Baker wrote of the natural setting, quoting Christopher Wren, required buildings constructed of local materials and with a minimum of decoration in order to do justice to their setting. Eventually, he came to build his mansions of native stone quarried from the piece of land on which a given house would eventually stand, and convinced other architects to do likewise. The walls that surrounded them were often built of the same local stone. Even today, they seem to rise from their location on the edge, and I can understand why he writes that they "rendered both the terrain and the European presence in it meaningful and comprehensible" (165).

I have no experience defending white racial privilege or questioning the wisdom of metropolitan investment in a far-flung colony, but I have smelled the veld and felt its sun. The corporeal engagements that I have had with these settings allows me to imagine what it might have been like for people who carried such thoughts in their heads, as Foster suggests, while they walked along rocky paths looking out to the thin skies of the Highveld. This small, admittedly minor experiment in geographic imagination convinces me at least to keep an open mind to matters that he admits are, in the end, almost impossible to put to proof. Foster is right, I believe, in urging us to take more seriously the bodily experiences that particular places make available to different groups of users. "Spatiotemporal undergoing and habitation lie at the heart of territorial meaning" (87), and landscapes disclose their meaning not to disembodied minds but to human bodies driven by expectations, sensations, memories, fears, and dreams.

Heath Massey Schenker
Melodramatic Landscapes: Urban Parks in the Nineteenth Century
Charlottesville: University of Virginia Press, 2009.
232 pages. 75 black-and-white illustrations.
ISBN 9780813928425, $35.00 (HB)

Review by Eliza Earle Ferguson

Heath Schenker's highly readable comparative study of nineteenth-century parks in Paris, Mexico City, and New York brings together a wealth of information concerning why and how these parks were created. Schenker finds that in all three cities, plans for massive new parks were informed by notions of melodrama, with the landscape designed to communicate clear moral messages about social harmony and the benefits of contact with nature for the edification of the lower classes. Drawing on primary sources such as contemporary guidebooks and published memoirs written by park planners, together with a range of secondary material, Schenker constructs a convincing case for the reformist intentions of park planners and government officials. However, the book also promises to investigate "how the public received and responded to those messages" of moral reform (19), and on this point of great social historical interest, the book is ultimately more suggestive than conclusive.

The book's three main chapters take each city and its parks in turn, beginning with the Parisian parks of the Second Empire. In Schenker's analysis, Napoleon III was motivated to create or renovate large parks throughout Paris in order to placate various political constituencies, whom Schenker identifies by their class status rather than their political views. While members of the bourgeoisie profited immensely through real estate speculation and enjoyed displaying their wealth on promenades in the parks, the working people of Paris were pushed to the periphery of the city, far from the nicest of the new parks. Schenker agrees with Zola's assessment in his 1872 novel *La Curée,* in which the parks are nothing more than a false backdrop for the empty ideals of the regime. The political spectrum of the Third Empire was far more nuanced than Schenker indicates, however, and the commitment of Napoleon III to improving the lives of the workers in his capital city was more sincere. The discussion of the Haussmannization of Paris would have been enriched by engagement with more recent scholarship as well as now-classic works dealing with Third Empire Paris by authors like François Loyer and David Jordan, not to mention the field of social history, which is represented here by outdated texts from the mid-twentieth century.

How the parks of Haussmann's Paris inspired the renovation of Chapultepec Park in Mexico City is an intriguing story outlined in chapter 2. The location of this park to the west of the city is rich in historical significance. Having once been a sacred site for the Aztecs, in 1530 it was designated as public property and a key source for Mexico City's water supply. By the nineteenth century, its springs were running dry, and the viceroy's former pleasure villa had been converted into a military academy. The Castle of Chapultepec saw a major battle in the Mexican-American War, where in 1847 the young cadets sacrificed themselves in a suicidal action against the invading Americans and became immortalized in the nationalist legend of *los niños héroes.* Thus the site of Chapultepec was already infused with political meaning when Emperor Maximilian I came to power in 1864 and dreamed of recreating Mexico City in the image of Paris. Though his regime was short-lived, his vision for Mexico City was not, and the new boulevard he cut from the city to Chapultepec would become "the spine of modern Mexico City" (85). The Porfiriato continued Maximilian's efforts to make Mexico City a European-style showplace in the last decades of the nineteenth century. As Schenker recounts, Chapultepec performed much

the same theatrical function as the Bois de Boulogne in Paris: the backdrop to a scene where well-to-do citizens enacted their social status and the state demonstrated its aspirations to modernize the city. Doubtless the wealthy citizens of Mexico City did use the park for this purpose, but the author's reliance on guidebooks as the main source of contemporary descriptions of the park may have unduly exaggerated its spectacular nature.

The thesis indicated by the book's title is best elaborated in chapter 3, where Schenker presents the development of Central Park as a purposeful antidote to New York's less refined (and lower-class) commercial pleasure gardens. Instead of the alcohol-fueled festivities of places like the Vauxhall Garden in the Bowery, contact with nature would uplift visitors to Central Park. "Like theatrical melodrama," Schenker argues, "urban parks were intended as a popular, morally edifying form of entertainment for 'the people'" (146). Although Schenker presents a concise description of the conventions of nineteenth-century melodrama, together with copious evidence of the reformist intentions of park promoters like Frederick Law Olmsted, this evidence does not permit a satisfactory answer to the question of the effectiveness of these moralizing efforts.

The intriguing vignette that opens the book provides a case in point. On December 28, 1877, the *New York Times* reported that a certain Officer Meaney discovered a man in Central Park who had built himself a hut of logs and branches and attracted the officer's attention with a bonfire with which he was warming himself. Schenker first proposes that this incident illustrates a disjuncture between the uses of the park as defined by its designers and as experienced by its visitors. Parks like this one, she writes, "were something of an enigma to their intended audience" (3). But then she suggests that the illusion of the countryside in the city had succeeded only too well with this one individual: "Wandering onto a stage set depicting

rural scenery, perhaps he mistook it for the real thing" (3). This anecdote sets up one of the central difficulties in Schenker's project, which is the relationship between the elites who created these parks and the ordinary people who visited them. Ultimately, the reception of the parks by the people appears in Schenker's text as a fairly straightforward and even successful transmission of values. Because melodrama was a "pervasive cultural discourse" (19), the author presumes that the working-class people who attended theatrical performances such as the very popular stage version of *Uncle Tom's Cabin* were equipped to read the messages encoded for them in the Central Park landscape. But the example of the bum who was disciplined by the police for mistaking the park for a real sylvan sanctuary suggests otherwise. Evidently, the law had to intervene when people did not adhere to the intended uses of the park.

As a social historian of nineteenth-century Paris, this reviewer is deeply interested the problem of the relationship between elite and popular culture, and perhaps it is unfair to expect a landscape architect to give answers that would fully satisfy a reader from another discipline. This is the risk of undertaking an interdisciplinary project like Schenker's. Still, a bit more due diligence might have helped the author avoid some errors, like the assertion that the naturalistic landscape planned by the Whig aristocrat Viscount Cobham at his estate Stowe in 1713 represented "the more 'natural' evolution of political reform accomplished in England without recourse to violent political revolution, such as the one that occurred across the channel in France, the specter of which haunted English politics throughout the century" (12). The French Revolution of course did not begin for more than seventy years after the garden at Stowe was designed; in the early eighteenth century the English would have had their own recent history of political violence more freshly in mind.

To expand the social historical dimension of the project, the author could have made much fuller use of the "sidebars" interspersed throughout the book. Offered with no introduction or analysis, these brief excerpts from contemporary texts such as newspapers and periodicals describe parks as far-flung as the Tiergarten in Berlin and the Promenade in Santiago. Along with the numerous illustrations in the book, they constitute an untapped reserve of primary source material that could serve the author well in developing her analysis of the social uses of the parks. For instance, an 1888 story from the *New York World* appears alongside an 1878 illustration from the *National Police Gazette* depicting the "Perils of the Park" (148–49). The story is about an "intrepid reporter" who gets into a cab with a man she encounters in the park, while the illustration depicts scenes of lovers on a bench, a gentleman being robbed at gunpoint, and an old man talking to a little girl. The story and the pictures offer evidence of activities that did not fit the moralizing agenda of park planners and city officials, and yet the reader is left to draw his or her own interpretations.

Schenker's book is valuable for its comparative perspective, demonstrating how different nineteenth-century regimes aimed to solve social and political problems through creating city parks. The social historical questions it leaves unanswered should inspire further research.

Randall Mason

The Once and Future New York: Historic Preservation and the Modern City

Minneapolis: University of Minnesota Press, 2009.

344 pages. 96 black-and-white illustrations.

ISBN 978-0-8166-5603-5, $84.00 (HB)

ISBN 978-0-8166-5604-2, $27.95 (PB)

Review by Carla Yanni

What was the defining moment in New York City's preservation history? The destruction of Penn Station? Not necessarily.

Randall Mason in *The Once and Future New York: Historic Preservation and the Modern City* lessens the historical rank of the demolition of Penn Station by demonstrating the importance of little-known St. John's Chapel and (spoiler alert!) narrating its ultimate demise. St. John's, designed by John and Isaac McComb and completed in 1809, was the center of a planned neighborhood east of Varick Street. The neighborhood was built by the Trinity vestry to include an urban park, a square on the model of those in London, and upscale townhouses. The chapel was demolished in 1918. Mason reveals this complicated story from every angle the archival record will allow: the nearby congregants, newspaper reporters, civic leaders, the church leaders of the Trinity vestry (who wanted to concentrate their members into a wealthier uptown parish), and others. In spite of the chapel's evocation of Old New York, a historical association linked to its Federal style, the church could not withstand a municipal street-widening program. The fate of St. John's Chapel is told in chapter 2 with drawings and photographs, carefully selected by Mason, that in themselves allow us to see how the arguments in favor of saving the chapel took shape over time. Supporters initially emphasized its importance as a local place of worship, but later advocates presented it as an architectural achievement.

The Once and Future New York focuses on a range of preservation issues from 1890 to 1920. Winner of the Antoinette Forrester Downing award from the Society of Architectural Historians in 2011, Mason's book describes many forceful New Yorkers who championed heritage-related activities as integral parts of urban development. Andrew Haswell Green appears frequently in the book. (I was struck by the thought that fifty years ago, at a different historiographic moment, this book might have taken the shape of a "Great Man" history of Green, positioning him as the founding father of preservation.) Green will be familiar to historians of New York because he played important roles in the

establishment of institutions such as the Metropolitan Museum of Art, the American Museum of Natural History, and the Bronx Zoo. In 1895, Green founded the American Scenic and Historic Preservation Society, demonstrating his dedication to the idea of historic sites as civic, patriotic symbols. Green saw the saving of monuments as part of a larger project of improving the city's aesthetics and moral tone: to restore a tidy colonial house on a bright parcel of land was not antithetical to urban planning; it was, rather, a necessary part of growth (6, 20). Mason concludes, therefore, that it is wrong to paint a picture of early preservationists as antiurban.

The American Scenic and Historic Preservation Society, as implied by its name, concerned itself with the conservation of natural ("scenic") settings and historical landmarks. Restored natural sites, mostly in the form of parks, and preserved buildings are deeply connected by the way they invite visitors to experience civic memory, however socially constructed that memory may be. These sites are valuable insofar as they cultivate shared identity. To frame his discussion of how places create memory, Mason has developed the useful idea of memory infrastructure. Infrastructure, in this formulation, is a system of fundamental amenities that must be in place for a city to function: "Memory infrastructure was intended to perform the important cultural function of building cultural identity by fusing celebrations of the past with optimism about the future" (xxv).

Memory infrastructure seems like an especially apt description of the Bronx River Parkway, a giant among infrastructures and the subject of chapter four. The Bronx River Parkway was many things to many people: a restored natural landscape, an engineering feat, a slum clearance initiative, a sewer improvement scheme, a suburban real estate deal, and a highway. By the close of the nineteenth century, the Bronx River and its tributaries were choked by pollution and wrecked by flooding. Residential sewage emptied into the river, which drained into the Bronx Zoo's lake, killing off some of the zoo's birds (184, 192). (Since the zoo was one of Green's pet projects, the dead critters may have had a disproportional impact on regional planning decisions.) Constructing the parkway and decontaminating the river went hand in hand. The state legislature established the Parkway Commission in 1905, and a business-like assembly of politicians and engineers commenced the "vast work of negotiating deals and condemning property and of cleaning, clearing, destruction, and construction" (182). Mason's prose perks up in this chapter, where he offers fine-grained details of the acquisition of lands for this remarkable thoroughfare. We learn about Anna and Domenico Disalvo's stables and bakeries, considered "tumbled down" by the appraisers hired by the Parkway Commission; we learn about delicatessen owners and bottle-stop makers, all driven out by the Parkway. In White Plains, the Church of Our Lady of Mt. Carmel was destroyed in spite of its stained-glass windows and fair construction, both of which the appraisers observed. The priest, Rev. Marinaro, did not even bother asking for his church to be spared: he merely tried to negotiate a fairer price (221). Mason persuades the reader that most of the buildings along the expressway's path were not blighted; more cruelly, although not surprisingly, the commissioners considered the German and Italian immigrants who lived in the environs of the river to be themselves sources of decrepitude, "part of the problem to be fixed" (223). Madison Grant, chief proponent of the road and its park-like setting, depicted the twenty-year improvement project as a heroic defense of American heritage. Attempts to build cultural identity through memory or physical infrastructure come at a great cost. Mason's account of the Bronx River Parkway casts aside two more myths: one, that preservationists were mere antiquarians, interested only in high-style edifices; and, two, that preservationists cared exclusively for individual buildings.

Some individual buildings do get care-ful attention from Mason, as they did from early-twentieth-century preservationists: the Morris-Jumel Mansion, Hamilton Grange, Fraunces Tavern, and City Hall are all set within the operational concept of memory infrastructure. Generally, Mason makes it clear that the history of preservation requires revision: the story is far more complex than the oft-told tale of the New York City Landmarks Commission rising like a phoenix from the ashes of Penn Station, thus catalyzing preservation in the Big Apple. Without denying the significance of those events, Mason constructs a longer, more nuanced history of preservation in New York, one that reveals the roots of the profession dating back to the 1890s (x). Capturing the tensions between building and demolition, between growth and the status quo, The Once and Future New York opens up a critical conversation about how early twentieth-century preservationists "spatialize[d] memory on an urban scale" (248).

Thomas G. Andrews
Killing for Coal: America's Deadliest Labor War

Cambridge, Mass.: Harvard University Press, 2008. 408 pages. 30 black-and-white illustrations, 4 maps. ISBN 978-0-674-04691-7, $18.95 (PB)

Review by Alison K. Hoagland

On April 20, 1914, unionist forces engaged in a day-long gun battle with the militia in the coalfields of Colorado. The site was a tent colony in Ludlow occupied by strikers who had been evicted from their company homes. Late in the afternoon, a fire of unknown origin swept the tent colony. When the smoke cleared, eighteen strikers were found dead, including two women and eleven children in a pit dug beneath a tent as shelter from the bullets. The incident, which rapidly became known as the Ludlow Massacre, was the piv-

otal event in what became the Ten Days' War, as unionists fought back with a ferocity that resulted in more than thirty deaths and the intervention of the U.S. Army.

Thomas G. Andrews uses this conflict as the starting point for *Killing for Coal: America's Deadliest Labor War,* winner of the Bancroft Prize as well as five other prestigious awards. In this book, Andrews marries environmental history with labor and industrial history, arguing that an event such as the Ludlow Massacre—its highly charged nomenclature indicating its partisan narrative—calls for a much broader context than this one tragic event has received. Accordingly, he places this coalfield conflict in a broad environmental history in which the nation's desire for fossil fuels is as culpable as the Rockefeller interests that controlled the largest coal company. In his account, Andrews discusses overarching environmental and industrial forces, synthesizing them into a compelling yet somewhat detached narrative.

Andrews begins with the gun battle of April 20, examines its one-sided reputation in leftist lore (i.e., "massacre"), and then introduces the reader to the rest of the story—the subsequent carnage of the Ten Days' War. Rather than parse the rights and wrongs of this polarizing conflict, though, Andrews spends the first six chapters of his book developing the environmental, labor, and corporate-paternalism stories. Only in the last and seventh chapter does he return to the strike of 1913–14.

The environmental story is wrapped up in the importance of coal for industrializing America. Although railroads are often identified as the force that opened up and developed the nation, Andrews points out that it was coal that not only fueled railroad engines but also provided energy to fabricate the thousands of miles of rails. Coal was also used to mine coal itself, powering the steam engines necessary for fans, hoists, pumps, and hauling. More significantly, coal shaped urban growth, making electricity and streetcar lines possible, fueling industry and smelters, helping produce brick and steel for buildings, and, not incidentally, casting a thick pall of pollution over the landscape. Coal also affected rural areas, providing energy for the railroads that took produce to market, mills that processed grain, and elevators that stored and moved the grain.

The labor story is connected to the nature of the work. Andrews devotes a chapter to the working conditions of the coal miners, especially underground. He introduces the term "workscape" to analyze the relationship between workers and the natural world—as it is changed by them and as it changes them (125). The workscape is particularly important in understanding the inherent danger in coal mining, from falling coal to explosions, noxious air, and fire. On average, about sixty men died each year in the Colorado coalfields, which employed about 15,000 in the early twentieth century. Another significant aspect of coal mining was the basic independence that colliers had because they worked for tonnage rates, not wages, and on their own schedule, not by the clock. This control of their workspace underground combined with the omnipresence of danger on the job, helping fuel the desire for an autonomous union.

In November 1913 Governor Elias Ammons brought representatives of the three big coal companies together with three union representatives in a private meeting. Andrews devotes several pages to this pivotal session, in which the various sides talked past one another. Anxious for resolution, the governor kept pointing out that all of the unionists' demands, such as an eight-hour day, pay for dead work (underground work that did not directly produce coal), checkweighmen selected by the miners, and so forth, were agreed to, except for one: recognition of the union. This missed the point, though, because recognition of the union went to the heart of how the miners thought about their jobs: they were experts, and the safety and fairness of their workplace could not be guaranteed unless they governed themselves. This fundamental split between workers, who insisted

on craft autonomy, and management, which attempted to gain control of production, was a division that echoed across the industrial landscape of early twentieth-century America.

The story of corporate paternalism comes closest to the interests of readers of this journal because it concerns the control of space. Andrews describes a fairly open company landscape initially—one of the original developers of the coalfields even hoped for an industrial utopia—but a strike in 1894 changed industrialists' attitudes. During that strike, the success of unionists in organizing communities where the miners owned the land caused the companies to develop mechanisms for controlling the landscape more effectively. After 1894, schools, churches, hospitals, and especially company-owned towns marked the landscape as one of corporate paternalism. The "closed" camps—those owned by the companies—were excessively controlled: fenced in by barbed wire and patrolled by guards (although it is unclear from Andrews's description if every closed camp was so controlled and how long such surveillance lasted). Companies heralded the company houses as far superior to the shanties built by the miners themselves. Company stores offered an array of goods, not necessarily at high prices, but the use of scrip— payment in currency redeemable only at company stores—was an obvious infringement on workers' freedom.

The policy of "containment" had two effects on the labor war of 1913–14. First, workers struck not only to obtain better working conditions, as they had in previous strikes, but with a new purpose added: to remove the hand of corporate paternalism. The oppression of company towns, scrip-dependent company stores, and the controlled landscape added to workers' sense of injustice. Secondly, the labor war played out spatially, with evicted strikers occupying tent colonies on non-company-owned land, which provided a visual image of their dispossession as well as their numerical strength.

Andrews's discussion of these spatial

issues lacks the kind of specificity that Vernacular Architecture Forum members find so beneficial. Although he includes three maps of the coalfields in order to show mines and communities highlighted in the ongoing conflict, he does not include any site plans of communities, which might have illustrated the control of access and egress. Although he discusses various kinds of housing for workers, both self-built and company-provided, the reader has only a few historic photographs, and no plans, with which to compare them. And although he comments wryly on the use of Spanish Colonial Revival–style designs for company stores, he does not picture them. Part of his difficulty with the material record is that so little of the built environment has survived. With the closure of the mines beginning in the 1930s, vast numbers of people left the region. None of the closed camps remains today, and only fragments of the open camps.

Andrews's environmental-history approach is rather detached, leaving him at a long remove from his story, as if Americans' thirst for fossil fuels made the conflict inevitable. People play an odd role in this history, more as subjects of broad forces than as actors in their own right. For a better understanding of corporate strategy and unionist infighting, one might turn to David A. Wolff's *Industrializing the Rockies: Growth, Competition, and Turmoil in the Coalfields of Colorado and Wyoming, 1868-1914* (Boulder: University Press of Colorado, 2003), which addresses company management and union leaders in much greater detail. Andrews's work is based on extensive primary research, especially company correspondence and contemporary observations, although he opts to quote these sources sparingly and play down the role of individuals. Similarly, his reluctance to analyze particular communities weakens his emphasis on the importance of corporate control. While rooted in the specific, Andrews's broad synthesis leads him to stick to the general, requiring the reader to trust his conclusions. Andrews casts this specific labor conflict not only as an inevitable result of a long struggle between workers and management but also, more provocatively, as an illustration of the relationship between physical energy and social power in early twentieth-century America.

Ellen Dunham-Jones and June Williamson
Retrofitting Suburbia: Urban Design Solutions for Redesigning Suburbs

Hoboken, N.J.: Wiley & Sons, Inc., 2008, updated 2011. 304 pages. 52 color plates, numerous black-and-white images throughout.
ISBN: 978-0-470-04123-9, $75.00 (HB)
ISBN: 978-0-470-93432-6, $49.95 (PB)

Review by Jason Alexander Hayter

Prior to the start of the Great Recession, with housing a magnet for equally intangible dreams and capital, the edges of our metropolises exploded with new exurbanization, center cities sprouted fresh skyline-lifting high-rises, and in between downtowns and the fringes infill and redevelopment projects churned the suburban landscape. *Retrofitting Suburbia*, by the architects Ellen Dunham-Jones of Georgia Tech and June Williamson of The City College of New York, is a cross-continent compendium of new building typologies and host morphologies in that churning landscape. Labeling them "retrofits," the authors' overarching belief is that these projects collectively comprise a process of "incremental metropolitanism" whereby a "large-scale approach" can, and in their minds should, "systematically and sustainably transform suburban form" (xiii).

Winner of the Association of American Publishers 2009 PROSE Award for Architecture and Planning, this is a book with much to recommend it. *Retrofitting Suburbia* covers a wide array of typologies being replaced or changed: garden apartments, commercial strips, regional malls, edge cities, and office and industrial parks. The content is useful.

Introductions to common suburban developments are provided. Case study backgrounds offer basic data on planners, architects, clients, and site size, among other subjects. Examples are drawn from a wide array of contexts, including Levittown, Cape Cod, Chicago, Atlanta, Denver, and Miami—with many of the delightful, but hideworn, usual suspects absent. Accompanying the text are helpful images, aerial photographs, site plans, and figure–ground diagrams, all of which are supplemented by a thirty-page color portfolio.

Morphological analyses throughout the work will be of particular interest to the readers of *Buildings & Landscapes*. This is because, first of all, intriguing comparisons are drawn, such as between Mizner Park in Florida, the Piazza Navona in Rome, and the 1951 Shopper's World outdoor mall in Massachusetts (125). But the book is most notably interesting because it contains separate comparative morphological analysis sections that usefully illustrate building footprints, roadbeds, and lot lines at multiple-decade intervals, and include descriptions of what Dunham-Jones and Williamson classify as *static, campus,* and *elastic tissues* (53).

It needs to be stated up front, however, that this work is not the "comprehensive guidebook for architects, planners, urban designers, developers, and elected officials" described on the back cover. Yet failing to match publisher puffery never renders a book hopelessly flawed—particularly when it comes to case-study collections. Instead, to genuinely appreciate the successes and challenges of *Retrofitting Suburbia*, one must consider it in terms of those works next to it on the shelf: namely, the genre of architecture books on the city, and, more problematically, the subgenre of New Urbanist writings.

When architects tackle the subject of the city, it provides them an opportunity to truly prove their intellectual mettle. But it also sets up the most brilliant of designers for their own literary Icarus moment. The difference between books at the heights and depths of

this genre often has to do with whether the author mistakenly conflates, first, the physical form of a city with its underlying social, economic, and ecological processes, and, second, the shorter-term, individual artistic process of architectural creation with the longer-term, collective policy, financial, and cultural processes of city building and morphogenesis. *Retrofitting Suburbia* avoids the first mistake, but partially makes the second.

Dunham-Jones and Williamson are refreshingly honest about their focus on form. They clearly define *suburb* "primarily in terms of physical form rather than location of governmental boundaries," and *urban* as "higher-density, mixed-use, walkable blocks of buildings supported by a continuous street network with well-defined public space" (viii). The authors acknowledge that cities are still decentralizing (10). They admit that what they investigate "are hybrids and reflect aspects of both centerness and decentralization" (13). Most impressively, they not only recognize, but even thoughtfully list the contradictions of suburban, single-developer, neo-traditional projects, such as "urban building types filled mostly with suburban chain retail outlets" (13).

Where this work stumbles is in how it addresses the relationships between matters of architecture and the cultural, infrastructural, policy, and financial aspects of the development process. On one hand, the authors do recognize these key facets of metropolitan morphological change, and such recognitions place this work ahead of many architecture books on their topic.

Dunham-Jones and Williamson describe the re-*chic*-ing of strip malls, notably La Grande Orange in Phoenix (70–71), the cycling of retail spaces into immigrant-serving uses (68), and the ethnic repositioning of entire malls (119). They also highlight public and community use conversions of retail buildings, as with a library in Denton, Texas, and with megachurches (69). Infrastructure issues, such as wastewater (99), bus systems (107), roadways (88), and light rail (throughout), are also mentioned. And they touch on the realities of the real estate business, such as REITs (Real Estate Investment Trusts) and why short-term profits matter to them (65, 115), and make frequent references to Tax Increment Financing (TIFs).

However, the authors do not adequately recognize the often project-defining relationships between these essential aspects of the development process and those tasks typically engaged in by architects. What's more, the text often centers on individual projects and architects, falsely implying that these other important factors are merely ancillary to a design-centered process. More distressingly, community responses and politics—as functionally and ethically central to redesigning suburbs as infrastructure or money—are often treated dismissively, with lines such as: "Perhaps you can take the shopping center out of the suburb, but you cannot take the suburban mind-set and building typologies out of the developers and city officials" (75). These shortcomings, while less than so many other texts in this genre, still hold this book back.

Then there is New Urbanism. The problem is this: regardless of one's opinion of its design philosophy, the subgenre of New Urbanist works often lack rhetorical professionalism, use predetermined design outcomes to drive collection and utilization of data, terms, history, and preexisting literature, and, like Modernism before it, have an obsession with demolition.

Retrofitting Suburbia is a New Urbanist work, regardless of whether its authors overtly claim it to be or not. Its argument rests heavily on that of the Congress for the New Urbanism's *Greyfields to Goldfields* publication, and while many of the developments covered in this book owe more conceptually to the evolution of Peter Calthorpe's Pedestrian Pocket into Transit Oriented Development designs, it is the DPZ SmartCode (38–40) used within the New Urbanist transect concept (37) that is given multipage treatment. And New Urbanist flaws are unfortunately prevalent throughout.

Curving suburban streets are proclaimed "dendritic," *cul-de-sac* is used as a pejorative term, and vacant properties are referred to as "dead." Generalized correlations are referenced as direct causations, as in: "Higher density residential patterns decrease the collective ecological footprint of the residents" (20). Terms such as *New Urbanism* and *Smart Growth* are incorrectly used as synonyms, and *sustainable* is used with no reference point at all. Urban history is artificially sweetened with lines such as: "Public spaces in cities have traditionally been designed to celebrate the community's collective aspirations of togetherness, memorializing great accomplishments, health and wealth" (60). And nods to preservation are awkward at best, such as with the mistitling of the neotraditional infilling of a modernist, Edward Durell Stone–designed property as "Completing a Job Started Almost a Half Century Ago" (219).

However, at times the authors also transcend this very problematic subgenre. Dunham-Jones and Williamson recognize the actual complexity of today's suburbs, citing census data as well as acknowledging suburbia's multifaceted history—tipping their hats to Robert Fishman and Kenneth Jackson as well as noting contemporary works such as Kevin Kruse and Thomas Sugrue's *The New Suburban History* (17). They also demonstrate nuance toward texts often treated, as with suburban form, as sacred or profane wholes. The authors admit that Jane Jacobs's observations about business cycling actually occurs in the "one-age construction" of suburbs (67–68), refer to Robert Putnam's *Bowling Alone* with recognition that his conclusions were not at all clear-cut about suburbanization (60), and concede that "time is proving [Joel] Garreau correct" in regard to some of his predictions about edge cities (173).

Overall, *Retrofitting Suburbia* is a fine book. While it does not claim to be an even-handed work, and it cannot claim to be a "comprehensive guidebook," it still casts its net wider, recognizes a broader array of metropolitan development factors, and treats suburbia with considerably more maturity

than those books it is likely to be categorized with. And most importantly, the case studies and background information provide a wonderful starter collection for those interested in these rapidly evolving typologies—making this work a solid contribution to any bookshelf.

Just as significantly, the text also provides a starter collection of examples of the broader city-building realities that the disciplinarily partisan and ideologically constrained among us must eventually internalize. In this way Dunham-Jones and Williamson have a created a work that offers more than their publisher may realize. For it is clear that the changing ways in which we rebuild our suburbs requires not only an appreciation of both the art of architecture and the realities of urban development but also a thorough understanding of how they relate to each other in equally complementary and contradictory ways. *Retrofitting Suburbia* begins to open the door to such an understanding for architects, New Urbanists, and students alike.

The Place Matters Project of City Lore and the Municipal Art Society
Census of Places That Matter
http://www.placematters.net/places

Review by Mike Christenson

Boy, the way Glenn Miller played
Songs that made the Hit Parade.
Guys like us, we had it made.
Those were the days!
  —Lyrics to "All in the Family"

The 1970s sitcom *All in the Family* opened with a sequence of views of New York City, moving from a high aerial view of Manhattan, through low-level aerial views of Queens, to street-level views of houses, and finally coming to rest on the double house presented as the home of the fictional Archie Bunker.

Although the exact location of the house was not identified in the show—Archie often quoted his address as 704 Hauser Street—the double house used in the title sequence stands at 89-70 Cooper Avenue in Queens. It is one of nearly seven hundred sites that appear on the Census of Places that Matter (www.placematters.net/places), an online repository of culturally significant sites in New York City. This census is the growing result of work begun in 1998 and cosponsored by New York's City Lore and the Municipal Art Society to "identify, celebrate, interpret and protect places that tell the history and anchor the traditions of New York's many communities." The content of the census is a mix of well-known landmark places (e.g. Governors Island, the Apollo Theater) and less familiar sites; it is a result of nominations from organizations and individuals. It is in reflecting the interests of ordinary people that I think the census takes on its greatest value. Without the Internet, this kind of project would likely require a central repository or document under the control of an individual or organization; it would lack the sense of unmediated participation that the census promises. But beyond simply organizing information and enabling ongoing updates—qualities in some degree present in every Web site—what makes the Census of Places that Matter uniquely valuable?

The census opens with an alphabetized list of sites across New York's five boroughs. Each entry indicates the site's neighborhood, its borough, and gives a one-line description. In most but not all cases, a linked page of additional information provides a brief background profile and one or more completed nomination forms of variable scope and quality. Several of the profiles include in-depth information concerning site histories, detailed descriptions, and discussions of significance with regard to a neighborhood, a borough, or the city as a whole. The information page for Governors Island is typical of these detailed entries, featuring a 1,600-word essay describing the site's location, history, physical characteristics, and cultural significance,

along with citations and links to additional resources and nomination forms from individuals testifying to the site's value with respect to diverse criteria (e. g., architecture, personal or family significance, and preservation efforts). If all of the sites in the census were supported with information of richness and depth similar to that provided for sites like Governors Island, or for the Skylight Gallery (a Brooklyn gallery "featuring work by artists from Africa and the Diaspora"), or for Manhattan Plaza ("Subsidized apartments for people in theater professions"), the Census of Places That Matter would be an invaluable and entirely unique resource for anyone interested in the cultural history of the city, whether professionally or casually. The dozen or so sites that cite interviews by Place Matters staff as a source clearly rise to the top of the census when considered in terms of the depth and breadth of information provided.

More typical of the census entries is Glaser's Bake Shop in Manhattan. Unlike Governors Island, Glaser's has no association with historical events of citywide significance; unlike Archie Bunker's House, Glaser's has no aura of media attention around it. Glaser's is not the kind of site likely to appear in a book chronicling the "official" history of New York (as Governors Island does).[1] It is also not likely to appear in an essay or review concerning relationships between media and culture.[2] Glaser's significance derives instead from its place in the daily lives and work of people in the Yorkville neighborhood in Manhattan. Indeed, sites such as Glaser's—that is, locally significant, "off-the-beaten-path" places—form the bulk of citations in the census. The stories and brief comments that appear on their respective information pages provide insights into the city's culture and history available in no other obvious way. Yet several sites on the census lack even rudimentary support information. There are entries for local businesses so casual in execution or minimal in scope as to be of dubious value, or at best of that kind of focused practical value that one could find more reliably by reading restaurant reviews (e.g., the supporting information

for one Brooklyn restaurant is limited to the single statement: "They give you a lot and the price is reasonable"). But to the degree that the census is understood as a dynamic and growing resource, the inclusion of such sites can't be discounted simply because supporting information is not yet present. The nature of the census is such that it supports participation at varying levels: an "Anonymous Nominator" might identify a favorite local restaurant or shop; other nominators might then add their own comments in support; and eventually, something like consensus may build up around a site to the degree that it draws attention from scholars, historians, and so on. Such a process—clearly enabled by the Internet—is entirely typical of what Henry Glassie has called "the transition from the unknown to the known," that process that begins when we isolate a "neglected architectural variety" and decide to call it vernacular.[3] It is precisely the isolation through the act of nomination of the neighborhood bakeries, beauty parlors, restaurants, and so on that begins the transition in this "Glassian" sense. It is really up to everyone, New Yorkers and visitors alike, to contribute to the census in order for it to reach its full potential.

While the content of the Census of Places That Matter is important insofar as it provides personalized narratives unavailable elsewhere, the importance of the project is not limited to its content. The potential of the Internet to change the way we understand the historical and cultural significance of places arises, I think, not primarily due to the kind of content that can be featured (e.g., text, images, videos, etc.), nor even because of the way ordinary people can contribute to this content. As critical as these attributes are to shaping historical or cultural significance, I think the provocation the Internet brings to this question resides in its ability to support dynamic links among distinctly organized or constituted bodies of information. Two such features of the Census of Places That Matter are worth mentioning here. First, each site in the census is linked to its location on Google Maps (maps.google.com). Because New York is extensively documented via the project known as Google Street View, it is possible to achieve fully panoramic, street-level views of every site on the census with only a few clicks from the master list. Even more importantly to the Places That Matter project, Google Street View supports "tags," i.e., user-provided comments and images related to specific locations, which constitute a parallel means of identifying cultural significance on a local level. The possibility of structuring an ever-more-closely-linked relationship between Google Street View and the Census of Places That Matter is tantalizing: the obvious first step in such a linkage would be to establish symmetry, making the census accessible via links from Google Street View. But even more promising is the idea that such links could extend the project of the census beyond the municipal boundaries of New York City.

Second, it's important to recognize the links between the Census of Places That Matter and the City of Memory project (www.cityofmemory.org), also supported by City Lore. The City of Memory is described on its home page as a "grand, new repository for New York City's stories and experiences." Like the Census of Places That Matter, the City of Memory supports user contribution of information, but in the form of narratives or stories. Although the linkage between the Census of Places That Matter and the City of Memory could be stronger—as of this writing, approximately ten sites are directly linked from the census to City of Memory—it's also important to acknowledge that the connection between narrative and place can be tenu-

ous: a story could conceivably be identified with a street address, with a whole neighborhood, or with a journey through the city. As with Google Street View, there is potential for an expanded linkage, and yet it's important to recognize that the value of the Internet is in *linking* distinct modes of organizing information and not *collapsing* them into each other.

Finally, we can ask about the Census of Places That Matter: *to whom*? Per the project's stated mission, its content is limited to places in New York City. A survey of the project reveals that certain individuals nominate sites more often than others (one nominator's name appears on perhaps a dozen sites); a significant share of the sites are nominated anonymously. While, historically, we might have depended on scholars to identify for us the "places that matter," sites like the census force the questions: Who are the new authorities? Who, today, decides whether a site is valuable or significant? Consider that, as of this writing, there are 21 "places that matter" on Staten Island, as compared to 68 in the Bronx, 69 in Queens, 166 in Brooklyn, and 353 in Manhattan—the smallest borough by area, though the most densely populated. Should we assume, then, that places in Manhattan matter more than places on Staten Island? (Or is it that Staten Island has fewer places?) And what about sites that arguably might matter more to tourists than to New Yorkers? Few tourists would visit New York without at least trying to go to the Statue of Liberty—and yet it doesn't appear on the census, except as something visible from other places in the city.

The observation brings the discussion full circle, back over Manhattan, circling over Queens, and stopping again in front of Archie Bunker's house. The importance of the house on Cooper Avenue is that its cultural significance is not due to what actually happened there, or because of its architecture, or even because it is a typical "vernacular" home in Queens. Instead, the site is significant precisely because of a story that was constructed about it, in which the *image* of the house rather than the house itself was central. In my view, the practice of establishing cultural or historical significance due to image as distinct from substance or event is no more or less valid than any other signifying practice, and yet it is a practice I see as being entirely characteristic of our time, and one that sites like the Census of Places That Matter—indeed the Internet in general—will only accelerate.

NOTES

1. As an example, see Edwin G. Burrows and Mike Wallace, *Gotham: A History of New York City to 1898* (New York: Oxford University Press, 1999), 320–22, etc.

2. Although the book *Hidden New York* doesn't discuss Glaser's, it does include in-depth discussion of several sites featured in the census. Marci Reaven and Steven J. Zeitlin, *Hidden New York: A Guide to Places That Matter* (New Brunswick, N.J.: Rivergate Books, 2006).

3. Henry Glassie, *Vernacular Architecture* (Bloomington: Indiana University Press, 2000), 20.

Contributors

Mike Christenson, AIA, is a registered architect and assistant professor of architecture at North Dakota State University in Fargo. Christenson's research examines the means through which architects make their ideas visible (via physical and digital representation), with a focus on developing media-based strategies suited for analytic and design-generative purposes. He has published his research nationally and internationally and is a member of the editorial board of the *International Journal of Architectural Computing*.

Eliza Earle Ferguson is associate professor of history at the University of New Mexico. She is the author of *Gender and Justice: Violence, Intimacy, and Community in Fin-de-Siècle Paris* (2010) and has published articles in the *Journal of Social History, Journal of Family History, Journal of Women's History*, and *Journal of Urban History*. Her current project is on working-class girls and sexuality in the Belle Epoque.

Rebecca Ginsburg is associate professor of landscape architecture at the University of Illinois at Urbana-Champaign, where she teaches courses in landscape and architectural history. She is author of *At Home with Apartheid: The Hidden Landscapes of Domestic Service in Johannesburg*. Her current research interests include carceral landscapes of the Atlantic slave trade.

John Hankey is a historian and curator who works primarily in the field of transportation heritage and historic preservation. He has three decades of engagement with Virginia's Shenandoah Valley.

Jason Alexander Hayter is a city planner, freelance writer, and doctoral candidate in the Department of City and Regional Planning at the University of California, Berkeley. His research explores how culture, design, and policy shape the interactions between the built and natural environments. His writings on landscape, politics, and urban design have been published in the *Oregonian, Dallas Morning News, Places*, and the *Berkeley Planning Journal*, as well as in other publications.

Barbara J. Heath is assistant professor of anthropology at the University of Tennessee, Knoxville. She received her PhD in American civilization with a specialization in historical archaeology from the University of Pennsylvania. She worked at Monticello from 1988–1991 and from 1992–2006 directed the department of archaeology and landscapes at Thomas Jefferson's Poplar Forest. Her interests include the social and material dimensions of New World plantations, African American landscapes and material culture, and the growth and development of Jefferson's plantation communities.

Alison K. Hoagland is professor emerita at Michigan Technological University, where she taught history and historic preservation for fifteen years. Her most recent book is *Mine Towns: Buildings for Workers in Michigan's Copper Country* (Minnesota, 2010). She chairs the Keweenaw National Historical Park Advisory Commission and is a past president of the Vernacular Architecture Forum.

Carl Lounsbury is senior architectural historian at the Colonial Williamsburg Foundation and adjunct associate professor of history at the College of William and Mary. He is a founding board member of the Vernacular Architecture Forum and past president. He has been a member of the English Vernacular Architecture Group since 1976. His most recent publication is *Essays in Early American Architecture: A View from the Chesapeake.*

Sara McDowell is a lecturer in human geography at the University of Ulster. Her research interests include the geography of conflict and commemoration. She has published in *Cultural Geographies, Gender, Place and Culture,* and *Memory Studies.*

Stephen E. Nepa is a PhD candidate and an adjunct professor of history and American studies at Temple University. He has also taught history at Bryn Mawr College, Rutgers University, and Rowan University. He is a contributing author to *America Goes Green: An Encyclopedia of Eco-friendly Practices in the United States* (forthcoming).

Tijen Roshko is currently assistant professor in the Department of Interior Design at the University of Manitoba. Roshko has earned both a master's degree in nuclear physics and a bachelor's degree in interior design. She is researching the vernacular architecture of Cambodia and the Islamic architecture of the Canadian prairies. Her teaching philosophy centers on the implementation of new methodologies and techniques, particularly in the areas of biodesign and intelligent materials.

Ryan K. Smith holds a PhD in American civilization from the University of Delaware. A Florida native, he is currently an associate professor of history at Virginia Commonwealth University, where he teaches American history, religion, and material culture. He is the author of *Gothic Arches, Latin Crosses: Anti-Catholicism and American Church Designs in the Nineteenth Century* (2006).

Catherine Switzer is the author of *Unionists and Great War Commemoration in the North of Ireland, 1914–39* (2007). Her research interests focus on the commemoration of conflict, particularly that of the First World War.

Chris Wilson is J. B. Jackson Chair of Cultural Landscape Studies at the University of New Mexico School of Architecture and Planning in Albuquerque, New Mexico, the author of *The Myth of Santa Fe: Creating a Modern Regional Tradition* (1997), and coeditor with Paul Groth of *Everyday America: Cultural Landscape Studies after J. B. Jackson* (2003).

Carla Yanni is professor of art history at Rutgers University and the author of *Nature's Museums: Victorian Science and the Architecture of Display* (2000) and *The Architecture of Madness: Insane Asylums in the United States* (Minnesota, 2007).

Join the Vernacular Architecture Forum

Please enroll me as a member of the Vernacular Architecture Forum. I understand that membership entitles me to two issues of the journal *Buildings & Landscapes,* and four issues of the *Vernacular Architecture Newsletter,* and that my newsletter subscription will begin with the next issue after the receipt of my dues. Membership also includes enrollment in our online listserv and members receive priority mailing for conferences (since field tours fill quickly).

*All receipts above the basic membership levels will be applied toward the giving category of your choice (please check one):

☐   Student and Professional Support Fund (including grants, fellowships, and awards)
☐   Publications Fund (including *B&L, VAN,* and special publications)
☐   VAF Endowment Fund

☐   Active, $45   ☐   Household, $65   ☐   Institution, $75   ☐   Contributing, $75

☐   Patron, $150   ☐   Lifetime, $2,000   ☐   Multiple Year _____ years x $45

☐   Student, $25 I am currently enrolled at _____

_____
NAME

_____
ADDRESS

_____
CITY   STATE/PROVINCE   ZIP

_____
COUNTRY

_____
EMAIL

☐   Check here if you do not wish to take part in our online listserv

Note: Memberships must be paid by check or money order in U.S. funds. VAF does not currently accept credit cards.

Please consider an additional gift in support of VAF programs.
$ _____ Student and Professional Support Fund
$ _____ Publications Fund
$ _____ VAF Endowment Fund

Please fill out this form and mail with payment to: Gabrielle M. Lanier, Secretary
                                                       Vernacular Architecture Forum
                                                       P.O. Box 1511
                                                       Harrisonburg, VA 22803-1511

VIRGINIA

At Home with Apartheid
The Hidden Landscapes of Domestic Service in Johannesburg
Rebecca Ginsburg
$35.00 | CLOTH

"At once modest in spirit and profound in effect. This is a major landmark in the growing field of race and space studies."—Dell Upton, University of California, Los Angeles

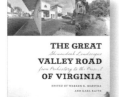

The Great Valley Road of Virginia
Shenandoah Landscapes from Prehistory to the Present
Edited by Warren R. Hofstra and Karl Raitz
$25.00 | PAPER

Winner of the Allen G. Noble Book Award of the Pioneer America Society: Association for the Preservation of Artifacts and Landscapes

Essays in Early American Architectural History
A View from the Chesapeake
Carl R. Lounsbury
$65.00 | CLOTH

"Reading these pages is to ride in the vanguard of early American architectural scholarship for the past forty years."
—Cary Carson, Colonial Williamsburg Foundation

 WWW.UPRESS.VIRGINIA.EDU

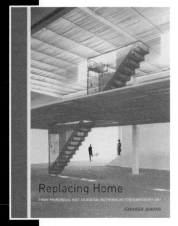
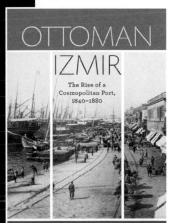
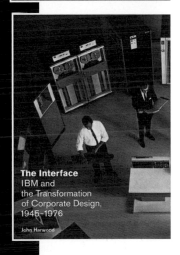